GCSE Edexcel
Music

There's a lot to get your ears around in Edexcel GCSE Music, and the new Grade 9-1 courses are tougher than ever. Luckily, help is at hand...

This brilliant CGP book explains everything you'll need to do well in your coursework and exams. Musical knowledge, set works, compositions — you name it.

What's more, each section has plenty of warm-up questions and exam-style practice. And to help you finish the course on a high note, we've even included a realistic practice exam at the end!

Complete
Revision & Practice

Everything you need to pass the exams!

Contents

Section One — The GCSE Course

What You Have To Do For GCSE Music 2
Component 1 — Performing.......................... 3
Component 2 — Composing 4
Component 3 — Appraising 7

Section Two — Reading and Writing Music

The Basics 8
Clefs... 10
Sharps, Flats and Naturals........................ 11
Time Signatures 12
Counting the Beat................................ 13
Rhythms and Metres 14
Warm-up and Exam Questions.................... 15
Notes and Rests 16
Dots, Ties and Triplets 17
Tempo and Mood 18
Dynamics and Articulation 19
More Instructions................................ 20
Warm-up and Exam Questions.................... 21
Revision Summary for Section Two 23

Section Three — Keys, Scales and Chords

Major Scales..................................... 24
Minor Scales..................................... 25
The Circle of Fifths............................... 26
Modes and Other Types of Scale.................. 27
Intervals.. 28
Examples 30
Practice Questions 31
Warm-up and Exam Questions.................... 32
Chords — The Basics 34
Triads 35
Fitting Chords to a Melody........................ 36
Inversions 37
Different Ways of Playing Chords 39
Examples and Practice 40
Using Decorations to Vary the Harmony.......... 41
Phrases and Cadences 42
Cadences.. 43
Modulation...................................... 44
Texture 45
Examples 48
Practice Questions............................. 49
Warm-up and Exam Questions.................... 51
Revision Summary for Section Three............... 53

Section Four — Structure and Form

Common Melodic Devices........................... 54
Common Forms................................... 56
Popular Song Forms.............................. 58
Warm-up and Exam Questions.................... 59
Revision Summary for Section Four 61

Section Five — Instruments

Brass Instruments................................ 62
Woodwind Instruments........................... 63
Orchestral Strings 64
Guitars 65
Keyboard Instruments 66
Percussion 67
The Voice 68
Wind, Brass and Jazz Bands....................... 69
Chamber Music 70
The Orchestra 71
Music Technology................................ 72
Timbre.. 74
Warm-up and Exam Questions.................... 76
Revision Summary for Section Five............... 79

Section Six — Instrumental Music 1700-1820

The Baroque Style................................ 80
Baroque Structures 81
Baroque Melody Patterns 83
Ornaments in Baroque Music 84
J.S. Bach — Brandenburg Concerto No.5 85
From Baroque to Classical 87
The Classical Orchestra 88
The Classical Style 89
Classical Structures.............................. 90
The Romantic Period 93
Beethoven — Sonata Pathétique 94
Warm-up and Exam Questions.................... 96
Revision Summary for Section Six............... 100

Section Seven — Vocal Music

Choral Music.. 101
Opera.. 102
Oratorios.. 103
Smaller Vocal Pieces.................................... 104
Romantic Songs — Lieder............................. 105
Purcell — Music for a While.......................... 106
Pop Music... 108
The Blues.. 110
Disco... 112
Rock.. 113
Queen — Killer Queen................................. 114
Warm-up and Exam Questions...................... 116
Revision Summary for Section Seven.............. 119

Section Eight — Music for Stage and Screen

Musicals... 120
Wicked — Defying Gravity............................ 122
Film Music.. 124
Star Wars: Episode IV — Main Title............... 128
Warm-up and Exam Questions...................... 130
Revision Summary for Section Eight............... 133

Section Nine — Fusions

World Music... 134
World Music and Fusion............................... 135
African Music.. 136
Celtic Music.. 138
Afro Celt Sound System — Release................. 140
Jazz.. 142
Improvisation.. 144
Samba... 145
Esperanza Spalding — Samba Em Preludio....... 146
Other Fusions.. 148
Warm-up and Exam Questions...................... 150
Revision Summary for Section Nine................ 153

Practice Exam... 154
Answers.. 172
Index and Glossary..................................... 180
Acknowledgements..................................... 188

Published by CGP

Editors: Caley Simpson, Ben Train, Ruth Wilbourne

Contributors: Catherine Baird, Christopher Dalladay, Faye Deane, John Deane, Elena Delaney, Rob Hall, Angela Major, Peter Maries, Mel McIntyre, Sam Norman, James Reevell.

With thanks to Hannah Totman and Karen Wells for the proofreading.
With thanks to Jan Greenway, Laura Jakubowski and Holly Poynton for the copyright research.

Audio CD edited and mastered by Neil Hastings.

For copyright reasons, this book can only be sold in the UK.

ISBN: 978 1 78294 615 1

Clipart from Corel®

Printed by Elanders Ltd, Newcastle upon Tyne.

Based on the classic CGP style created by Richard Parsons.

What You Have To Do For GCSE Music

Music GCSE doesn't cover every single aspect of music — if it did it would take forever.
Instead you focus on four main 'Areas of Study' (AoS for short).

You Learn About **Four Areas of Study**

For each Area of Study you'll learn the basics of that style or period — e.g. the musical
structures, the instruments used, the context the music was originally created in, etc.
You'll also have to give your opinions on the music — using appropriate musical terms.

You have to look at set pieces for each Area of Study:

> **AoS1 — INSTRUMENTAL MUSIC 1700-1820** (covered in Section 6)
> Your set pieces are the 3rd Movement from J. S. Bach's *Brandenburg Concerto No. 5 in D Major*
> and the 1st Movement from Beethoven's *Piano Sonata No. 8 in C minor 'Pathétique'*.

> **AoS2 — VOCAL MUSIC** (covered in Section 7)
> Your set pieces are Henry Purcell's 'Music for a While' and
> Queen's 'Killer Queen' from the album *Sheer Heart Attack*.

> **AoS3 — MUSIC FOR STAGE AND SCREEN** (covered in Section 8)
> Your set pieces are Stephen Schwartz's 'Defying Gravity' from *Wicked* and John Williams'
> 'Main Title/Rebel Blockade Runner' from the soundtrack for *Star Wars Episode IV — A New Hope*.

> **AoS4 — FUSIONS** (covered in Section 9)
> Your set pieces are Afro Celt Sound System's 'Release' from the album *Volume 2: Release*
> and Esperanza Spalding's 'Samba Em Preludio' from the album *Esperanza*.

They Test You With **Coursework...**

The coursework is work done during the course. Obviously. It's split into two chunks:

PERFORMING

worth 30% of the total marks

1) You do two performances.
2) One has to be a solo performance. This can be a piece you play or sing,
   and it can be an improvisation or a realisation (see p.3).
3) For the other, you have to perform as part of an ensemble. There must
   be 2 or more players in the ensemble, with distinct and separate parts.

COMPOSING

worth 30% of the total marks

1) You compose two pieces. One is based on a composition brief set by the exam board.
   There'll be composition briefs for each Area of Study and you can choose which one you do.
2) Your second composition can be anything you like — it's a free composition.

...and a **Listening Exam**

worth 40% of the total marks

At the end of Year 11 you do an exam called the Appraising exam. You listen to extracts from the
set works from all four Areas of Study (and a mystery piece) and answer questions on what you hear.

Err, Miss... is it too late to change to Physics?

Welcome to the wonderful world of GCSE Music. Breathe in the cool clear air. Listen to the birds. Relax.

Component 1 — Performing

Pick your pieces carefully and practise till your neighbours beg for mercy.

You Have To Do Two Performances

Each performance has to be at least one minute long (you can play more than one piece for each performance) — and the combined time must be at least four minutes. If it's less than four minutes, you won't get any marks. There's no maximum time, but six minutes in total will probably be enough.

SOLO PERFORMANCE

You simply play one (or more) solo piece(s) of your own choice. It can be a traditional performance, an improvisation or a realisation. A realisation is a performance that can't be assessed using the same criteria as the others — such as using music technology or music that's been passed down orally. Your solo can be accompanied (if it was written with an accompaniment, you have to perform it with accompaniment) — but the accompaniment can't double your part (see p.45).

ENSEMBLE PERFORMANCE

For your ensemble piece, there must be at least two of you playing or singing, and your part can't be doubled by any other part. Like the solo performance, this can be a traditional performance or an improvisation. You have to play a different piece than the one you played for your solo.

For both performances, you have to hand in a score, professional recording or commentary of your piece, or for an improvisation, the stimulus used (e.g. the chord pattern you used). You also have to hand in the recordings on a CD or USB stick. You can do each performance on a different instrument if you want.

You Get Marks for the Quality of Your Playing...

In each performance, you need to show off your 'musicality'. You get marks for:

1) **TECHNIQUE:** This is how well you play your instrument — things like breath control (on a wind instrument), diction (if you're singing) and coordination (e.g. on a piano or string instrument). You'll get marks for sonority (the quality of your tone) as well.

2) **EXPRESSION AND INTERPRETATION:** Your performance needs to be expressive — to make the audience feel something. Pay attention to stuff like dynamics, tempo, mood, articulation and phrasing. It's all about how well you communicate — i.e. how you interpret the music.

3) **ACCURACY AND FLUENCY:** Learn the notes, play them in time and in tune. Most importantly, keep going — your performance needs to be fluent. Lots of stopping and starting or slowing down for tricky bits will lose you marks. Don't worry about the odd slip, but start off well prepared.

When you're playing in an ensemble, there are other things that you'll get marks for. Play in time and in tune with the other players. Really listen to the other parts, so you know when you should be part of the background and when you should make your part stand out — the ensemble should be balanced.

...and Marks for the Difficulty of the Piece

1) It's obvious really — a very simple piece will get fewer marks for difficulty than a complicated piece. But there's no point trying to play something that you're not capable of and then messing it up...

2) Choose your pieces carefully — ideally they should be the hardest level that you can play well. If you pick something too easy, you'll be throwing away difficulty marks. If you pick something too hard, you won't be able to play your best, and you'll lose marks for musicality. Get your music teacher or instrument teacher's advice on what to play.

3) If you choose an easy piece, you won't be able to get as many marks for the areas described above.

Practice makes perfect...

No doubt people have been going on at you about practising since you were knee-high to a piccolo. It gets boring after a while. I expect you know that you need to do lots of practice. So I'll say no more.

Component 2 — Composing

When you write your GCSE pieces you can't just write whatever you like. Well, you can for one of them — but for the other, you have to follow a composition brief. Read on to find out more...

You Have to Write **Two Pieces** for **Coursework**

1) Each piece you compose has to be <u>at least one minute</u> long, and the <u>total</u> time for both pieces has to be <u>at least three minutes</u> (you won't get <u>any</u> marks if they're <u>less</u> than three minutes). The suggested <u>maximum</u> time for both pieces is <u>five minutes</u> (but you <u>won't</u> lose marks if you go over this time).

2) You <u>don't</u> have to perform your compositions <u>yourself</u> (but you can if you want to). You have to spend at least <u>5 hours</u> composing (supervised by your <u>teacher</u>) — but you can take as <u>long</u> as you want.

3) You can compose for <u>any</u> combination of <u>instruments</u> or <u>voices</u> (unless the composition brief tells you otherwise).

4) One piece you write has to follow a <u>composition brief</u>. This will be given to you by the <u>exam board</u>. There will be <u>different</u> composition briefs for each of the <u>areas of study</u>, and you can <u>choose</u> which one you do (though your <u>teacher</u> might suggest which one you pick). Here's an <u>example</u> of what you might be asked to do for <u>each</u> of the four areas of study:

> **Instrumental Music 1700-1820**
> The composition brief might ask you to write a piece in <u>rondo form</u>.

> **Vocal Music**
> You might be asked to set a <u>poem</u> to music.

> **Music for Stage and Screen**
> You might be given a description of a <u>scene</u> and have to write music to go with it.

> **Fusions**
> The composition brief might give you <u>two musical styles</u> and ask you to create a fusion of both of them.

5) You'll be given the composition brief <u>halfway</u> through your GCSE course — by which point, you should have <u>studied</u> the different areas (and looked at the <u>set pieces</u>) in detail.

6) The other piece you write is a <u>free composition</u> — it can be in <u>any style</u> you like.

Each Piece is Marked on **Three** Different **Categories**

Each composition is worth <u>30 marks</u>, based on three different categories (there are up to <u>10 marks</u> available for each category).

> 1) **DEVELOPING IDEAS:** You'll get marks for <u>coming up with</u>, <u>developing</u> and <u>extending</u> musical <u>ideas</u>. If you're writing in a particular <u>style</u>, your piece needs to reflect this <u>style</u>, and be suitable for the <u>purpose</u> or <u>audience</u> for which it was written. For the composition based on the <u>brief</u>, you'll get marks here if your piece <u>meets</u> the brief in a <u>secure</u> and <u>imaginative</u> way.
>
> 2) **TECHNICAL CONTROL:** You need to show that all the <u>musical features</u> work <u>together</u> and <u>fit</u> the <u>style</u> of the piece. The parts need to be <u>suitable</u> for the <u>instruments</u> they're written for (i.e. within an instrument's <u>range</u> and making full use of its playing <u>techniques</u>). You should also vary the <u>textures</u> within your compositions (as long as it fits with the <u>style</u>).
>
> 3) **COHERENCE:** This is a fancy word that just means how well your piece works as a <u>whole</u>. It looks at things like <u>structure</u>, <u>fluency</u>, use of <u>contrast</u> and if the piece has a sense of <u>direction</u>.
>
> *There are more details on all of these areas on the next page.*

You have to hand in a <u>recording</u> of each composition, as well as a <u>written version</u>. There's more information about these on p.6.

Composition briefs aren't a special type of underwear...

The music you study for the four topics is more than just exam fodder — you need it for your compositions too. So it's doubly important that you get <u>listening</u> and <u>learning</u> about it (it's covered in Sections 6-9).

Component 2 — Composing

Well, the good news is — the compositions you have to do for GCSE only need to be a total of <u>between 3 and 5 minutes</u> long. No one's expecting an opera. Something short will do.

To get **Top Marks** Think About...

DEVELOPING YOUR MUSICAL IDEAS

Don't just use a good idea once and then forget about it. <u>Build up</u> and <u>develop</u> the good bits —
e.g. by changing the <u>rhythm</u> from short notes to long notes or the <u>key</u> from major to minor.
See Sections 3 and 4 for loads more <u>techniques</u> and <u>devices</u> for developing your ideas.

MAKING THE STYLE CONVINCING

Listen to <u>lots</u> of music from the style you're composing in.
Make your piece sound like 'the real thing' by using <u>similar musical ideas</u> —
e.g. in a Baroque gigue, use a lively tempo, steady beat and a harpsichord.

THE POTENTIAL AND LIMITS OF YOUR RESOURCES

Once you've chosen the instruments, think about <u>all</u> the ways they can make
<u>interesting</u> and <u>contrasting</u> sounds — e.g. <u>pizzicato</u> bits for strings.
But also remember the <u>limitations</u> — e.g. clarinet players need <u>time to breathe</u>.
Think about the <u>highest</u> and <u>lowest</u> notes your chosen instruments can
play — there's no point composing a brilliant piece if <u>no one can play it</u>.

One of your pieces will have to meet the composition brief, so there'll be extra things you have to bear in mind to match the brief.

STRUCTURE

Organise your music with a <u>clear</u>, <u>definite structure</u> (there's lots of information on
different structures throughout this book). Even if your composition doesn't follow
a <u>traditional form</u>, you'll need to make sure it doesn't just <u>ramble on aimlessly</u>.

When You're Composing, Make Plans **Before** You Start

1) Making a <u>musical plan</u> helps to <u>organise</u> your ideas — it's a bit like writing an essay plan.

2) Music's got to be organised, or it just sounds like a load of <u>random notes</u>. The <u>most basic</u>
   bit of organisation is the timing (<u>beats in a bar</u>). The next biggest chunk is the <u>phrasing</u>.

3) The <u>overall shape</u> is called the <u>structure</u> or <u>form</u>. The structure could be the <u>verses</u> and
   <u>chorus</u> in a pop song, or the <u>movements</u> of a symphony. Composers usually <u>decide</u>
   on the <u>structure</u> of a piece of music <u>before</u> they get into the detail.

4) It's OK to <u>design your own</u> musical plan, but a lot of people use 'tried and tested' structures
   like the ones described throughout this book — because they know they'll work.

5) 'Tried and tested' structures are like <u>templates</u>. The <u>general organisation</u>
   of your ideas is decided for you — you just need to add the <u>details</u>.

6) For the piece that follows the <u>composition brief</u>, it's probably a <u>good idea</u> to use a 'tried
   and tested' structure as your composition will need to be in a particular <u>style</u> or <u>form</u>.

7) Your plan should include ways to <u>vary</u> the different <u>sections</u>
   — have a look on the next page for some ideas.

Clarinet players need time to breathe? Amateurs...

So the main thing to take away from this page is 'be organised'. I'm not expecting you to be
organised in all aspects of your life, just in your compositions — and planning really helps.

Component 2 — Composing

There are lots of things you need to think about when composing. This is not a complete list (just a few general ideas), but it'll give you a few things to bear in mind.

Most Music Uses **Repetition** Repetition Repetition...

1) Repetition means using a musical idea — a chunk of tune — more than once.
2) Repeating bits is a really good way of giving music shape. A recognisable tune works like a landmark — the audience recognises that tune later in the piece. That's how choruses work.
3) If you're planning your own piece of music, try repeating the best part of the tune.
4) You can even repeat whole sections — in rondo form (see p.92), one section is repeated lots of times.

...and **Contrast**

Repetition is really important — but constant repetition is boring. Good compositions balance repetition with contrast. The aim is to do something different from the repeated bits to add variety. Here are some ways you can vary your compositions:

PITCH AND TONALITY

You can create contrast by changing the organisation of pitch — e.g. changing the melody from a high register to a low register, and swapping between conjunct and disjunct tunes (see p.28). You can also change the tonality (key) by modulating between major and minor keys.

TEMPO AND RHYTHM

Changing speed from fast to slow (or vice versa) is a good way of creating contrast. You can also change the rhythms — try a mix of dotted and straight rhythms, or long and short notes. You can change the articulation too — try legato, staccato, slurs and accents to vary your piece.

DYNAMICS

Changes in dynamics (loud to soft and vice versa, and crescendos and diminuendos) will instantly create contrast.

TEXTURE

Changing between a thin, monophonic texture to a thicker homophonic or polyphonic texture (see p.45) will create contrast.

Decide How To **Hand In** Your Work

For each piece, you give in two things — a written version and a recording (though you won't be marked on the quality of the recording, just the composition). There are a few options for how you present them.

The **WRITTEN VERSION** can be either...
- a score — either handwritten or computer generated. It can be in any appropriate format, e.g. a full score, a lead sheet or chord chart.
- OR a written commentary (up to 500 words long) with detailed performance directions and a description of the composition process.

Give as much information as possible. Dynamics, tempo, expression and articulation will all improve your mark. There should be enough detail for someone else to be able to recreate your piece.

The **RECORDING** can be on CD or USB stick.

Even though you don't get marks for the quality of the recording, good recordings are easier to mark. It's also in your best interests to produce an accurate one.

I'm going to submit my work by telepathy...

On the one hand, you've got plenty of time to get these compositions sorted. On the other hand, if you don't start ASAP you might just find yourself running out of time. Best get on with it.

Component 3 — Appraising

At the end of the course, you have the joy of a <u>listening exam</u>. All <u>1 hour and 45 minutes</u> of it.

The **Appraising Exam** Tests All Four **Areas of Study**

1) The Appraising Exam is worth <u>80 marks</u> in total (<u>40%</u> of your total mark). You listen to music from a CD and answer <u>written questions</u> about it. It's divided into <u>two</u> sections — <u>Section A</u> and <u>Section B</u>.

2) You're given <u>extracts</u> to listen to — <u>each one</u> has its own set of questions. You'll be told <u>what</u> each piece is and <u>how many times</u> it'll be played. You're given <u>reading</u> and <u>writing</u> time for each question.

3) Section A is worth <u>68 marks</u>, and has <u>8</u> questions. <u>6</u> of the questions will be on the <u>set pieces</u>, and most of them only need <u>short answers</u>. There'll also be a <u>musical dictation</u> question, and one on an <u>unfamiliar piece</u> (that might be <u>related</u> to the set pieces in some way).

4) Section B is worth <u>12 marks</u> and only has <u>one</u> question that needs a <u>longer answer</u>. You'll be asked to <u>compare</u> one of the <u>set pieces</u> with an <u>unfamiliar piece</u> (you'll be given the <u>scores</u> for both pieces). You might have to compare <u>musical elements</u> (e.g. tonality, structure, etc.), <u>instrumentation</u> or <u>context</u>, and you could be asked for your own <u>opinions</u>. You can mention <u>other related pieces</u> in your answer.

Some Questions are **Multiple Choice**

Don't mess these up by <u>rushing</u> — read all the options <u>carefully</u>.

If you're stuck — <u>guess</u> the answer. There's a <u>chance</u> of getting it right.

What is the texture of this extract? Put a cross in the correct box. *[1 mark]*

☐ homophonic   ☐ monophonic   ☐ contrapuntal   ☐ antiphonal

Some Questions Just Need a **Short Answer**

These questions are only worth a few marks so don't waste time writing your answer out in a nice long sentence — just write down <u>one good word</u> for <u>each mark</u>.

Name two instruments playing the theme in this extract. *[2 marks]*

For questions worth 3 or 4 marks, you'll have to write a bit more. You might be asked to compare different bits of the extract.

They Sometimes Give You an **Outline** of the Music

You'll be given an <u>outline</u> of part of the music called a 'skeleton score'. It will just show <u>part</u> of the music — the melody, rhythm or lyrics, say. The skeleton score will help you with answering the question. You might be asked to <u>fill in</u> the pitch, rhythm or chords of a short section of the music.

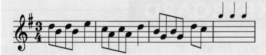

Fill in the missing notes in bar 4. The rhythm is given above the stave. *[3 marks]*

The Question in **Section B** Needs a **Longer Answer**

This is a question where you have to write a <u>longer</u> answer — a few <u>paragraphs</u> of writing. Make sure you cover all the <u>key points</u> of the question in your answer.

Compare the ways in which both pieces of film music effectively create a sense of heroism and drama. You should mention musical elements, instrumentation and context. *[12 marks]*

 Shiver me timbers — 'tis the skeleton score...
Concentrate on answering just a <u>few</u> of the questions each time the music's played — it's less confusing. Have a go at the Practice Exam on p.154 to give you an idea of what it'll be like.

The Basics

These two pages give the essential basics you'll need to get through Music GCSE. Make sure you know everything here before you go on into the rest of the book.

1 CLEF

These symbols at the start of a line tell you how high or low to play the notes. All the different clefs are covered on page 10.

2 NOTE

Each note is shown by a separate oval. The symbol also tells you how long or short the note is. The symbols are shown on page 16.

3 TWO LINES OF MUSIC

The top line of music has got a tune — it's the melody. The bottom line is the accompaniment.

7 TIME SIGNATURE

The numbers tell you about the beats in a bar. Time signatures are covered on page 12.

8 BEATS

Each bar has the same number of beats. Beats, bars and rhythm are covered on pages 13, 14, 16 & 17.

9 KEY SIGNATURE

There are no flats or sharps, so this piece is in the key of C. Keys and scales are covered in Section Three.

THE PIANO KEYBOARD

Some of the diagrams in this book make more sense if you know what's what on a piano keyboard. The white keys play natural notes.

F G A B C D E F G A B C D E

Note: The white notes from C to C make the scale of C major (p.24).

The black keys play SHARPS and FLATS. Sharps and flats are covered on page 11. The C in the middle of a piano keyboard is known as MIDDLE C.

The Basics

5 STAVE

The five lines are called a stave. Notes can go on or between the lines, or on separate short lines above or below.

4 BAR

The vertical bar lines split the music into bars.

bar line

6 TRIPLETS

The '3' and the curved line show these notes are triplets. They're explained on page 17.

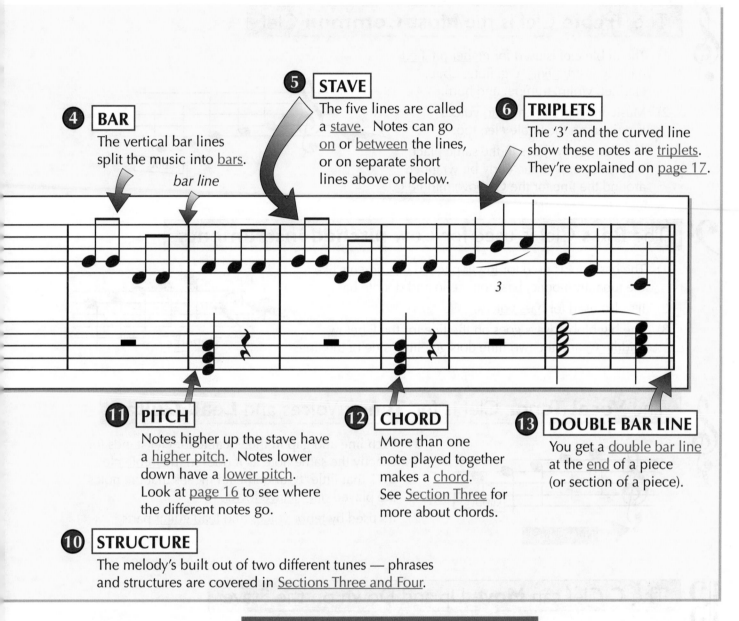

3

11 PITCH

Notes higher up the stave have a higher pitch. Notes lower down have a lower pitch. Look at page 16 to see where the different notes go.

12 CHORD

More than one note played together makes a chord. See Section Three for more about chords.

13 DOUBLE BAR LINE

You get a double bar line at the end of a piece (or section of a piece).

10 STRUCTURE

The melody's built out of two different tunes — phrases and structures are covered in Sections Three and Four.

TONES AND SEMITONES

Tones and *semitones* are the gaps between notes.

On a piano, a semitone is the gap between any key, black or white, and its immediate neighbour.

The gap from any key to a key two semitone steps above or below is called a tone.

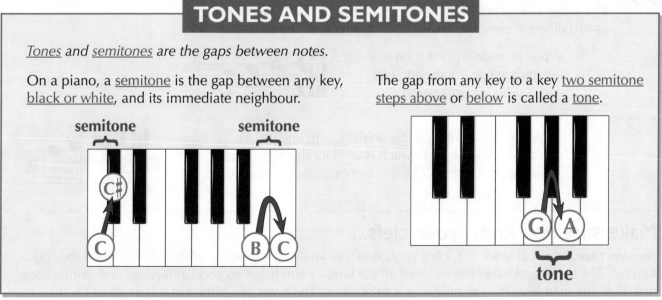

semitone   semitone

C#   C   B   C

G   A

tone

Clefs

Clefs are the <u>curly symbols</u> that you find right at the <u>start</u> of most written music. The treble clef is used for high-pitched music. The bass and alto clefs are used for lower-pitched music.

The **Treble** Clef is the **Most Common** Clef

1) The treble clef is used for <u>higher-pitched melody instruments</u>, e.g. flute, oboe, clarinet, violin, trumpet and horn.

2) Music for <u>soprano</u> and <u>alto</u> voices is written on the treble clef, too.

3) The sign always goes in the same place on the stave, with the curly bit wrapped around the line for the <u>G above middle C</u>.

MIDDLE C

The **Bass** Clef is used for **Low-pitched Instruments**

1) The bass clef is used for <u>lower-pitched instruments</u> like the tuba, trombone, bassoon, cello and double bass.

2) It's also used for <u>bass voices</u>.

3) The big blob always goes on the line for the <u>F below middle C</u>, and the two little dots go either side of the line.

MIDDLE C

The **Vocal Tenor** Clef is for **Tenor** Voices and **Lead Guitar**

MIDDLE C

Here's the 8.

1) Each line and gap in the vocal tenor clef stands for exactly the same note as it does in the <u>treble clef</u>, BUT that little '<u>8</u>' underneath means that the notes are played <u>one octave lower</u>.

2) It's used by <u>tenor voices</u> and <u>lead guitar</u> parts.

The **C** Clef can **Move** Up and Down on the Stave

The C clef always has its <u>middle point</u> on <u>middle C</u>. It can be used as two different clefs, depending on its <u>position</u> on the stave.

1) When its middle point is on the <u>middle line</u>, it's the <u>alto clef</u> and is used for <u>viola</u> parts.

MIDDLE C

2) When the middle point is on the <u>fourth line up</u>, it's called the <u>tenor clef</u>, which is used for the <u>higher notes</u> in <u>bass instruments</u> like trombones, bassoons and cellos.

MIDDLE C

Make sure you know your clefs...

You don't see the vocal tenor or C clefs very often, but you've got to know what they are when they <u>do</u> turn up. The treble and bass clefs are used all the time — aim to get so good at reading and writing them that it's easier than English. The only way is to practise. The notes are written in full on page 16.

Sharps, Flats and Naturals

On a piano, <u>natural</u> notes are the <u>white</u> ones. <u>Sharps</u> are the <u>black</u> notes to the <u>right</u> of the white notes. <u>Flats</u> are the blacks to the <u>left</u> of the whites. So each black is both sharp <u>and</u> flat.

♯ A **Sharp** Makes a Note One Step **Higher**

1) A sharp sign next to a note tells you to play it <u>one semitone higher</u>.

When you're writing on the stave, put sharps, flats and naturals before the note they affect. If you're writing text, put them afterwards — F♯.

2) A <u>double sharp</u> — ✖ — makes a note <u>two semitones higher</u>. If you see <u>C✖</u> you play <u>D</u> — it's the <u>same note</u> going by a different name. The fancy name for notes that sound the same but have different names is <u>enharmonic equivalents</u>.

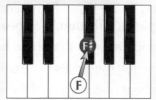 

♭ A **Flat** Makes a Note One Step **Lower**

1) A flat symbol next to a note means you have to play it <u>one semitone lower</u>.

 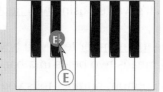

2) A <u>double flat</u> — ♭♭ — makes a note two semitones (a tone) lower.

 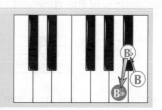

The **Key Signature** is Shown with Sharps or Flats

This key signature's got one sharp — on the F line. You have to play every F in the piece as an F♯.

1) Sharps or flats written at the <u>start</u> of a piece, straight after the clef, tell you the <u>key signature</u>.

2) The key signature makes notes sharp or flat <u>all the way through</u> a piece of music.

3) Sharps and flats that you see by individual notes — but not in the key signature — are called <u>accidentals</u>. Once an accidental has appeared in a bar, it applies to all notes of the same pitch for the rest of the bar, unless it's cancelled out by a <u>natural sign</u>...

There's more about key signatures on p.24-26.

♮ A **Natural** Sign **Cancels** a Sharp or Flat

A <u>natural</u> sign before a note <u>cancels</u> the <u>effect of a sharp or flat</u> sign from earlier in the bar or from a key signature. You <u>never</u> see natural signs in the key signature, only in the music, as accidentals.

This stuff should all come naturally in no time...

Double sharps and flats are uncommon and quite peculiar — it doesn't seem that <u>logical</u> to write C✖ when you could write D, but sometimes you just have to, I'm afraid. It all depends what key you're in.

Time Signatures

Those <u>two numbers</u> at the beginning of a piece of music tell you <u>how many beats</u> there are in a bar and <u>how long</u> they are. Whatever you're playing, don't ignore them.

Music has a **Regular Beat**

1) You can tap your foot along to the <u>beat</u> of any piece of music, as long as it hasn't got a horribly complicated rhythm. The beat is also called the <u>pulse</u>.

2) If you listen a bit harder, you can hear that some beats are <u>stronger</u> than others.

3) The strong beats come at <u>regular intervals</u> — usually every <u>2</u>, <u>3</u> or <u>4</u> beats.

4) The strong beat is the <u>first</u> beat of each <u>bar</u>. If the strong beat comes every 3 beats, then the piece of music you're listening to has <u>three beats</u> in a bar.

The **Time Signature** Shows **How Many** Beats are in a Bar

1) There's always a <u>time signature</u> at the beginning of a piece of music.

2) It goes to the <u>right</u> of the clef and the key signature.

3) It's written using <u>two numbers</u>.

TOP NUMBER
goes between the middle line and the top line

BOTTOM NUMBER
goes between the middle line and the bottom line

The <u>top number</u> tells you <u>how many beats</u> there are in each bar, e.g. a '2' means two beats in a bar, a '3' means three beats in a bar and so on.

The <u>bottom number</u> tells you <u>how long</u> each beat is (see <u>page 16</u> for the names of the different notes).

If you see a big '**C**' in place of the time signature, it stands for 'common time', which means it's in $\frac{4}{4}$. If it's ¢, then it's 'cut common time' — $\frac{2}{2}$.

A <u>2</u> at the bottom means each beat is <u>1 minim</u> long.

$2 = \textrm{𝅗𝅥}$

A <u>4</u> at the bottom means each beat is <u>1 crotchet</u> long.

$4 = \textrm{𝅘𝅥}$

An <u>8</u> at the bottom means each beat is <u>1 quaver</u> long.

$8 = \textrm{𝅘𝅥𝅮}$

A <u>16</u> at the bottom means each beat is <u>1 semiquaver</u> long.

$16 = \textrm{𝅘𝅥𝅯}$

If the **Beat Changes**, the **Time Signature Changes**

1) The time signature usually <u>stays the same</u> all the way through a piece of music. If it does, it's written just <u>once</u>, at the beginning.

2) Sometimes the beat <u>changes</u> during a piece. If it does, the new time signature's written in the bar where it <u>changes</u>.

3) Not all pieces start on the first beat of the bar — some start on an <u>unaccented beat</u> called an <u>anacrusis</u> (or <u>upbeat</u>).

You can practise listening for the beat any time...

Every time you listen to music, practise <u>listening for the beat</u> and work out the time signature.

Counting the Beat

Counting the beat's fairly easy, but it's a crucial skill. It can help you work out how to <u>play</u> a new piece and how to <u>write a tune down</u> when you've only heard it on a CD or in your head.

In **Simple Time** You Count **All the Beats**

1) <u>Simple</u> time signatures have <u>2</u>, <u>3</u> or <u>4</u> as their <u>top</u> number.

2) In simple time, if you're counting to the music, you count <u>every beat</u>. For $\frac{4}{4}$ you'd count, "<u>One, two, three, four.</u>" For $\frac{3}{2}$, you'd count, "<u>One, two, three.</u>"

3) If you want to count out the rhythm of <u>smaller notes</u> as well as the beats, try using "<u>and</u>", "<u>eye</u>" and "<u>a</u>" — it seems to make the rhythm come out just right.

> Count "<u>One and two and</u>" for quavers, and "<u>One eye and a</u>" for semiquavers.

4) Any shorter notes are usually a <u>half</u>, a <u>quarter</u>, an <u>eighth</u> or a <u>sixteenth</u> of the main beat.

In **Compound Time** Only Count the **Big Beats**

1) Compound time signatures have <u>6</u>, <u>9</u> or <u>12</u> as their <u>top</u> number — you can always divide the top number by <u>three</u>.

2) If the music is fairly fast, it's too <u>awkward</u> to count to nine or twelve for every bar. You end up with so many little beats that the rhythm sounds <u>mushy</u>.

3) To make the rhythm <u>clear</u>, you can just count the <u>main beats</u>:

4) If you were counting out the main beats in $\frac{6}{8}$, you'd count "One, two". $\frac{9}{8}$ would go "One, two, three".

5) To count the <u>in-between notes</u>, use "<u>&</u>" and "<u>a</u>".

6) Shorter notes are made by dividing by three — so they're <u>thirds</u>, <u>sixths</u>, <u>twelfths</u>, etc. of the main beat.

7) Music in compound time <u>sounds different</u> from music in simple time because the beat is divided into threes — <u>practise</u> spotting the difference.

The **Patterns** the Beats Make are Called the **Metre**

Depending on the time signature, the beats make different <u>patterns</u>.
The pattern is known as the <u>metre</u>. Metre can be:

Regular	Irregular	Free
The strong beats make the <u>same pattern</u> all the way through. <u>two</u> beats per bar = <u>duple</u> metre <u>three</u> beats per bar = <u>triple</u> metre <u>four</u> beats per bar = <u>quadruple</u> metre	There could be <u>five</u> beats in a bar grouped in twos and threes, or <u>seven</u> beats in a bar grouped in threes and twos or fours.	Music with <u>no particular metre</u>. This one's fairly unusual.

You can describe a time signature based on its beat and metre — e.g. a piece in $\frac{4}{4}$ is in simple quadruple time, and a piece in $\frac{6}{8}$ is in compound duple time.

One and a, two and a, three and a, four and a...

Counting the beat's not really that hard. The tricky bit on this page is the stuff about <u>metre</u>. You could get asked about the metre of a piece in your listening exam, so learn <u>all three sorts</u>.

Rhythms and Metres

When <u>different rhythms</u> are played at the <u>same time</u>, some of them <u>fit together</u> well, but some of them <u>don't</u>. Rhythms that <u>don't fit</u> can create interesting and crazy <u>effects</u>.

Hemiola Gives the Impression of a Different Metre

1) <u>Hemiola</u> is a <u>rhythmic device</u> used to create <u>contrast</u> within a piece. Music <u>written</u> in <u>duple</u> metre (see p.13) is temporarily <u>accented</u> to make it <u>feel</u> like it's in <u>triple</u> metre, or <u>vice versa</u>.

2) In $\frac{6}{8}$ time there are <u>two beats</u> in a bar, each the length of a dotted crotchet. <u>Hemiola</u> is created by playing a bar of <u>three crotchets</u>, giving the impression of $\frac{3}{4}$ time instead.

3) In $\frac{3}{4}$ time, <u>hemiola</u> is created by <u>accenting every other</u> <u>beat</u> for <u>two bars</u>. This gives the impression of <u>three bars</u> of $\frac{2}{4}$ time, rather than two bars of $\frac{3}{4}$.

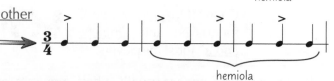

Different Rhythms Can be Played at the Same Time

1) When two or more <u>contrasting rhythms</u> are played at the <u>same time</u>, the music is <u>polyrhythmic</u>. A polyrhythm made up of just <u>two</u> different rhythms is known as a <u>bi-rhythm</u>. Lots of <u>African</u> music is polyrhythmic — see p.137.

2) <u>Polyrhythms</u> can be created by a number of performers playing <u>different instruments</u>. A drummer can also create polyrhythms by playing a <u>different rhythm</u> with <u>each hand</u>.

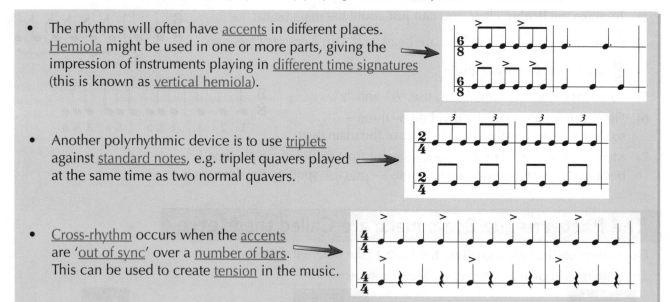

- The rhythms will often have <u>accents</u> in different places. <u>Hemiola</u> might be used in one or more parts, giving the impression of instruments playing in <u>different time signatures</u> (this is known as <u>vertical hemiola</u>).

- Another polyrhythmic device is to use <u>triplets</u> against <u>standard notes</u>, e.g. triplet quavers played at the same time as two normal quavers.

- <u>Cross-rhythm</u> occurs when the <u>accents</u> are '<u>out of sync</u>' over a <u>number of bars</u>. This can be used to create <u>tension</u> in the music.

Drum Fills are Little Drum Solos

1) <u>Drum fills</u> are fairly <u>short</u> — they often only last for a <u>few beats</u>.
2) Fills are normally used to <u>build</u> the music up, or to <u>change</u> between <u>sections</u>.
3) They give the drummer a (very short) chance to <u>show off</u>.
4) Most <u>rock</u>, <u>pop</u> and <u>jazz</u> pieces will have drum fills in them.

Rhythms make me very cross...

Have a listen to 'Dragon Days' by Alicia Keys and see if you can pick out the drum fills.

Warm-up and Exam Questions

Now have a crack at some questions to see how much you've learnt so far.

Warm-up Questions

1) Draw the symbols for a treble clef, bass clef, vocal tenor clef and C alto clef.

2) Explain what a sharp sign, a flat sign and a natural sign do.

3) Draw a time signature describing three minim beats per bar.

4) How many beats are there per bar if the time signature is $\frac{9}{8}$?

5) What's the difference between simple and compound time?

6) Name the three main types of metre.

Exam Question

This is the type of question you could get in your listening test. You'll need a track from the CD for this question. Use it to test your understanding of the last few pages and as practice for the real thing.

Play the following extract **four** times. Leave a short pause between each playing of the extract.

 Track 1

It's a good idea to read the whole question through before you listen to the track.

a) Fill in the **8 missing notes** from the vocal part, using the rhythm supplied.

Listen carefully for the direction of the notes — this really isn't as difficult as it seems at first.

[8 marks]

b) Draw a circle around the key signature.

[1 mark]

c) Fill in the time signature.

[1 mark]

d) Here is another part of the same extract.

Label the following features:

• the note A♯
• two notes a tone apart
• two notes a semitone apart

[3 marks]

Notes and Rests

Let's face it, you'd be a bit lost reading music if you didn't know what all those funny little dots and squiggles meant. Make sure you know all this stuff <u>better than the alphabet</u>.

The **Symbols** Tell You **How Long** Notes and Rests Are

1) <u>Notes</u> tell you how many beats to hold a <u>sound</u> for.

2) <u>Rests</u> tell you how many beats to hold a <u>silence</u> for.

3) Notes and rests have <u>names</u>, depending on how long they are.
Two beats is a <u>minim</u> note or rest. A half-beat is a <u>quaver</u> note or rest.

The length of a note or rest is also called its duration.

Learn this table now — you need to know exactly how to <u>write</u> these out, and how to <u>play</u> them.

NAME OF NOTE	NUMBER OF CROTCHET BEATS	NOTE SYMBOL	REST SYMBOL
semibreve	4	𝅝	▬
minim	2	𝅗𝅥	▬
crotchet	1	♩	𝄽
quaver	½	♪ or 𝅘𝅥𝅮𝅘𝅥𝅮 *if there are 2 or more*	𝄾
semiquaver	¼	𝅘𝅥𝅯 or 𝅘𝅥𝅯𝅘𝅥𝅯 *if there are 2 or more*	𝄿

The **Position** of the Note Tells You the **Pitch**

<u>Just in case</u> you don't know, this is where the notes go in the <u>bass</u> and <u>treble</u> clefs:

In the <u>bottom</u> half of the stave, the tails on the notes go <u>upwards</u>.

There is some overlap — e.g. these are the same note written in different clefs.

In the <u>top</u> half of the stave, the tails on the notes go <u>downwards</u>.

The tail of the note on the <u>middle line</u> can go <u>up</u> or <u>down</u>.

These lines are called <u>ledger lines</u>. You use them to work out how <u>high</u> or <u>low</u> notes <u>above</u> and <u>below</u> the stave are.

'Leger lines' is an alternative spelling for 'ledger lines'.

There's no excuse for not knowing this stuff...

Those of you who were playing the church organ before you could crawl might be feeling a bit like you know this stuff already and you don't need to be told. It's still worth <u>checking over</u> though, I reckon.

Dots, Ties and Triplets

You can only get so far with the note lengths from <u>page 16</u>. If you use <u>dot</u>, <u>tie</u> and <u>triplet</u> symbols you can create more complicated, interesting and sophisticated rhythms.

A **Dot** After a Note or Rest Makes It **Longer**

1) A dot just <u>to the right</u> of a note or rest makes it <u>half as long again</u>.

$$\text{♩} = \frac{1}{\text{beat}} \quad \begin{array}{c} 1 \div 2 = \frac{1}{2} \\ \longrightarrow \\ 1 + \frac{1}{2} = 1\frac{1}{2} \end{array} \quad \text{♩.} = \frac{1\frac{1}{2}}{\text{beats}} \qquad\qquad \text{𝅗𝅥} = \frac{2}{\text{beats}} \quad \begin{array}{c} 2 \div 2 = 1 \\ \longrightarrow \\ 2 + 1 = 3 \end{array} \quad \text{𝅗𝅥.} = \frac{3}{\text{beats}}$$

2) A <u>second</u> dot adds on another <u>quarter</u> of the original note length.

$$\text{♩..} = \mathbf{1\frac{3}{4}} \text{ beats} \qquad\qquad \text{𝅗𝅥..} = \mathbf{3\frac{1}{2}} \text{ beats}$$

Count these really carefully when you're playing — don't just "add a bit on".

3) In <u>dotted quaver rhythms</u>, you have a <u>dotted quaver</u> (worth $\frac{1}{2} + \frac{1}{4} = \frac{3}{4}$ of a beat) followed by a <u>semiquaver</u> (worth $\frac{1}{4}$ of a beat). Dotted quaver rhythms are common in <u>marches</u>. They're usually written like this:

¾ beat   ¼ beat

4) In a <u>Scotch snap</u>, the rhythm is the <u>other way round</u> — the <u>semiquaver</u> is on the <u>beat</u> (and <u>accented</u>), followed by the <u>dotted quaver</u>, like this: Scotch snaps are used in <u>Scottish music</u> (e.g. <u>dances</u>) — hence the name.

A **Tie Joins Two Notes** Together

1) A tie is a <u>curved line</u> joining two notes of the <u>same pitch</u> together.

2) It turns them into <u>one note</u>.

3) Ties are often used to make a long note that goes over the <u>end of a bar</u>.

...sounds the same as...

...sounds the same as...

Ties are not the same as slurs. See page 19.

A **Triplet** is **Three Notes** Played in the Time of **Two**

1) A triplet is <u>three</u> notes, all the <u>same length</u>, squeezed into the time of <u>two</u>.

2) Triplets are marked with a '<u>3</u>' above or below the <u>middle</u> of the three notes. Sometimes there's a <u>square</u> bracket or a <u>curved</u> line as well as the three.

3) The notes don't all have to be <u>played</u> — part of a triplet can be <u>rests</u>.

Stick with it, even the tricky bits...

Triplets look so straightforward on the page, but they can be tricky to get just right. The only way to make sure you're playing them properly is to practise with a metronome. Have a go right now.

Tempo and Mood

Composers don't just tell you the notes — they tell you <u>how fast</u> to play them, and what the <u>atmosphere</u> of the piece should be too. You need to understand all the different <u>terms</u> they use.

The **Tempo** is the **Speed** of the Music

Tempo is Italian for "<u>time</u>". In a lot of music the instructions for how fast to play are written in Italian too. Here are the words you're <u>most</u> likely to come across:

<u>60</u> beats a minute means each crotchet lasts <u>one</u> second. <u>120</u> beats a minute means each crotchet lasts <u>half</u> a second. And so on...

Italian word	What it means	Beats per minute
largo	broad and slow	40-60
larghetto	still broad, not so slow	60-66
adagio	bit faster than largo	66-76
andante	walking pace	76-108
moderato	moderate speed	108-120
allegro	quick and lively	120-168
vivace	very lively — quicker than allegro	168-180
presto	really fast	180-200

This is where you put the <u>tempo</u> and <u>beats per minute</u> on the stave. ♩ = 112 means there are 112 crotchet beats per minute. This is called a <u>metronome marking</u>.

Moderato (♩ = 112)

These words tell you how to <u>vary</u> the speed. The <u>words</u> go <u>underneath</u> the stave. The <u>pause</u> symbol goes <u>above</u>.

Rubato means '<u>robbed time</u>' — you can <u>slow</u> some bits down and <u>speed</u> others up.

Italian word	Abbreviation	What it means
accelerando	accel.	speeding up
rallentando	rall.	slowing down
ritenuto	rit.	holding back the pace
allargando	allarg.	slowing down, getting a bit broader
rubato	rub.	can be flexible with pace of music
⌢		pause — longer than a whole beat
a tempo		back to the original pace

To give the <u>impression</u> that the tempo has changed (without actually changing it), composers can use <u>augmentation</u> or <u>diminution</u>. Augmentation is where note lengths are <u>increased</u> in a melody (e.g. by <u>doubling</u> the length of every note — so a <u>crotchet</u> becomes a <u>minim</u>). This has the effect of making the music sound <u>slower</u>. Diminution is the <u>opposite</u> — note lengths are <u>shortened</u>, so the music sounds <u>faster</u>.

Mood is the **Overall** Feel of a Piece

The <u>mood</u> of a piece is usually described in Italian too.

Sometimes parts are marked <u>obbligato</u>, which means they are <u>really important</u> and can't be missed out (obbligato means '<u>obligatory</u>').

Italian word	What it means
agitato	agitated
alla marcia	in a march style
amoroso	loving
calmato	calm
dolce	sweetly
energico	energetic

Italian word	What it means
giocoso	playful, humorous
grandioso	grandly
pesante	heavy
risoluto	strong, confident, bold
sospirando	sighing
trionfale	triumphant

To describe the <u>overall mood</u> put the word at the beginning of the piece.

Andante Grandioso (♩ =100)

To describe a <u>change of mood</u> write the word under the stave.

giocoso

Yes, you do have to learn it all — even the Italian bits...

When you're learning this page, start with words that sound a bit like English — they're easy.

Dynamics and Articulation

More ways for composers to tell players <u>exactly</u> how they want their music to sound...

Dynamic Markings Tell You How Loud or Quietly to Play

Music that was all played at the <u>same volume</u> would be pretty dull.
To get a <u>variety</u> of different volumes you can use these symbols:

Symbol	Stands for	What it means
pp	pianissimo	very quiet
p	piano	quiet
mp	mezzopiano	fairly quiet
mf	mezzoforte	fairly loud
f	forte	loud
ff	fortissimo	very loud
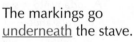	crescendo	getting louder
	diminuendo	getting quieter

You might also see dynamics combined together in other ways.
E.g. ***fp*** means you play a sudden loud bit followed by a sudden quiet bit.

For more extreme dynamics, composers might use ***ppp*** or ***fff*** (or even ***pppp*** or ***ffff***).

The markings go <u>underneath</u> the stave.

Crescendos and diminuendos are sometimes called <u>hairpins</u> when they're written like this.

Articulation Tells You How Much to Separate the Notes

In theory all the notes of a bar should add up to one <u>continuous</u> sound — but actually there are <u>tiny gaps</u> between them. If you <u>exaggerate</u> the gaps you get a <u>staccato</u> effect. If you smooth the gaps out, the notes sound <u>slurred</u>.

STACCATO — All the dotted notes are played slightly short.

SLUR — All the notes below or above the slur are played smoothly, with no breaks between.

<u>Tenuto</u> marks (<u>lines</u> above or below a note) tell you that a note should be held for its <u>full length</u>, or even played slightly <u>longer</u>.

If the articulation goes <u>all the way through</u> a piece, there's an overall instruction at the <u>beginning</u>.

If this piece was marked <u>legato</u> you would have to play smoothly all the way through.

Staccato

Nothing to do with articulated lorries then...

Don't just learn the symbols, learn what they're <u>called</u> too — it'll sound far more impressive if you write about the "dynamics" and "articulation" in your listening exam rather than "loudness and quietness".

More Instructions

Once a composer has told you how <u>fast</u> and how <u>loud</u> to play and how to <u>articulate</u> it, they sometimes put in <u>extra instructions</u>. Things like <u>accents</u>, <u>sforzandos</u> and <u>bends</u> make the music more <u>interesting</u>.

An **Accent Emphasises** a Note

1) An <u>accent</u> is a type of articulation that tells you to <u>emphasise</u> (or <u>stress</u>) a note.

2) On a <u>wind</u> instrument, this is often done by <u>tonguing</u> a note <u>harder</u> than normal.

3) Accents are usually written like this **>** or like this **∧**.

4) If a whole <u>section</u> should be accented, it can be marked '*marcato*' (which means 'marked').

5) A <u>sforzando</u> is a <u>strongly accented</u> note. It's shown by writing **sfz** or **sf** underneath the note.

6) A sforzando is often a <u>sudden</u> accent — e.g. a <u>very loud</u> note in a <u>quiet section</u> of a piece. This makes the music more <u>dramatic</u>.

A **Glissando** is a **Slide** Between Notes

A portamento is similar to a glissando — it's more common in singing and on string instruments.

1) A <u>glissando</u> is a <u>slide</u> from one note to another. Usually you're <u>told</u> which notes to <u>start</u> and <u>finish</u> on.

2) A glissando can be played <u>effectively</u> on a <u>violin</u> (or other <u>string</u> instrument), <u>piano</u>, <u>harp</u>, <u>xylophone</u> (or similar instrument), <u>timpani</u> and <u>trombone</u>. Other instruments can play them too, but they often <u>won't</u> sound as <u>good</u>.

3) On some instruments (e.g. piano, harp and xylophone), <u>every note</u> is played in the glissando. Think about it — if you were to play a glissando on a xylophone, you'd run your beater over every note, so they'd all be played.

4) On other instruments, like the trombone and strings, the notes you hear <u>aren't fixed notes</u> — the glissando covers all the <u>tiny differences</u> in pitch between the two notes. For example, you <u>can't</u> pick out <u>individual notes</u> in a glissando on the trombone.

5) A glissando can be shown by writing *gliss.* underneath the stave, or by putting a <u>line</u> between <u>two notes</u>.

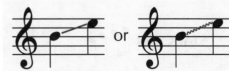

Notes can be **Bent**

1) A <u>bend</u> (or <u>bent note</u>) changes the <u>pitch</u> of the note slightly — it sounds a bit like a <u>wobble</u>.

2) They're often played by starting just <u>above</u> or <u>below</u> the note then <u>bending</u> to it.

3) Bends are often used in <u>jazz music</u>.

4) Bent notes can be played on <u>most</u> instruments — including <u>guitars</u>, <u>trumpets</u>, <u>trombones</u> and <u>harmonicas</u>. <u>Singers</u> can bend notes too.

COMPOSING TIP

Roundabouts, swings, climbing frames, glissandi...

All the things on this page are little <u>extras</u> composers can add to their music to make it more <u>interesting</u> — you could try adding some to your compositions too. I do love a good sforzando.

Warm-up and Exam Questions

Get your brain going with these warm-up questions before tackling the exam question below.

Warm-up Questions

1) Draw a 4-beat note, and write down its full name.

2) Draw a 4-beat rest.

3) Name the following notes and give the time value of each of them.

♩. ♪ ♩.

4) Explain the difference between a tie and a slur.

5) Look at the tempo words below. Write them out in order, fastest first.

Andante   **Largo**   **Presto**   **Moderato**   **Allegro**

Exam Question

Here's another exam-style question for you to try.

Play the following extract **three** times. Leave a short pause between each playing of the extract.

(Track 2)

a) Listen to the rhythm of the opening melody.
    Tick one feature that matches what you hear.

Staccato notes   ☐

Triplets   ☐

Dotted notes   ☐

[1 mark]

Turn over

Exam Question

b) Which word best describes the tempo of this piece of music? Underline your answer.

largo　　　**adagio**　　　**andante**　　　**allegro**

[1 mark]

c) Which word describes the dynamic at the opening? Underline your answer.

pianissimo　　　**piano**　　　**forte**　　　**fortissimo**

[1 mark]

d) Which of the following describes the mood of this extract? Tick the box.

agitato ☐

dolce ☐

energico ☐

pesante ☐

[1 mark]

Revision Summary for Section Two

You'll find a page of questions like this at the end of every section. They're <u>not</u> here just to fill up space — they're here to <u>help you</u> test yourself. The basic idea is, if you can answer all the Revision Summary questions without looking back through the section, you can be pretty sure you've understood and remembered all the important stuff. Look back through the section the first and second time you try the questions (if you must), but by the third time you do the questions, you should be aiming to have all the answers <u>off by heart</u>.

1) Does a clef tell you:
   a) how wide the stave is, b) what instrument it's for, or c) how high or low the notes on it are?

2) Draw a stave with a treble clef at the beginning.

3) Draw a stave with a bass clef at the beginning.

4) Which voices read music from the treble clef?

5) Name two instruments that read music from the bass clef.

6) What's the difference between the symbol for a treble clef and the symbol for the vocal tenor clef?

7) Where does middle C go on a vocal tenor clef?

8) Draw staves showing the C clef in both positions and write the correct name by each one.

9) Draw a sharp sign, a flat sign and a natural sign.

10) What does a sharp do to a note?

11) What does a flat do to a note?

12) Draw each of these signs and explain what you do if you see them by a note:
    a) a double sharp   b) a double flat

13) Draw a treble clef stave and add a key signature with one sharp.

14) What do you call a sharp, flat or natural sign when it's in the music but not in the key signature?

15) One beat in the bar usually feels stronger than the others. Which one?

16) What do you call the two numbers at the start of a piece of music?

17) What does the top number tell you about the beats?

18) What does the bottom number tell you about the beats?

19) When a time signature changes in a piece of music, where's the new one written?

20) What's the difference between simple and compound time?

21) What's the difference between regular and irregular metre?

22) What is meant by a cross-rhythm?

23) Draw the symbol for each of the following notes and write down how many crotchet beats it lasts:
    a) semibreve   b) semiquaver   c) crotchet   d) quaver   e) minim

24) What does a dot immediately after a note or rest do?

25) What's the time value of:
    a) a dotted crotchet   b) a dotted minim   c) a dotted semibreve   d) a double dotted minim?

26) What does a 'tie' do?

27) How much time, in crotchet beats, does a crotchet triplet take up?

28) Where do you put the tempo marking on a stave?

29) Which is slower, *allegro* or *moderato*?

30) Where would you write the word *agitato* on the stave?

31) How does a composer show on the written music that the notes should be played smoothly?

32) How are accents usually indicated in a piece of music?

33) What's a glissando?

Major Scales

There are two main types of scales — <u>major</u> and <u>minor</u>. Once you've got the hang of how scales are put together, you should find keys and chords start to make a lot more sense.

Ordinary Scales have **Eight Notes**

The gap between the bottom and top notes of a scale is called an <u>octave</u>. See p.28.

1) An ordinary major (or minor) scale has <u>8 notes</u>, starting and ending on notes of the <u>same name</u>, e.g. C major goes C, D, E, F, G, A, B, C.

2) Each of the eight notes has a <u>name</u>.

1st note	2nd note	3rd note	4th note	5th note	6th note	7th note	8th note
tonic	supertonic	mediant	subdominant	dominant	submediant	leading note	tonic
I	II	III	IV	V	VI	VII	VIII

3) You can just use the <u>numbers</u> or the <u>Roman numerals</u> to name the notes too.

Major Scales Sound **Bright** and **Cheery**

Whatever note they start on, all major scales sound <u>similar</u>, because they all follow the same <u>pattern</u>. This pattern is a set order of <u>tone</u> and <u>semitone</u> gaps between the notes:

I tone II tone III semitone IV tone V tone VI tone VII semitone VIII

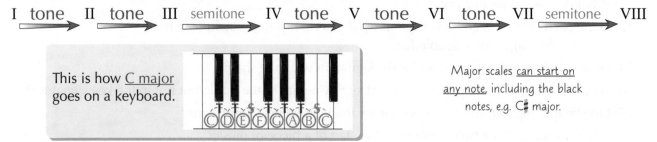

This is how <u>C major</u> goes on a keyboard.

Major scales <u>can start on</u> <u>any note</u>, including the black notes, e.g. C♯ major.

All Major Scales Except C have **One or More Black Notes**

<u>C major</u> is the <u>only</u> major scale with <u>no black notes</u>.

<u>All the others</u> need <u>at least one black note</u> to stick to the 'tone-semitone' pattern.

1) <u>G major scale</u> — you have to change <u>F to F♯</u> to make the notes fit the major scale pattern.

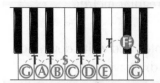

2) <u>F major scale</u> — you have to change <u>B to B♭</u> to make the pattern right.

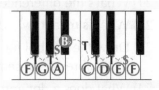

The **Set of Notes** in a **Scale** is Called a **Key**

The key signature goes between the clef and the time signature.

1) The <u>key</u> tells you what <u>sharps and flats</u> there are (if any).

2) Most music sticks to one key. To show what key it's in, all the <u>sharp</u> or <u>flat</u> signs from the scale are written on the beginning of every stave of the piece. This is called the <u>key signature</u>.

3) A key signature can have <u>sharps or flats</u> but <u>NEVER both</u>.

4) If a piece <u>changes</u> key, it's called a <u>modulation</u> — see p.44.

G major's got <u>one</u> <u>sharp</u> note — F♯. You put a <u>sharp</u> symbol on the <u>F line</u>.

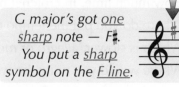

Scales — dull but important...

Try playing some major scales starting on <u>different notes</u>. Even if you don't "<u>know</u>" them, you should be able to <u>work out</u> what the notes are, using the <u>tone-semitone</u> pattern and the <u>sound</u>. Give it a go.

Minor Scales

Minor scales have fixed patterns too. There are <u>three</u> different kinds you need to know.

Minor Scales All Sound a Bit Mournful

Minor scales sound <u>completely different</u> from major scales, because they've got a different tone-semitone pattern. There are <u>three</u> types of minor scale, and all of them sound a bit <u>mournful</u>.

1) The Natural Minor has the Same Notes as the Relative Major

These are easy. Start from the <u>sixth</u> note of any major scale. Carry on up to the same note an octave higher. You're playing a <u>natural minor scale</u>.

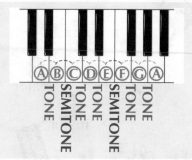

The sixth note of <u>C major</u> is <u>A</u>. If you play from <u>A to A</u> using the notes of C major, you're playing <u>A natural minor</u> (usually just called '<u>A minor</u>').

Pairs of keys like <u>A minor and C major</u> are called "<u>relative</u>" keys.
A minor is the <u>relative minor</u> of C major.
C major is the <u>relative major</u> of A minor.

<u>All the notes</u> in a natural minor are <u>exactly the same</u> as the ones in the <u>relative major</u>. The <u>key signature's</u> exactly the same too.

2) The Harmonic Minor has One Accidental

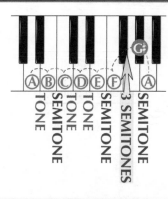

1) The <u>harmonic minor</u> has the same notes as the relative major, except for the <u>seventh note</u>.

2) The <u>seventh</u> note is always raised by <u>one semitone</u>.

3) You use the harmonic minor when you're writing <u>harmonies</u>. That <u>sharpened seventh note</u> makes the harmonies work much better than they would with notes from a natural minor. It's probably because it feels like it wants to move up to the <u>tonic</u>.

3) The Melodic Minor has Two Accidentals

1) The <u>melodic minor</u> is just like a natural minor, using the notes from the relative major scale, <u>except for notes 6 and 7</u>.

2) On the way <u>up</u>, notes <u>6</u> and <u>7</u> are each <u>raised</u> by <u>one semitone</u>.

3) On the way <u>down</u>, the melodic minor goes just like the natural minor.

4) The melodic minor is used for writing <u>melodies</u>. The accidental on note 6 makes tunes sound <u>smoother</u> by avoiding the big jump between notes 6 and 7 in the harmonic minor.

And not forgetting the Morris Minor...

All these scales have a <u>minor third</u> between the first and third notes in the scale — that's why they sound melancholy. You need to learn <u>all three</u> — names, notes and what they're used for.

The Circle of Fifths

The circle of fifths looks complicated but it's very <u>useful</u> once you understand how it works — it tells you <u>all the keys</u>, all the <u>relative keys</u> and their <u>key signatures</u>.

The **Circle of Fifths** Shows **All the Keys**

1) Altogether there are <u>12 major keys</u>. They're all shown on the <u>circle of fifths</u>.

2) Don't expect to fully get it if this is the first time you've seen it. Just <u>have a look</u>, then read on.

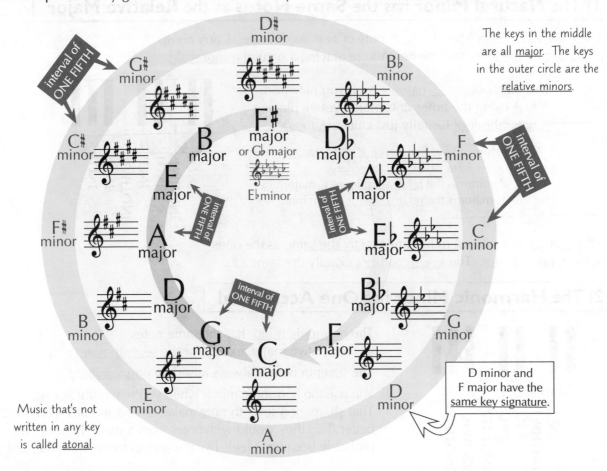

The keys in the middle are all <u>major</u>. The keys in the outer circle are the <u>relative minors</u>.

D minor and F major have the <u>same key signature</u>.

Music that's not written in any key is called <u>atonal</u>.

Each Key **Links** to the Next One

1) The circle <u>starts</u> with <u>C major</u> at the bottom. The next key round is <u>G</u>. G's the <u>fifth note</u> of C major.

2) The fifth note of G major is D, the <u>next</u> key on the circle. This pattern repeats <u>all the way round</u>. That's why the chart's called the circle of fifths.

3) As you go round the circle the number of <u>sharps</u> in the <u>key signature</u> goes up <u>one</u> for each key.

4) When you get to <u>F♯ major</u> at the top there are <u>six sharps</u>. From here, you start writing the key signature in <u>flats</u> — you don't need as many so it's clearer to read.

5) The number of <u>flats</u> keeps going <u>down</u> until you get back to C major, with no sharps and no flats.

The <u>relative minors</u> in the outer circle work just the same way as the major keys — the <u>fifth note</u> of <u>A minor</u> is <u>E</u> and the next minor key's <u>E minor</u>... and so on. Don't forget you can always work out the relative minor by counting up or down to the <u>sixth note</u> of a major scale (see p.25), or the relative major by counting up to the <u>third note</u> of the minor scale.

REVISION TIP

Don't worry if it's making your head spin...

You need to be familiar with key signatures with <u>up to four sharps</u> or <u>four flats</u> (both <u>major</u> and <u>minor</u>). Don't worry too much about the others (but there's no harm in learning them too).

Modes and Other Types of Scale

Most music uses notes from a <u>major</u> or a <u>minor scale</u> — and they're the <u>most important</u> ones to learn, but there are a few <u>more unusual scales</u> and <u>modes</u> that you need to know about too.

Modes Follow **Different Patterns** of **Tones** and **Semitones**

Just like scales, you can start a <u>mode</u> on any note.

1) The most common mode is the one you get by playing a <u>major scale</u> (e.g. C major — just play the white notes on a keyboard from C to C). The pattern is <u>tone-tone-semitone-tone-tone-tone-semitone</u>.

2) Another mode can be formed by playing the notes of the same major scale, starting from the <u>second note</u>, e.g. D to D:

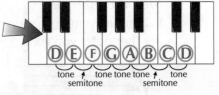

3) Starting on E gives you another mode...

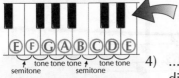

This one is used a lot in flamenco music.

4) ...<u>and so on</u>. Each forms its own semitone / tone pattern and they all have different names. You don't need to know them all though — it's more important that you <u>know what they sound like</u>. (E.g. playing the white notes starting from G forms a mode that sounds quite bluesy.)

5) For some examples of pieces written in modes, have a listen to the folk song <u>Scarborough Fair</u>, the theme tune to <u>The Simpsons</u> and REM's <u>Losing My Religion</u>.

Pentatonic Scales are Used a Lot in **Folk** and **Rock Music**

Pentatonic scales use <u>five</u> notes. They're really easy to compose with, because there are <u>no semitone steps</u> — <u>most combinations</u> of notes sound fine. There are <u>two types</u> of pentatonic scale.

1) The <u>major pentatonic</u> uses notes 1, 2, 3, 5 and 6 of a <u>major</u> scale.

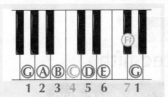

2) The <u>minor pentatonic</u> uses notes 1, 3, 4, 5 and 7 of the <u>natural minor</u> scale.

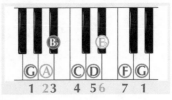

Whole Tone and **Chromatic Scales** Sound **Spooky**

Whole tone scales

Whole tone scales are pretty simple to remember — <u>every step is a tone</u>. From bottom to top there are only <u>six notes</u> in a whole tone scale.

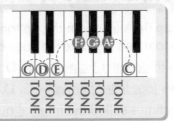

Major and minor scales are known as <u>diatonic scales</u>.

Chromatic scales

Chromatic scales are fairly easy too. On a keyboard you play <u>every white and black note</u> until you get up to an octave above the note you started with. From bottom to top there are <u>12 notes</u>. Basically, <u>every step</u> of a chromatic scale is <u>a semitone</u>.

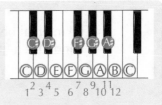

You know the score...

You <u>could</u> get a piece of music in your <u>listening</u> that's written in a <u>mode</u> or one of the other <u>scales</u>. And you could get <u>asked</u> what kind of scale it's written with. So you'd better learn this page.

Intervals

Not the break halfway through a concert, but the <u>distance</u> between two notes.

An **Interval** is the **Gap** Between **Two Notes**

An interval is the <u>musical word</u> for the <u>gap</u> or <u>distance</u> between <u>two notes</u>.

Notes <u>close together</u> make <u>small</u> intervals. Notes <u>further apart</u> make <u>larger</u> intervals.

There are <u>two ways</u> of playing an interval.

Melodic interval
When one note <u>jumps</u> up or down to another note, you get a <u>melodic interval</u>.

ASCENDING interval   DESCENDING interval

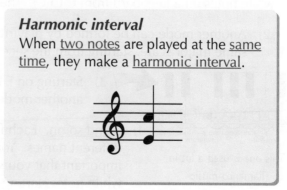

Harmonic interval
When <u>two notes</u> are played at the <u>same time</u>, they make a <u>harmonic interval</u>.

1) You can use the <u>melodic intervals</u> to describe the <u>pattern</u> of a <u>melody</u>.

2) In some melodies, there are only <u>small</u> intervals between the notes — no bigger than a <u>tone</u>.

3) When the notes are <u>close together</u> like this, the melody can be called <u>stepwise</u>, <u>conjunct</u> or <u>scalic</u> (because it moves up and down the notes of a <u>scale</u>).

4) Tunes with <u>big</u> melodic intervals (larger than a tone) are called <u>disjunct</u>.

An Interval has **Two Parts** to its Name...

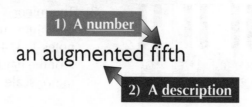

1) A <u>number</u>

an augmented fifth

2) A <u>description</u>

The **Number** Tells You **How Many Notes** the Interval Covers

1) You get the number by counting up the stave from the bottom note to the top note. You <u>include</u> the bottom and top notes in your counting.

2) C to E is a <u>third</u> because it covers <u>three letter names</u> — C, D and E.

3) C to F is a <u>fourth</u> because it covers <u>four letter names</u> — C, D, E and F.

4) The number of an interval is sometimes called the <u>interval quantity</u>.

The "description" bit is covered at the top of the next page...

The interval between G and D is a <u>fifth</u>.

G	A	B	C	D
1	2	3	4	5

An interval covering <u>eight letters</u> (e.g. A to A) is called an <u>octave</u>.

The interval between D and F sharp is a <u>third</u> (you can just <u>ignore</u> the accidentals when counting).

D	E	F♯
1	2	3

Intervals

The **Description** Tells You How the Interval **Sounds**

There are <u>five names</u> for the five main sounds:

| perfect | major | minor | diminished | augmented |

1) To work out the <u>description part</u> of an interval's name, think of the <u>lower note</u> of the interval as the <u>first</u> note of a <u>major scale</u>.

2) If the top note of the interval is part of that major scale it's either <u>perfect</u> or <u>major</u>:

PERFECT **unison** MAJOR **2nd** MAJOR **3rd** PERFECT **4th** PERFECT **5th** MAJOR **6th** MAJOR **7th** PERFECT **octave**

The perfect intervals are the ones that sound 'best' — the notes go together very cleanly.

3) If the top note <u>doesn't</u> belong to the major scale, then it's <u>minor</u>, <u>diminished</u> or <u>augmented</u>.
   If the interval is <u>one semitone LESS</u> than a <u>major interval</u>, then it's <u>minor</u>.
   If the interval is <u>one semitone LESS</u> than a <u>minor</u> or a <u>perfect interval</u>, then it's <u>diminished</u>.
   If the interval is <u>one semitone MORE</u> than a <u>major</u> or a <u>perfect interval</u>, then it's <u>augmented</u>.

Work Out the **Full Name** of an Interval **Step by Step**

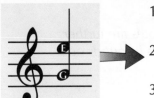

1) **HOW MANY LETTER NAMES DOES IT COVER?**
   <u>Six</u> — G, A, B, C, D and E. So the <u>quantity</u> is a <u>sixth</u>.

2) **ARE THE NOTES FROM THE SAME MAJOR SCALE?**
   The bottom note's G. E <u>is</u> in G major — it's the <u>sixth</u> note.

3) **WHAT TYPE OF INTERVAL IS IT?**
   It's the <u>sixth note</u> of G major, and the sixth note always gives a major interval — so it's a <u>major sixth</u>.

1) **HOW MANY LETTER NAMES DOES IT COVER?**
   <u>Three</u> — C, D and E flat. So the <u>quantity</u> is a <u>third</u>.

2) **ARE THE NOTES FROM THE SAME MAJOR SCALE?**
   No.

3) **WHAT TYPE OF INTERVAL IS IT?**
   A third in the major scale is a <u>major</u> interval.
   This interval's one semitone smaller, so it's a <u>minor third</u>.

The **Tritone** Interval **Sounds Odd**

1) The tritone is an interval of <u>three tones</u>. It's <u>dissonant</u> — i.e. it sounds awkward, some would say terrible. It's used in some twentieth century Western art music.

2) <u>Diminished fifths</u> (e.g. G to D flat) and <u>augmented fourths</u> (e.g. G to C♯) are both <u>tritones</u>.

3) Try playing some, so you know what they <u>sound</u> like.

Take it one step at a time and you'll get there in the end...

The tritone interval used to be called '<u>the Devil's interval</u>' — because it has such an awkward, clashing sound. It's supposed to be unlucky, so use it in your composition at your own risk...

Examples

You need to <u>hear</u> the difference between different types of scales and chords. Tracks 3-9 are practical examples of the theory on pages 24-29. Listen to the tracks as you read the info below.

Examples

Track 3 A <u>major scale</u>, with <u>F♯</u> as the tonic, played over two octaves. *(see p.24)*
Try writing out the notes of the scale on a stave. Remember — TTSTTTS.

Track 4 The <u>three</u> different types of <u>minor scale</u> with <u>D</u> as the tonic. *(see p.25)*
  a) The <u>natural minor</u> scale
  b) The <u>harmonic minor</u>
  c) The <u>melodic minor</u>

Track 5 The two different types of pentatonic scale. *(see p.27)*
  a) <u>Major pentatonic</u> scale starting on <u>C</u>
  b) <u>Minor pentatonic</u> scale starting on <u>A</u>
These are relative scales, and because they're pentatonic all the notes are the same.

Track 6 A <u>whole tone</u> scale. *(see p.27)*
It starts off like the major scale, but the 4th and 5th notes are further apart (<u>harmonically distant</u>) than in a major scale, so it sounds odd.

Track 7 A <u>chromatic</u> scale. *(see p.27)*
This one starts on <u>G</u>, but all <u>chromatic</u> scales use all the notes, so they sound nearly the same.

Track 8 The <u>major</u> and <u>perfect</u> intervals. *(see p.29)*
They're played at the same time so they're <u>harmonic</u>.

Track 9 The <u>minor</u> and <u>diminished intervals</u>. *(see p.29)*
  a) Minor 2nd
  b) Augmented 2nd / minor 3rd
  c) Augmented 4th / diminished 5th
  d) Augmented 5th / minor 6th
  e) Augmented 6th / minor 7th

Practice Questions

Now check you've got the hang of it all with these practice questions.

Practice Questions

Track 10 Listen to the four different types of scale. What are they?

a) ....

b) ....

c) ....

d) ....

You can play these tracks more than once — some of them are quite tricky.

Track 11 What type of scale does this tune use?

....

Track 12 Listen to these harmonic intervals. Write down what each of them is called.

a) .... b) ....

c) .... d) ....

e) .... f) ....

g) .... h) ....

Track 13 Now name these melodic intervals.

a) .... b) ....

c) .... d) ....

e) .... f) ....

g) .... h) ....

Warm-up and Exam Questions

Time for another round of questions...

Warm-up Questions

1) How many notes would you find in a normal scale?

2) What does a key or key signature tell you about the music?

3) What do the scales of C major and A minor have in common?

4) Name the **three** types of minor scales.

5) Which scale uses only notes 1, 2, 3, 5 and 6 from the major scale?

6) Why is a chromatic scale unusual?

7) What type of interval is formed when two notes are played together at the same time?

8) Which is smaller, a minor 7th or a diminished 7th?

Exam Question

This exam-style question includes a couple of questions on intervals to test your knowledge.

Play the extract **three** times. Leave a short pause between each playing.

a) Here are the first three bars.

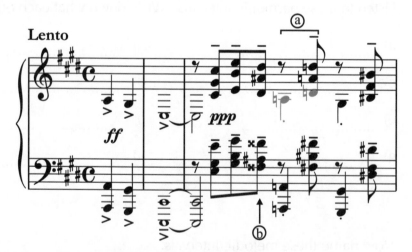

Exam Question

i) How many beats are there in a bar?

....

[1 mark]

ii) What is the interval between the notes highlighted in red at letter **a**?

....

[1 mark]

iii) What is the interval between the two lower notes in the
left-hand chord indicated at letter **b**?

....

[1 mark]

b) What key is this extract in?

....

[1 mark]

c) What does the mark ‾ above a note tell the performer to do?

....

[1 mark]

Chords — The Basics

A <u>chord</u> is two or more notes played together. Chords are great for writing <u>accompaniments</u>.

Only **Some** Instruments **Play Chords**

1) A lot of instruments only play <u>one note at a time</u> — flutes, recorders, trumpets, clarinets, trombones... You can't play a chord with one note, so these instruments <u>don't</u> play chords.

2) You can <u>only</u> play chords on <u>instruments</u> that play <u>more than one</u> note at a time. <u>Keyboards</u> and guitars are both great for playing chords — you can easily play several notes together.

3) Other <u>stringed instruments</u> like violins and cellos can play chords, but not very easily, so chords are only played from time to time.

Don't play chords.

Do play chords.

Some Chords Sound **Great**, Others Sound **Awful**

1) The notes of some chords <u>go together</u> really well — like apple pie and ice-cream.

When you have nice-sounding chords it's called <u>CONCORDANCE</u> or <u>CONSONANCE</u>.

2) Other chords have <u>clashing notes which disagree</u> — more like apple pie and pickled eggs.

When you have horrible-sounding chords it's called <u>DISCORDANCE</u> or <u>DISSONANCE</u>.

The **Best-Sounding** Chords are Called **Triads**

1) You can play <u>any</u> set of notes and make a chord — but most of them sound <u>harsh</u>.

2) An <u>easy, reliable</u> way of getting nice-sounding chords is to play <u>triads</u>.

3) Triads are chords made up of three notes, with <u>set intervals</u> between them.

4) Once you know the intervals, you can easily play <u>dozens</u> of decent chords.

How to make a triad...

1) On a piano, start with any white note — this is called the <u>root note</u>. You <u>build</u> the triad <u>from the root</u>.

2) Count the root as 'first' and the next white note to the <u>right</u>, as 'second'. The <u>third</u> note you reach is the <u>third</u> — the middle note of the triad.

3) Keep counting up and you get to the <u>fifth</u> — the final note of the triad.

4) The intervals between the notes are <u>thirds</u>.

5) If the root note's a <u>B</u>, then you end up with a <u>B triad</u>. If the root note's a <u>C</u>, you end up with a <u>C triad</u>.

6) You can build triads on black notes too, so long as the intervals between notes are <u>thirds</u>.

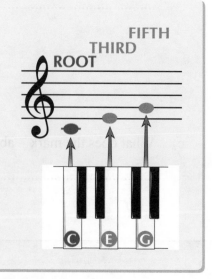

ROOT THIRD FIFTH

C E G

COMPOSING TIP

Good things come in threes...

The next six pages will be useful when it comes to writing your compositions. You'll need to think about which instruments can play chords, and which notes sound nice together.

Triads

There's more than one type of triad...

Triads Use Major and Minor Thirds

1) All triads have an interval of a third between each pair of notes.

2) The intervals can be major or minor thirds.

A major third is four semitones.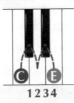

A minor third is three semitones.

3) Different combinations of major and minor thirds give different types of triad:

Major triads

- Major triads have a major third followed by a minor third.
- The major third goes between the root and the third.
- The minor third goes between the third and the fifth.

Minor triads

- Minor triads use a major and a minor third too, but in the opposite order.
- The minor third goes between the root and the third.
- The major third goes between the third and the fifth.

DIMINISHED TRIADS use two minor thirds.
AUGMENTED TRIADS use two major thirds. ⬅ These two kinds aren't nearly as common as major and minor triads.

You Can Add a Note to a Triad to Get a 7th Chord

1) 7th chords are triads with a fourth note added — the seventh note above the root.
2) The interval between the root and the 7th can be a major seventh or a minor seventh — see p.29.

These Symbols Stand for Chords

A special notation is used to represent the various chords. For a triad starting on a C:

C = C major
Caug or **C+** = augmented C chord
C7 = C major with added minor 7th
Cmaj7 = C major with added major 7th

Cm = C minor
Cdim or **C-** or **Co** = diminished C chord
Cm7 = C minor with added minor 7th
Cm maj7 = C minor with added major 7th

For chords other than C, just change the first letter to show the root note.

It's not as hard as it looks and it's VERY useful...

If you play the guitar or play in a band you need to learn these symbols right now. Even if you only ever play classical music they're still worth learning — they're really useful as shorthand.

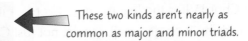

Fitting Chords to a Melody

There are some basic rules about fitting chords to a melody:
No.1: All the notes in the chords have got to be in the <u>same key</u> as the notes in the melody.

The **Melody** and **Chords** Must be in the **Same Key**

1) A melody that's composed in a certain key <u>sticks</u> to that key.

2) The chords used to <u>harmonise with</u> the melody have got to be in the <u>same key</u> or it'll <u>clash</u>.

3) As a <u>general rule</u> each chord in a harmony should <u>include</u> the note it's accompanying, e.g. a <u>C</u> could be accompanied by a <u>C chord</u> (C, E, G), an <u>F chord</u> (F, A, C) or an <u>A minor chord</u> (A, C, E).

There's a Chord for **Every Note** in the **Scale**

You can make dozens of triads using the notes of <u>major</u> and <u>minor</u> scales as the <u>roots</u>. <u>Every note</u> of <u>every chord</u>, not just the root, has to belong to the scale. This is how <u>C major</u> looks if you turn it into chords:

The odd accidental or ornament in a different key is OK — see p.41.

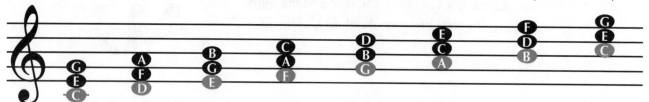

Chord I	Chord II	Chord III	Chord IV	Chord V	Chord VI	Chord VII	Chord I
Tonic	Supertonic	Mediant	Subdominant	Dominant	Submediant	Leading Note	Tonic

1) Chords I, IV and V are <u>major triads</u>. They sound <u>bright and cheery</u>.
    A <u>7th</u> can be added to <u>chord V</u> to give a <u>dominant 7th</u> chord (written V^7).

2) Chords II, III and VI are <u>minor triads</u>. They sound more <u>gloomy</u>.

3) Chord VII is a <u>diminished triad</u>. It sounds <u>different</u> from the major and minor chords. Another name for Chord VII is the <u>leading note chord</u> — it sounds like it should lead on to another chord.

4) Chords built on <u>any</u> major scale, not just C major, follow the <u>same pattern</u>.

5) A <u>series</u> of chords is known as a <u>harmonic progression</u> (also called a <u>chord progression</u> or <u>chord sequence</u>).

6) The <u>speed</u> at which the chords <u>change</u> is called the <u>harmonic rhythm</u>.

The **Primary Chords** are Most **Useful**

1) The three major chords, <u>I</u>, <u>IV</u> and <u>V</u>, are the <u>most important</u> in <u>any</u> key. They're called <u>primary chords</u>. Between them, the primary chords can harmonise with <u>any note</u> in the scale.

2) This is how it works in <u>C major</u>:

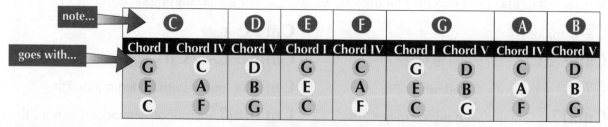

Minor Chords Make Harmony **More Interesting**

1) Primary chords can get a bit <u>boring</u> to listen to after a while — the harmonies are fairly <u>simple</u>.
2) Composers often mix in a few of the other chords — <u>II</u>, <u>III</u>, <u>VI</u> or <u>VII</u> — for a <u>change</u>.
3) Instead of just having endless major chords, you get a mixture of minor and diminished chords too.

Inversions

Inverting triads means changing the order of the notes. It make accompaniments more varied.

Triads with the **Root at the Bottom** are in **Root Position**

These triads are all in root position — the root note is at the bottom.

● = fifth
● = third
● = root

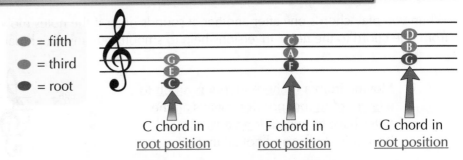

C chord in root position

F chord in root position

G chord in root position

First Inversion Triads have the **Third** at the **Bottom**

These chords are all in first inversion. The root note's moved up an octave, leaving the third at the bottom.

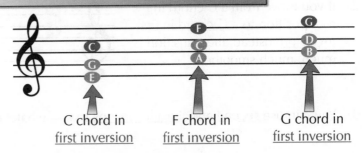

C chord in first inversion

F chord in first inversion

G chord in first inversion

Second Inversion Triads have the **Fifth** at the **Bottom**

Chords can be played in second inversion too.

From the first inversion, the third is raised an octave, leaving the fifth at the bottom.

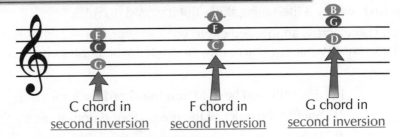

C chord in second inversion

F chord in second inversion

G chord in second inversion

7th Chords Can Go into a **Third Inversion**

1) 7th chords can be played in root position, first inversion or second inversion — just like triads.

2) But there's also a third inversion — where the 7th goes below the standard triad. They have a third inversion because they're four-note chords.

There's a **Symbol** for Each **Inversion**

This means a C chord with E at the bottom.

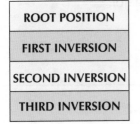
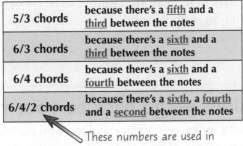
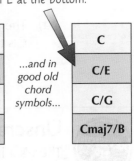

ROOT POSITION	...also known as...	5/3 chords	because there's a fifth and a third between the notes	Ia	C
FIRST INVERSION		6/3 chords	because there's a sixth and a third between the notes	Ib	C/E
SECOND INVERSION		6/4 chords	because there's a sixth and a fourth between the notes	Ic	C/G
THIRD INVERSION		6/4/2 chords	because there's a sixth, a fourth and a second between the notes	Id	Cmaj7/B

...and in Roman numerals...

...and in good old chord symbols...

These numbers are used in figured bass — see page 57.

Inversions

So now you know what inversions <u>are</u>. Now get to grips with what to <u>do</u> with them too...

Inversions are Handy for **Moving Between Chords**

When you play chords one after another, it sounds <u>nicer</u> if the notes move <u>smoothly</u> from one chord to the next. Inversions help to smooth out any rough patches...

1) Moving from a <u>C chord in root position</u> to a <u>G chord in root position</u> means <u>all</u> the notes have to jump a <u>long way</u>. It sounds <u>clumsy</u> and not all that nice.

2) If you move from a C chord in root position to a <u>G chord</u> in <u>first inversion</u> instead, the transition is much, much smoother.

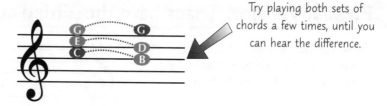

Try playing both sets of chords a few times, until you can hear the difference.

3) You can use <u>second</u> and <u>third inversions</u> too — whatever sounds best.

Unscramble the Inversion to Work Out the **Root Note**

This isn't exactly a life-saving skill. But it's <u>dead useful</u>...

If you come across an inverted chord you can <u>work out</u> which is the <u>root note</u>. Once you know that, and you know what <u>key</u> you're in, you can tell whether it's chord IV, VII, II or whatever.

1) Basically you have to turn the chord back into a <u>root position triad</u>.
2) Shuffle the order of the notes around until there's a <u>third interval</u> between each one.
3) When the notes are arranged in <u>thirds</u>, the root will <u>always</u> be at the <u>bottom</u>.

B to D is a THIRD, but D to G is a FOURTH.
You need to <u>move the G</u> to find the root chord.

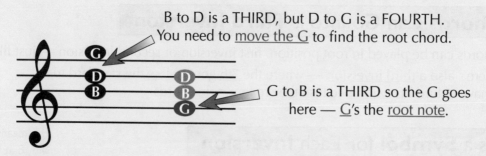

G to B is a THIRD so the G goes here — <u>G</u>'s the <u>root note</u>.

4) There are no sharps or flats in the key signature, so the piece is in C major. G's the fifth note of C major, so this is <u>chord V</u>.

Unscramble inversions — go back to your roots...

There's a lot to take in when it comes to inversions. Don't go racing through this page — go over it one bit at a time, letting all the facts sink in. Playing the chords for yourself will help.

Different Ways of Playing Chords

So far, the chords in this section have all been written as three notes. It sounds dull if you do it all the time. To liven things up there are chord figurations — different ways of playing the chords.

Block Chords are the Most Basic

This is probably the easiest way to play chords. The notes of each chord are played all together and then held until the next chord.

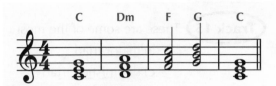

Rhythmic Chords Give You Harmony and Rhythm

1) Rhythmic chords are chords played to a funky rhythm.

2) You play all the notes of each chord at the same time, like you do for block chords.

3) You don't hold the notes though — you play them to a rhythm that repeats in each bar.

4) Rhythm guitar and keyboards often play rhythmic chords.

In Broken and Arpeggiated Chords the Notes are Separate

Accompanying chords don't have to have to be played at all once. You can play the notes separately.

1) Here's one way of doing it — it goes root, fifth, third, root.

2) This pattern was really popular around the time Mozart was alive (last half of the 1700s). It's called Alberti bass after the composer Domenico Alberti — it usually goes root, fifth, third, fifth.

3) The notes of a chord are sometimes played in order (e.g. root, third, fifth, root) going up or coming down. This is called an arpeggio (are-pedge-ee-o).

4) In an arpeggiated chord, you play the notes one at a time, but in quick succession (imagine strumming a harp). On a piano, you hold down each key as you build up the chord. They're usually written with a wiggly line, like this:

5) A walking bass usually moves in crotchets, often either in steps (see p.28) or arpeggios.

6) A drone is a long, held-on note, usually in the bass, that adds harmonic interest.

7) Pedal notes are a bit different — they're repeated notes, again usually in the bass part. However, the harmony on top of a pedal note changes (whereas a drone sets up the harmony for the whole piece).

Think about using an Alberti bass in your composition...

When you get chord symbols over the music you can play the chords any way you like. Try all these ways of playing chords and think about using them in your compositions.

Examples and Practice

Read on for some more examples of the different kinds of chords.

Examples

Track 15 These are some of the most <u>common</u> chords — learn to recognise them.

a) <u>major</u> triad   b) <u>minor</u> triad

c) <u>diminished</u> triad   d) <u>augmented</u> triad

e) <u>major</u> triad with a <u>major</u> 7th   f) <u>major</u> triad with a <u>minor</u> 7th

g) <u>minor</u> triad with a <u>major</u> 7th   h) <u>minor</u> triad with a <u>minor</u> 7th

Track 16 A <u>sequence</u> of chords, showing different <u>inversions</u>:

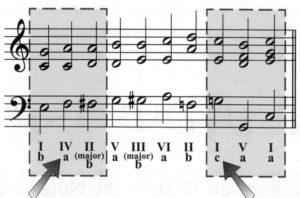

What <u>inversion</u> a chord is depends on which note is on the <u>bottom</u> — it doesn't matter how the other notes of the triad are arranged on top.

In these first <u>three</u> chords, chords in the <u>first inversion</u> lead nicely on to <u>root chords</u> a <u>perfect 4th</u> up. The <u>semitone</u> steps in the bass make these progressions sound smooth and logical.

At the <u>end</u> of the sequence, listen out for the <u>third from last</u> note (<u>second inversion</u> of <u>chord I</u>), which leads into the <u>cadence</u> that ends the phrase (see p.42-43 for more on cadences).

How well do you know your chords... Find out by answering these practice questions.

Practice Questions

Track 17 Describe each of the eight chords on the track, using one of the following words:

major	minor	diminished	augmented

You can play these tracks more than once.

a) ....   b) ....   c) ....

d) ....   e) ....   f) ....

g) ....   h) ....

Track 18 For each of the following you'll hear a root note, and then an inversion. Which inversions are they?

a) ....   b) ....   c) ....

d) ....   e) ....   f) ....

g) ....   h) ....

Use Decorations to Vary the Harmony

If you want to <u>liven things up</u> in a harmony you can add a sprinkle of <u>melodic decoration</u>.

Melodic Decoration **Adds Notes** to the Tune

1) <u>Decorative notes</u> are <u>short notes</u> that move between notes or create <u>fleeting clashes</u> (<u>dissonance</u>) with the accompanying chord. They make things sound <u>less bland</u>.

2) Decoration that belongs to the key of the melody (e.g. B in C major) is called <u>diatonic</u>.

3) Decoration that <u>doesn't</u> belong to the key (e.g. F♯ in C major) is called <u>chromatic</u>.

4) There are <u>four</u> main ways of adding melodic decoration.

1) **Auxiliary** Notes are **Higher** or **Lower** than the Notes **Either Side**

1) An auxiliary note is either a <u>semitone</u> or <u>tone</u> <u>above</u> or <u>below</u> the notes either side.

2) The two notes before and after the auxiliary are always the <u>same pitch</u>, and always belong to the accompanying chord.

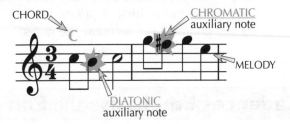

2) **Passing** Notes **Link** the Notes **Before** and **After**

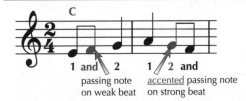

1) A passing note <u>links</u> the notes before and after. They either belong to the same chord or link one chord with another.

2) They're usually put on <u>weak beats</u>. When they <u>are</u> on the strong beat they're called '<u>accented passing notes</u>'.

3) **Appoggiaturas Clash** with the Chord

1) An appoggiatura <u>clashes</u> with the accompanying chord. It's written as a <u>little note</u> tied to the note of the chord, and takes <u>half the value</u> of the note it's tied to.

2) The note <u>before</u> it is usually quite a <u>leap</u> away (jumps between notes of more than a <u>2nd</u> are called <u>leaps</u>).

3) The note after the appoggiatura is always <u>just above</u> or <u>below</u>. It's called the <u>resolution</u>. The <u>resolution</u> has to be from the <u>accompanying chord</u>.

4) Appoggiaturas usually fall on a <u>strong beat</u>, so the resolution note falls on a <u>weaker beat</u>.

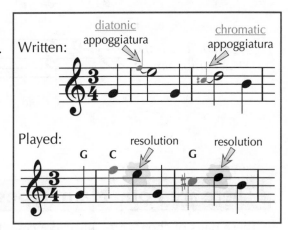

4) **Suspensions Clash** then Go Back to **Harmonising**

A suspension is a series of three notes called the <u>preparation</u>, <u>suspension</u> and <u>resolution</u>.

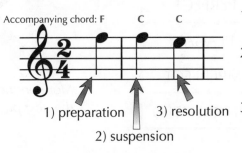

1) The <u>preparation</u> note belongs to the accompanying chord. It's usually on a weak beat.

2) The <u>suspension</u> is the <u>same pitch</u> as the preparation note. It's played at the same time as a <u>chord change</u>. It <u>doesn't go</u> with the new chord, so you get <u>dissonance</u>.

3) The <u>resolution</u> note moves up or down (usually down) from the suspension to a note in the accompanying chord. This <u>resolves</u> the dissonance — everything sounds lovely again.

Phrases and Cadences

Notes in a melody fall into 'phrases' just like the words in a story are made up of sentences.
A cadence is the movement from the second-to-last to the last chord of a phrase — it finishes it off.

A **Phrase** is Like a Musical **'Sentence'**

There should be clear phrases in any melody. A tune without phrases would
sound odd — just like a story with no sentences wouldn't make much sense.

1) Phrases are usually two or four bars long.

2) Phrases are sometimes marked with a curved
line called a phrase mark, that goes above
the stave. Not all music has phrase marks but
the phrases are always there. Don't confuse
phrase marks and slurs. A phrase mark
doesn't change how you play the notes.

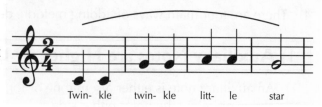

Twin- kle   twin- kle   litt- le   star

Cadences Emphasise the **End of a Phrase**

1) A cadence is the shift between the second-to-last chord and the last chord in a phrase.

2) The effect you get from shifting between the two chords works like a comma or a full stop.
It underlines the end of the phrase and gets you ready for the next one.

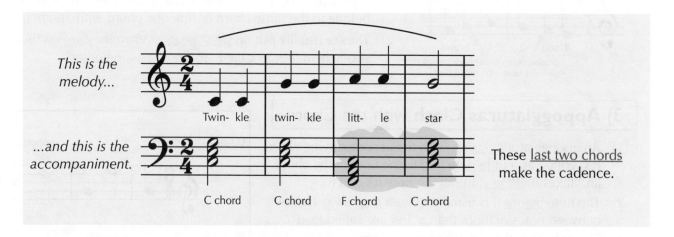

This is the melody...

Twin- kle   twin- kle   litt- le   star

...and this is the accompaniment.

C chord   C chord   F chord   C chord

These last two chords
make the cadence.

There are **Four Main Types** of Cadence

These pairs of chords are only cadences when they come at the end of a phrase.
Anywhere else in a phrase, they're just chords.

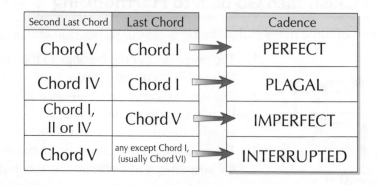

Second Last Chord	Last Chord		Cadence
Chord V	Chord I	→	PERFECT
Chord IV	Chord I	→	PLAGAL
Chord I, II or IV	Chord V	→	IMPERFECT
Chord V	any except Chord I, (usually Chord VI)	→	INTERRUPTED

More on these on the next page...

Cadences

Learning the <u>names</u> of the different cadences is no use unless you also learn what they're <u>for</u>.

Perfect and Plagal Cadences Work Like Full Stops

1) A <u>perfect cadence</u> makes a piece of music feel <u>finished or complete</u>.

2) It goes from <u>Chord V</u> to <u>Chord I</u> — in C major that's a <u>G chord</u> to a <u>C chord</u>.

3) This is how a perfect cadence goes at the <u>end</u> of 'Twinkle, Twinkle, Little Star':

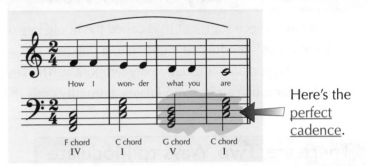

Here's the <u>perfect cadence</u>.

4) A <u>plagal cadence</u> sounds really different from a perfect cadence but it has a <u>similar effect</u> — it makes a piece of music sound finished.

5) A plagal cadence in C major is an <u>F chord</u> (IV) to a <u>C chord</u> (I). Play it and see what it sounds like. The plagal cadence gets used at the <u>end</u> of lots of <u>hymns</u> — it's sometimes called the '<u>Amen</u>' cadence.

Imperfect and Interrupted Cadences are Like Commas

<u>Imperfect</u> and <u>interrupted</u> cadences are used to end <u>phrases</u> but <u>not</u> at the end of a piece. They work like <u>commas</u> — they feel like a <u>resting point</u> but not an ending.

An <u>imperfect cadence</u> most commonly goes from chord <u>I</u>, <u>II</u> or <u>IV</u> to <u>V</u>. Here's one going from <u>chord I</u> to <u>chord V</u> at the end of the <u>third line</u> of 'Twinkle, Twinkle':

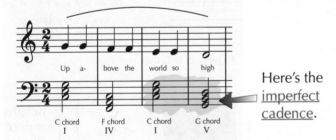

Here's the <u>imperfect cadence</u>.

In an <u>interrupted cadence</u> chord V can go to any chord except I, but it usually goes to chord VI. You expect it to go to chord I — so it sounds "interrupted". In C major an interrupted cadence may go from a <u>G chord</u> (V) to an <u>Am chord</u> (VI).

Some Minor pieces Finish with a Tierce de Picardie

1) If a piece of music is in a <u>minor key</u>, you'd expect it to <u>finish</u> with a <u>minor chord</u>.

2) However, some composers (especially <u>Baroque</u> composers) finish a <u>minor piece</u> with a <u>major chord</u>, by using a <u>major third</u> in the last chord. This is known as a <u>Tierce de Picardie</u> (or <u>Picardy third</u>).

This extract is from <u>Scarlatti's Piano Sonata in G Minor</u> (<u>Cat's Fugue</u>). Even though the piece is in <u>G minor</u>, it finishes with a <u>G major chord</u>.

You need to listen to cadences to understand them...

Cadences probably won't make much sense unless you try playing them. <u>Play</u> the cadences for yourself (or listen to Track 19 — see p.48) until you can <u>hear</u> the differences between them.

Modulation

Most of the notes in a piece of music come from one key — but to vary the melody or harmony you can <u>modulate</u> (change key). It can happen just once, or a few times. It's up to the composer.

The **Starting Key** is Called '**Home**'

1) The key a piece <u>starts out in</u> is called the <u>home key</u> or <u>tonic key</u>.

2) If the music's modulated it goes into a <u>different key</u>.

3) The change of key is usually only <u>temporary</u>. The key <u>goes back</u> to the home key after a while.

4) However much a piece modulates, it usually <u>ends</u> in the home key.

There are **Two** Ways to Modulate

1) Modulation by **Pivot Chord**

1) A pivot chord is a chord that's in the home key <u>and</u> the key the music modulates to.

2) <u>Chord V</u> (G, B, D) in <u>C major</u> is exactly the same as <u>chord I</u> in <u>G major</u> — so it can be used to <u>pivot</u> between C major and G major.

3) Sometimes, the <u>key signature</u> changes to show the new key. More often, <u>accidentals</u> are written in the music where they're needed.

The home key here is <u>C</u>. At the end of the <u>first bar</u> the accompaniment uses the chord <u>G, B, D</u> to pivot into G major:

Pivot chord

F♯ belongs to G major.

This is called a V/I pivot because it uses <u>V</u> from the home key and <u>I</u> from the key it modulates to.

Related keys...

1) It sounds best if you modulate to <u>related keys</u>.

2) The <u>closest</u> keys are (major) keys <u>IV</u> and <u>V</u> and the <u>relative minor</u>.

3) The <u>next closest</u> are the relative minors of keys IV and V.

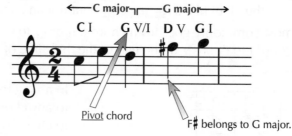

2) **Abrupt** Modulation

1) In abrupt modulation there's <u>no pivot chord</u>, and no other preparation either. It just happens.

2) Often the modulation is between two keys just <u>one semitone apart</u>, e.g. from <u>C major</u> to <u>C♯ major</u>.

3) <u>Pop songs</u> often modulate <u>up</u> one semitone. It creates a <u>sudden</u>, <u>dramatic effect</u> — it's meant to give the music an <u>excited</u>, <u>uplifting</u> feeling.

You can choose related keys but you can't choose your family...

If you see <u>accidentals</u> it often means the music's modulated, but <u>not always</u>. The accidental could also be there because: 1) the music's written in a <u>minor key</u> — harmonic or melodic (see p.25); or 2) the composer fancied a spot of <u>chromatic</u> decoration (see p.41). That's composers for you...

Texture

Here's one last way composers vary the harmony — by changing the <u>texture</u>. Texture's an odd word to use about music — what it means is how the different parts (e.g. chords and melody) are <u>woven together</u>.

Texture is How the parts Fit Together

1) An important part of music is how the <u>different parts</u> are <u>woven together</u>.
   This is known as <u>texture</u> — it describes how the <u>melody</u> and <u>accompaniment</u> parts <u>fit together</u>.

2) <u>Monophonic</u>, <u>homophonic</u> and <u>polyphonic</u> are all different types of texture.

3) Some textures are made up of the <u>same</u> melodic line that's passed round <u>different parts</u>.
   <u>Imitation</u> and <u>canons</u> are good examples of this.

Monophonic Music is the Simplest

1) In <u>monophonic</u> music there's <u>no harmony</u> — just one line of tune (e.g. a <u>solo</u> with <u>no accompaniment</u>).

2) Parts playing in <u>unison</u> or <u>doubling</u> each other (i.e. the same notes at the same time) are also monophonic.

3) Monophonic music has a <u>thin texture</u>.

Polyphonic Music Weaves Tunes Together

1) <u>Polyphonic</u> music gives quite a complex effect because there's <u>more than one tune</u> being played at once.

2) It's sometimes called <u>contrapuntal</u> music.

3) Parts that move in <u>contrary motion</u> (one goes <u>up</u> and another goes <u>down</u>) are polyphonic.

4) <u>Two-part music</u> (with two separate melodic lines) is also polyphonic.

In Homophonic Music, the Parts Move Together

1) If the lines of music move at more or less the <u>same time</u>, it's <u>homophonic</u> music.

2) A <u>melody with accompaniment</u> (the accompaniment is often <u>chordal</u>) is a good example of homophonic music.

3) <u>Parallel motion</u> (when parts move with the <u>same interval</u> between them, e.g. parallel 5ths) is also homophonic.

In Heterophonic Music the Instruments Share the Tune

In heterophonic music there's <u>one tune</u>. <u>All</u> the instruments play it, but with <u>variations</u>, and often at <u>different times</u>.

<u>Polyphonic</u>, <u>homophonic</u>
and <u>heterophonic</u> music all
have quite a <u>thick texture</u>.

You might have to write about texture in the exam...

Make sure you use the proper terms in your exam — you won't get the marks for saying something has a thick or thin texture (you'd have to say polyphonic or monophonic).

Texture

When there's <u>one</u> part, the music's <u>pure</u> and <u>simple</u>, but put <u>more parts in</u> and it's much more <u>complex</u>.

Imitation — Repeat a Phrase With **Slight Changes**

1) In <u>imitation</u> a phrase is repeated with <u>slight changes</u> each time.

2) It works particularly well if one instrument or voice imitates <u>another</u> and then <u>overlaps</u>.

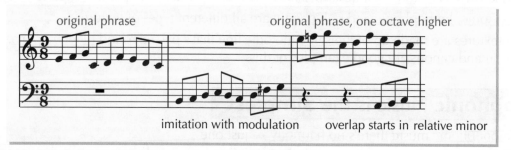

Canon — **Same Melody** Different Parts

1) In a <u>canon</u>, each part plays the <u>same melody</u>, but they come in <u>separately</u> and at <u>regular intervals</u>. The parts <u>overlap</u>.

2) A canon is also known as a <u>round</u>. There are some really well-known rounds, e.g. '<u>London's Burning</u>'.

3) Canons are an example of <u>contrapuntal</u> (or <u>polyphonic</u>) music (see previous page).

4) Composers from the <u>Baroque</u> period (1600-1750) like <u>Bach</u> and <u>Vivaldi</u> used lots of canons.

This extract comes from 'Spring' from Vivaldi's Four Seasons. The solo violin and first violin often play in canon.

Another common Baroque texture is the <u>continuo</u> (or <u>basso continuo</u>) — see p.57.

Looping and Layering are Modern Techniques

1) In the <u>1960s</u> and <u>70s</u>, composers like <u>Steve Reich</u> started developing <u>new techniques</u> in their music.

2) They took recordings of sections of <u>music</u>, <u>words</u>, <u>rhythms</u> and <u>other sounds</u> and <u>repeated</u> them over and over again. These are called <u>loops</u>.

3) The loops were often created by <u>cutting</u> pieces of <u>tape</u> and <u>sticking</u> the ends together so they could be played over and over again — this is <u>looping</u>.

4) If there are lots of <u>different loops</u> being played at the <u>same time</u> it's called <u>layering</u>.

A layer of fruit, a layer of sponge, a layer of custard...

There are a few more words on this page that'll be useful if you need to write about musical texture in the listening exam — imitation, canon, looped and layered. Make sure you know what they mean.

Texture

Composers use different textures to vary their music. They can change the number of instruments and whether they play the same notes or in harmony. They can also split tunes between different instruments.

More Than One Part Can Play the Same Melody

1) If there's just one part playing with no accompaniment, there's just a single melody line.

2) If there's more than one instrument playing the same melody at the same pitch, they're playing in unison.

3) If there's more than one instrument playing the same notes but in different ranges, they're playing in octaves.

All of these are examples of monophonic textures.

Some Instruments Play Accompanying Parts

1) The instruments that aren't playing the melody play the accompaniment. Different types of accompaniment give different textures.

2) If the accompaniment is playing chords underneath the melody (or the same rhythm of the melody but different notes), the texture is homophonic. It sounds richer than a single melody line, unison or octaves.

3) If there are two choirs singing at different times, the music is antiphonal. The two choirs will often sing alternate phrases — like question and answer or call and response. A lot of early religious vocal music was antiphonal. You can also get the same effect with two groups of instruments.

Group 1
Group 2

4) If there's more than one part playing different melodies at the same time, the music is contrapuntal (or polyphonic). Contrapuntal parts fit together harmonically.

The examples on this page use the melody from Handel's 'Water Music'.

REVISION TIP

Would you care to accompany me to the cinema...

There are quite a few tricky textures to learn on this page. Listen to the different types, and try and recognise what they sound like so that you can describe them if they come up in the exam.

Examples

Track 19 should help you get a better idea about cadences, and Track 20 gives you some different examples of modulation. Listen to them lots of times until you can recognise them straight away.

Examples

Track 19 You'll hear this bar played **four** times, followed by a different cadence each time.

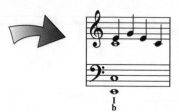

a) The perfect cadence sounds totally complete — perfect, in fact. You can't imagine it moving on to any other chord.

b) The plagal cadence is sometimes called the "amen cadence" — it sounds peaceful and reassuring.

c) The imperfect cadence is the opposite of the perfect cadence. Instead of bringing things to a close, it seems to open up loads of possibilities.

d) The interrupted cadence starts off like a perfect cadence but ends with a more open, melancholy feel.

Track 20 Listen to these **three** short extracts. Each one is a different example of a modulation from one key to another. In each extract the pattern goes like this:

Note 1 Original key

Note 2 Original key

Note 3 Pivot chord (in the original key and the new key)

Note 4 New key

Practice Questions

Practise your hard-won knowledge of chords, modulation and texture with the questions on this page and the next. Listen to each track a few times to make sure you've heard it properly.

Practice Questions

Track 21 This question is about identifying cadences.
You will hear eight phrases, a)-h), all starting like this:

Write down whether the final cadence is perfect, plagal, imperfect or interrupted.

a) .... b) .... c) ....

d) .... e) .... f) ....

g) .... h) ....

Track 22 *For each of the following tracks, fill in the missing notes in the melody, then answer the questions.*

a)

b) The chord in the fourth bar has an A in the bass.
What inversion of chord I is this?

....

c) What type of cadence does the passage end with?

....

Track 23 a)

b) In this passage, the harmony tends to move in time with the melody.
What is the name of this type of musical texture?

....

c) What type of cadence does the passage end with?

....

d) Which note is sustained in the bass in the second-to-last bar?

....

50

Practice Questions

 a)

b) In the first chord in bar 2, the left hand plays the major of chord II. Which note in this chord is not in the scale of the home key?

....

c) What type of cadence does the passage end with?

....

 a)

b) Circle each auxiliary note in the passage, and say whether each is diatonic or chromatic.

c) Which one of the following best describes the chord in bar 4? Ring your answer.

1st inversion   **harmonic**   **relative minor**   **suspension**

 a)

b) What key does this passage start in?

....

c) What key does it finish in?

....

d) The B-flat chord at the start of bar 3 comes before the dominant chord of the new key. Give the name of a chord in this position in a modulation.

....

e) Fill in the blanks in the sentence below with the appropriate Roman numerals:

The B-flat chord is chord .... in the home key

and chord .... in the final key.

Warm-up and Exam Questions

Warm-up Questions

1) Name **two** instruments that are frequently used to play chords.

2) Which **three** chords in a major key produce major triads?

3) If the *root* of a chord is on the top, and the *third* of the chord is on the bottom, which inversion is the chord in?

4) Name **three** different ways of playing chords.

5) What do you call a melodic decoration that belongs to the same key as the main melody?

6) List **three** ways melodies can be decorated to vary the harmony within a piece of music.

7) At what point in a piece of music would you expect to find an imperfect or interrupted cadence?

8) What's another name for the texture known as polyphonic?

Exam Question

Now practise your exam technique with the question below and over the page.

Track 27

Play the extract **four times** then answer the questions on the next page.

Leave a short pause for writing time before each playing.

Here is the complete score for the extract:

Exam Question

a)   What instrument is playing this piece?

....
                                                                                                                    [1 mark]

b)   How would you describe the way the left hand is playing at **1**?

....
                                                                                                                    [1 mark]

c)   Which of the following best describes the cadence at **2**?
     Circle your choice from the options below.

                perfect   **plagal**   **imperfect**
                                                                                                                    [1 mark]

d)   Which key is this extract in?

....
                                                                                                                    [1 mark]

e)   Look at the key of the piece. How would you explain the sharpened note at **3**?

....
                                                                                                                    [1 mark]

f)   What term is used to describe the dots above the notes at **4**?

....
                                                                                                                    [1 mark]

g)   Which of these options best describes the texture of this music?
     Circle your choice.

           monophonic   **homophonic**   **heterophonic**
                                                                                                                    [1 mark]

Revision Summary for Section Three

There's a lot to remember here: four types of triad, four types of triad inversion, cadences, different ways of using decoration with chords, modulation, the something-phonic words... It's too much to tackle all in one go. Test yourself a page at a time and make sure you really know it. You'll know you've done it properly when you can answer all these questions <u>without</u> looking back.

1) How many notes are there in a major scale? How many notes are there in a minor scale?

2) Write out the names of the notes of a scale in words, numbers and Roman numerals.

3) Write down the tone-semitone pattern for a major scale.

4) Which major scale only uses the white notes on the keyboard?

5) What does a key signature tell you?

6) How do you find the 'relative minor' of a major scale?

7) D major has two sharps — F and C. What's the key signature of the relative minor?

8) Write out A minor in each of the three types of minor scale and label the tone and semitone gaps.

9) How many major scales are there altogether?

10) How many minor scales are there altogether?

11) Write down all the major scales in order around the circle of fifths, starting with C major.

12) Write out two common modes.

13) What's a pentatonic scale? What types of music often use pentatonic scales?

14) What are the notes in a G major pentatonic scale?

15) What's a chromatic scale? How many notes are there in a chromatic scale?

16) What's a whole tone scale?

17) What's the difference between a melodic and a harmonic interval?

18) Give the name and number of each of these intervals: a) A to C   b) B to F   c) C to B   d) D to A

19) What's a tritone?

20) What do you call chords with: a) clashing notes   b) notes that sound good together?

21) What are the two most common types of triad? Describe how you make each one.

22) What makes a 7th chord different from a triad?

23) Write down the letter symbols for these chords:
   a) G major   b) A minor   c) A minor with a major 7th   d) D diminished triad

24) Draw the scale of G major on a stave, then build a triad on each note. *(Don't forget the F sharps.)*

25) Which three chords of any major or minor scale are known as the 'primary' chords?

26) Write out the notes of the three primary chords in C major, G major and D major.

27) Where do the root, third and fifth go in: a) a first inversion chord   b) a second inversion chord?

28) Are these chords in root position, first inversion, second inversion or third inversion?
   a) 6/4   b) C/E   c) IVa   d) 6/4/2

29) Name and describe four different chord figurations.

30) What's the difference between a 'diatonic' decoration and a 'chromatic' decoration?

31) Explain the following terms: a) auxiliary note   b) passing note   c) appoggiatura

32) What is a musical phrase and what job does a cadence do in a phrase?

33) How many chords make up a cadence?

34) Write down the four different types of cadence and which chords you can use to make each one.

35) What do you call it when a piece in a minor key ends on a major chord?

36) What do people mean when they talk about the 'texture' of music?

37) Explain the difference between monophonic music, homophonic music and polyphonic music.

Common Melodic Devices

Melodic devices are methods that composers use to construct melodies.
You need a few good technical words to describe them — like conjunct, disjunct, triadic and scalic.

Melodies can be Conjunct or Disjunct

1) Conjunct (or stepwise) melodies move mainly by step — notes that are a tone or a semitone apart.

2) The melody doesn't jump around, so it sounds quite smooth.
   This example shows a conjunct melody:

This extract's from 'The Silver Swan' by Orlando Gibbons.

3) Disjunct melodies move using a lot of jumps — notes that are more than a major 2nd (a tone) apart.

4) The melody sounds quite spiky as it jumps around a lot.

5) Disjunct melodies are harder to sing or play than conjunct ones.
   This example shows a disjunct melody:

This one's from 'Nessun Dorma' by Puccini.

6) The distance between the lowest and highest notes in any melody is called the range (or compass).

Triadic Melodies Use the Notes of a Triad

1) Triads are chords made up of two intervals of a third on top of each other — so triadic melodies usually move between the notes of a triad. (There's more on triads on page 35.)

2) For example, a C major triad is made up of the notes C, E and G. There's a major third between C and E, a minor third between E and G and a perfect fifth between C and G. There's more on intervals on pages 28-29.

3) This example shows a triadic melody:

This extract is from the first movement of Haydn's Trumpet Concerto.

Scalic Melodies Use the Notes of a Scale

1) A scalic melody moves up and down using the notes of a scale.

2) Scalic melodies are similar to conjunct melodies, but they can only move to the next note in the scale. Conjunct melodies can have a few little jumps in them.

3) Like conjunct melodies, scalic melodies sound quite smooth. Here's an example of a scalic melody (it's also from the first movement of Haydn's Trumpet Concerto):

Some melodies contain all of these melodic devices...

These different types of melody are pretty easy to spot if you have the music in front of you, but it's a bit harder if you're listening to them. Listen out for them in all types of music and practise identifying them.

Common Melodic Devices

Call and response is used a lot in blues, rock and pop, as well as African and Indian music — so it's important that you know what it is. It's used in both instrumental and vocal music.

Call and Response is Like a Musical Conversation

1) Call and response is a bit like question and answer. It takes place either between two groups of musicians, or between a leader and the rest of the group.

2) One group (or the leader) plays or sings a short phrase. This is the call. It's then answered by the other group. This is the response.

3) The call ends in a way that makes you feel a response is coming — e.g. it might finish with an imperfect cadence (see page 43).

4) Call and response is very popular in pop and blues music. Often the lead singer will sing the call and the backing singers will sing the response.

In a 12-bar blues structure (see p.111), the usual pattern of a call and response would be A, A1, B:

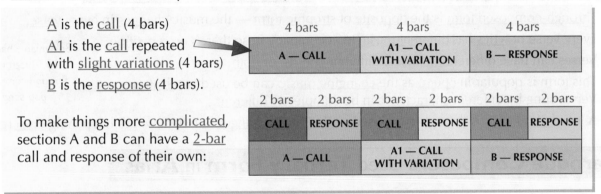

A is the call (4 bars)

A1 is the call repeated with slight variations (4 bars)

B is the response (4 bars).

To make things more complicated, sections A and B can have a 2-bar call and response of their own:

Indian and African Music Use Call and Response

1) In Indian music, call and response is usually used in instrumental music. One musician will play a phrase and it'll either be repeated or improvised upon by another musician.

2) African music uses call and response in religious ceremonies and community events. The leader will sing first and the congregation will respond.

3) Call and response is also used in African drumming music (see p.136-137). The master drummer plays a call and the rest of the drummers play an answering phrase.

Some Melodies Form an Arch Shape

1) If a melody finishes in the same way it started, then the tune has an arch shape.

2) The simplest example of this is ABA — where the first section is the same as the last section of the piece. This is extended in some pieces to ABCBA, or even ABCDCBA.

3) This gives a symmetrical melody because the sections are mirrored. It makes the whole piece feel more balanced.

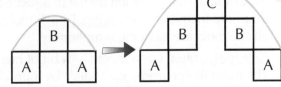

Call and response is used in a lot of music...

... so make sure you can spot it if it comes up in the listening exam — remember to listen out for it in both instrumental and vocal music. Keep your ears pricked for arch-shaped melodies too.

Section Four — Structure and Form

Common Forms

Form or structure is the way a piece of music is organised as a whole. Strophic form, through-composed form and da capo arias are all song structures. Cyclic form is found in large works like symphonies.

In **Strophic Form** Each **Verse** has the **Same Tune**

1) In strophic form, the same section of music is repeated over and over again with virtually no changes.

2) Strophic form is used in Classical, folk, blues and pop music.

3) In strophic songs, the music for each verse is the same, but the lyrics change in every verse. Hymns are a good example of this.

4) Strophic form can be thought of like this: A, A1, A2, A3, etc. — the same section is repeated but with a small change (the lyrics).

5) The first part of Led Zeppelin's 'Stairway to Heaven' is in strophic form.

In **Through-Composed Form** Each **Verse** is **Different**

1) Through-composed form is the opposite of strophic form — the music changes in every verse.

2) Every verse of lyrics has different music to accompany it, so there's no repetition.

3) Verses can have different melodies, different chords, or both.

4) This form is popular in opera, as the changing music can be used to tell stories. Verses sung by different characters can be completely different.

5) A lot of film music is through-composed — the music changes to reflect what's happening on-screen.

'Bohemian Rhapsody' by Queen is a through-composed pop song.

Baroque Composers Used **Ternary Form** in **Arias**

1) An aria is a solo in an opera or oratorio (see p.102).

2) Arias from the Baroque period (1600-1750) are often in ternary form (see p.81). Arias like this are called 'da capo arias'. Handel wrote lots of these.

After repeating Section A and Section B you come to the instruction da capo al fine. It means "go back to the beginning and play to where it says fine". The fine is at the end of Section A. That's where the piece finishes.

Works in **Cyclic Form** Have a **Common Theme**

1) Pieces in cyclic form have common themes in all the movements. These themes link the movements together.

2) Big works like sonatas, symphonies and concertos are sometimes in cyclic form.

3) The linking themes vary in different ways, e.g. they might be played on different instruments, played faster or slower, or played in a different key in different movements. You'll still be able to recognise them though.

4) An example of a common theme in a piece in cyclic form is the four-note theme of Beethoven's Fifth Symphony. It appears in all the movements of the symphony.

5) Film music often has a theme — a bit of melody that keeps popping up throughout the film. The main theme from 'Star Wars®' by John Williams (see p.128-129) is really easy to recognise.

Don't mind me — I'm just passing through...

Make sure you're completely sorted with the definitions and proper names of all these forms.
Have a listen to the suggested pieces, and check you can spot the features of the forms they're written in.

Common Forms

Continuo and ground bass are both types of bass part. A cadenza is played by a soloist.

A **Continuo** is a **Bass Part**

1) A continuo (or basso continuo) is a continuous bass part. Most music written in the Baroque period has a continuo that the harmony of the whole piece is based on. There are continuos in the set pieces 'Brandenburg Concerto No.5' by J. S. Bach (p.85-86) and 'Music for a While' by Purcell (p.106-107).

2) The continuo can be played by more than one instrument, but at least one of the continuo group must be able to play chords (e.g. a harpsichord, organ, lute, harp, etc.). A cello, double bass or bassoon could also be used. The most common combination was a harpsichord and a cello.

3) Continuo parts were usually written using a type of notation called figured bass. Only the bass notes were written on the stave, but numbers underneath the notes told the performers which chords to play. The continuo players would then improvise using the notes of the chord.

4) If there weren't any numbers written, the chord would be a normal triad (the root, the third and the fifth). A 4 meant play a fourth instead of the third, and a 6 meant play a sixth instead of the fifth. A 7 meant that a 7th should be added to the chord.

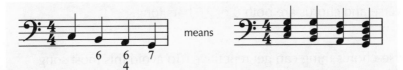
means

Some versions of Handel's Water Music still have the continuo written in figured bass.

5) The improvisation is called a realization — the performer would 'realize' a continuo part.

Ground Bass Pieces Have **Repetition AND Variety**

1) A ground bass is a repeated bass part that's usually four or eight bars long. It can be played by the left hand on a harpsichord or piano, or by the cello and double bass in a chamber orchestra. A ground bass is a type of ostinato — a short pattern of notes repeated throughout a piece of music.

2) The tune is played over the ground bass part. First you hear the main tune, then a load of variations. The variations are played as one continuous piece — there are no gaps between them.

3) The ground bass part can be varied too. You change the starting note but keep the pattern the same.

First time round, the ground bass tune starts on C.

Later on you get the same tune starting on G.

4) The ground bass piece gets more and more complex as it goes on. It can be developed by adding extra, decorative notes to the melody, using more advanced harmonies and adding more instruments to give a richer texture.

A **Cadenza** is Where a **Soloist** can **Show Off**

1) A cadenza is a bit of music that's played by a soloist, usually in the middle of a concerto (see p.90).

2) Almost all concertos have a cadenza — it allows the soloist to show off their technique.

3) Cadenzas started out as improvisations on the main themes of a piece, but now most of them are written out by the composer. However, different musicians will interpret the cadenza in their own way.

Right, that's this page done — better continuo onto the next one...

Listen to a couple of different musicians' performances of Haydn's Trumpet Concerto in E♭ major — the cadenzas will sound different in each one, even though the soloists are playing the same notes.

Popular Song Forms

It's not just <u>Classical</u> music that follows set <u>structures</u> — <u>pop songs</u> do as well.

Pop Songs Usually Have an Intro

Pop tunes almost always start with an <u>intro</u>. It does <u>two jobs</u>:

- It often uses the best bit from the rest of the song to <u>set the mood</u>.
- It grabs people's <u>attention</u> and makes them <u>sit up and listen</u>.

Most Pop Songs Have a Verse-Chorus Structure

<u>After</u> the intro, the structure of most pop songs goes <u>verse-chorus-verse-chorus</u>.

- All the verses usually have the <u>same tune</u>, but the <u>lyrics change</u> for each verse.
- The chorus has a <u>different tune</u> from the verses, usually quite a catchy one. The lyrics and tune of the chorus <u>don't change</u>.
- In a lot of songs the verse and chorus are both <u>8 or 16 bars long</u>.

'Killer Queen' by Queen (see p.114-115) has a verse-chorus structure.

The old verse-chorus thing can get repetitive. To avoid this most songs have a <u>middle 8</u>, or <u>bridge</u>, that sounds different. It's an <u>8-bar section</u> in the <u>middle</u> of the song with <u>new chords</u>, <u>new lyrics</u> and a whole <u>new feel</u>.

The song ends with a <u>coda</u> or <u>outro</u> that's <u>different</u> to the verse and the chorus. You can use the coda for a <u>big finish</u> or to <u>fade out gradually</u>.

Pop Songs Can Have Other Structures Too

For example:

CALL AND RESPONSE

This has <u>two bits</u> to it. <u>Part 1</u> is the call — it asks a musical <u>question</u>. <u>Part 2</u>, the response, responds with an <u>answer</u> (p.55).

RIFF

A <u>riff</u> is a <u>short section</u> of music that's <u>repeated</u> over and over again (a bit like an <u>ostinato</u> — see p.83). Riffs can be used to build up a <u>whole song</u>. <u>Each part</u>, e.g. the drums or bass guitar, has its own riff. All the riffs <u>fit together</u> to make one section of the music. They often <u>change</u> for the <u>chorus</u>.

'Take a Bow' by Rihanna is an R&B ballad.

BALLADS

These are songs that tell <u>stories</u>. Each verse usually has the <u>same rhythm</u> and <u>same tune</u>.

32-BAR SONG FORM

This breaks down into <u>four 8-bar sections</u>. Sections 1, 2 and 4 all have the <u>same melody</u>, but may have different lyrics. Section 3 has a <u>contrasting melody</u>, making an AABA structure. The 32 bars may be repeated. The song 'Somewhere Over the Rainbow' from the film 'The Wizard of Oz' has this form.

Verse — chorus — verse — chorus — tea break — chorus...

Songs from <u>musicals</u> follow these structures too. Have a listen to '<u>Any Dream Will Do</u>' from '<u>Joseph and the Amazing Technicolour Dreamcoat</u>', '<u>Mama, I'm a Big Girl Now</u>' from '<u>Hairspray</u>' and the set piece '<u>Defying Gravity</u>' from '<u>Wicked</u>' (see p.122-123), and look for the structures.

Warm-up and Exam Questions

Warm-up Questions

1) Describe each of the following melody structures:

   Conjunct   **Disjunct**   **Triadic**   **Scalic**

2) What is through-composed form?

3) What is a ground bass, and what instruments often play these parts?

Exam Question

If there are bits you get stuck on in this question, reread the last few pages, then try again.

Play the extract **four** times, leaving a short pause between each playing.

Track 28

a) i) The key signature of the extract is shown below.
        What key is the extract in?

....

[1 mark]

   ii) What is the interval between the notes shown on the right?
       Circle your answer.

   Major third   **Minor third**   **Diminished fourth**

[1 mark]

b) At the very beginning of the extract, the singer's lines are answered by
    a group of instruments. What is this back-and-forth movement called?

....

[1 mark]

c) Which of these examples is the music that these answering instruments play?
    Tick the box next to your choice.

A:

B:

[1 mark]

Exam Question

Play the extract **four** times, leaving a short pause between each playing.

Track 29

a) What musical period was this piece composed in?

....

[1 mark]

b) Name two instruments that play in the extract.

....

....

[2 marks]

c) The melody at the start of the extract is shown below.

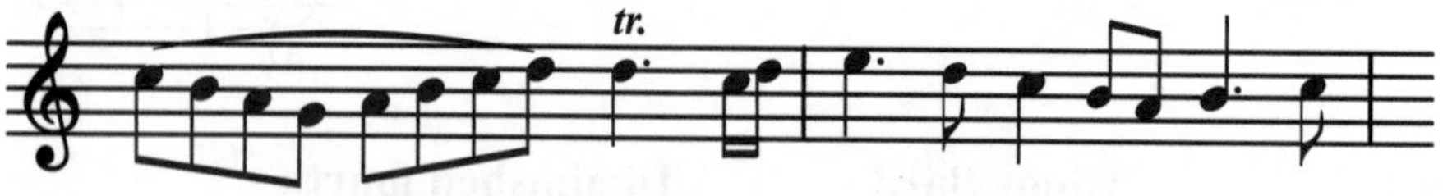

i) Fill in the missing notes in bars 3 and 4.
The rhythm is given above the stave.

[7 marks]

ii) Which word best describes the melodic style in this excerpt?
Circle your choice from the options below.

        Conjunct   **Disjunct**   **Triadic**

[1 mark]

d) What type of bass part is used in this piece?

....

[1 mark]

e) Give one instrument that plays the bass part.

....

[1 mark]

Revision Summary for Section Four

You need to know a lot more about melodies and structures than being able to whistle a few tunes — you'll need to be familiar with all the terms used in this section so you can use them when you need to describe melodies and musical structures in the exam. If you're not sure about any, go back and have another look over the section. And then to really cement this knowledge into your head, go through these questions until you can answer them without looking back.

1) Explain what is meant by each of the following words that are used to describe melodies:
    a) conjunct,
    b) disjunct,
    c) triadic,
    d) scalic.
2) What is call and response?
3) Name two types of music that use call and response.
4) Explain what is meant by an arch-shaped melody.
5) What's the difference between strophic and through-composed form?
6) Give an example of a type of music that's often written in through-composed form, and explain why this form is used.
7) What's a da capo aria?
8) What is cyclic form?
9) What is basso continuo?
10) Explain how figured bass works.
11) Describe the structure of a ground bass piece.
12) What's a cadenza?
13) Why do pop songs have an introduction?
14) Describe verse-chorus structure.
15) What is a bridge?
16) What is a riff?
17) What is the structure of a song in 32-bar form?
18) Name two structures (other than 32-bar form) often used in pop songs.

Brass Instruments

You probably know a lot about <u>your</u> instrument. It's also a good idea to know about the instruments other people play so you can understand what they're up to. <u>Brass</u> first.

Brass Instruments are All Made of Metal

trumpet

French horn

1) Brass instruments include <u>horns</u>, <u>trumpets</u>, <u>cornets</u>, <u>trombones</u> and <u>tubas</u>.

2) They're all basically a length of <u>hollow metal tubing</u> with a <u>mouthpiece</u> (the bit you blow into) at one end and a <u>funnel shape</u> (the <u>bell</u>) at the other.

3) The different <u>shapes</u> and <u>sizes</u> of these parts gives each brass instrument a different tone and character.

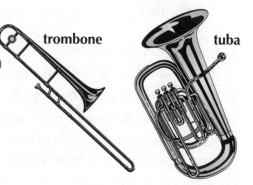
trombone   tuba

4) Brass instruments often play <u>fanfares</u> (short musical <u>flourishes</u>) in orchestral pieces. They're most commonly played on the <u>trumpet</u>, and can be accompanied by <u>percussion</u>. A fanfare might also be played as part of a <u>ceremony</u>.

You Get a Noise by 'Buzzing' Your Lips

1) To <u>make a sound</u> on a brass instrument, you have to make the air <u>vibrate</u> down the tube.

2) You do it by '<u>buzzing</u>' your lips into the <u>mouthpiece</u>. You <u>squeeze</u> your lips together, then <u>blow</u> through a tiny gap so you get a <u>buzzing noise</u>.

3) You have to squeeze your lips together <u>tighter</u> to get <u>higher notes</u>.

4) Notes can be <u>slurred</u> (played together <u>smoothly</u>) or <u>tongued</u> (you use your tongue to <u>separate</u> the notes).

Brass Instruments Use Slides and Valves to Change Pitch

1) Squeezing your lips only gets a <u>limited range</u> of notes. To get a decent range, brass instruments use <u>slides</u> (like on a trombone) or <u>valves</u> (like on a trumpet).

2) The <u>slide</u> on a trombone is the <u>U-shaped tube</u> that moves in and out of the main tube. Moving it <u>out</u> makes the tube <u>longer</u> so you get a <u>lower</u> note. Moving it in makes the tube <u>shorter</u> so you get a <u>higher</u> note.

3) <u>Horns</u>, <u>trumpets</u> and <u>cornets</u> use three buttons connected to <u>valves</u>. The valves <u>open</u> and <u>close</u> different sections of the tube to make it <u>longer</u> or <u>shorter</u>. Pressing down the buttons in <u>different combinations</u> gives you all the notes you need.

Brass Players use Mutes to Change the Tone

1) A <u>mute</u> is a kind of <u>bung</u> that's put in the <u>bell</u> of a brass instrument. It's used to make the instrument play more <u>quietly</u> and change the <u>tone</u>. You wouldn't usually use one all the way through a piece — just for a <u>short section</u>.

2) <u>Different shapes</u> and <u>sizes</u> of mute change the tone in different ways, e.g. the <u>wah-wah</u> mute gives the instrument a wah-wah sound.

EXAM TIP

Brass instruments aren't always made of brass...

If you get brass in a listening test and need to say what instrument it is, remember that bigger instruments generally play lower notes and smaller instruments usually play higher notes.

Woodwind Instruments

Some people get woodwind and brass muddled up. If you're one of them, <u>learn the difference</u>.

Woodwind Instruments Used to be **Made of Wood**

<u>Woodwind</u> instruments got their name because they all use <u>air</u> — wind — to make a sound and once upon a time were all made of <u>wood</u>. Nowadays some are still made of <u>wood</u>. Others are made of <u>plastic</u> or <u>metal</u>. These are the main ones:

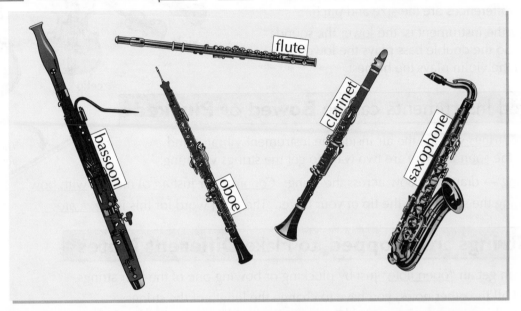

Woodwind Instruments **Make Sound** in **Different Ways**

To get a <u>sound</u> from a <u>wind</u> instrument, you have to make the <u>air</u> in its tube <u>vibrate</u>. There are <u>three different ways</u> woodwind instruments do this:

1) <u>Edge-tone instruments</u> — <u>flutes</u> and <u>piccolos</u>. Air is blown across an <u>oval-shaped hole</u>. The <u>edge</u> of the hole <u>splits</u> the air. This makes it <u>vibrate</u> down the instrument and make the sound.

2) <u>Single-reed instruments</u> — <u>clarinets</u> and <u>saxophones</u>. Air is blown down a <u>mouthpiece</u> which has a <u>reed</u> (a thin slice of wood/reed/plastic) clamped to it. The reed <u>vibrates</u>, making the air in the instrument <u>vibrate</u>, and creating the sound.

3) <u>Double-reed instruments</u> — <u>oboes</u> and <u>bassoons</u>. The air passes between <u>two reeds</u>, tightly bound together and squeezed between the lips. The reeds <u>vibrate</u> and you get a sound.

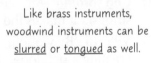

Like brass instruments, woodwind instruments can be <u>slurred</u> or <u>tongued</u> as well.

Different Notes are Made by **Opening** and **Closing Holes**

1) Wind instruments are covered in <u>keys</u>, <u>springs</u> and <u>levers</u> (or just holes for some instruments). These operate little <u>pads</u> that <u>close</u> and <u>open</u> holes down the instrument.
2) Opening and closing holes effectively makes the instrument longer or shorter. The <u>shorter</u> the tube, the <u>higher</u> the note. The <u>longer</u> the tube, the <u>lower</u> the note.

I can't see the woodwind for the clarinets...

Flutes and saxophones are made of metal but they're still woodwind instruments. If you're still confused, remember that woodwind instruments sound more breathy than brass instruments.

Orchestral Strings

Orchestral strings are the <u>heart</u> of the orchestra — or so string players would have you believe.

The **Double Bass**, **Cello**, **Viola**
and **Violin** are Very Alike

violin

double bass

viola

cello

These are all <u>made</u> and played in a <u>similar way</u>. The main differences are the <u>size</u> and <u>pitch</u>.

The <u>bigger</u> the instrument is, the <u>lower</u> the sounds it makes. So the double bass plays the lowest notes and the violin plays the highest.

bow (made of wood and hair). The hair is drawn across the strings.

Stringed Instruments can be **Bowed** or **Plucked**

When the <u>strings vibrate</u>, the air inside the instrument <u>vibrates</u> and amplifies the <u>sound</u>. There are two ways to get the strings vibrating:

1) <u>Bowing</u> — drawing a bow across the string. <u>*Con arco*</u> (or just <u>*arco*</u>) means '<u>with bow</u>'.

2) <u>Plucking</u> the string with the tip of your finger. The posh word for this is <u>*pizzicato*</u>.

The **Strings** are '**Stopped**' to Make **Different Notes**

1) You can get an "<u>open note</u>" just by plucking or bowing one of the four strings.

2) To get all the other notes, you have to change the <u>length</u> of the strings. You do this by <u>pressing down</u> with your finger. It's called <u>stopping</u>.

3) If you stop a string <u>close to the bridge</u>, the string's short and you get a <u>high</u> note.

4) If you stop a string <u>further away</u> from the bridge, the string's longer and you get a <u>lower</u> note.

5) <u>Double-stopping</u> is when <u>two</u> notes are played at the same time. Both strings are <u>pressed</u> (not open).

6) If you just <u>touch</u> a string <u>lightly</u> at certain points (instead of stopping), you can produce a series of <u>higher</u>, <u>fainter-sounding notes</u> called <u>harmonics</u>.

You Can Get **Very Varied** Effects with Stringed Instruments

mute

strings

bridge

1) **Tremolo** The bow's moved <u>back and forth</u> really <u>quickly</u>. This makes the notes sort of trembly. It's a great effect for making music sound <u>spooky</u> and <u>dramatic</u>.

2) **Col legno** The <u>wood</u> of the bow (instead of the hair) is tapped on the strings. This makes an <u>eerie</u>, <u>tapping</u> sound.

3) **Con sordino** A <u>mute</u> is put over the <u>bridge</u> (the piece of wood that supports the strings). It makes the strings sound <u>distant</u> and <u>soft</u>. Mutes are made of <u>wood</u>, <u>rubber</u> or <u>metal</u>.

4) **Vibrato** By <u>wobbling</u> the finger used to stop a string, a player varies the <u>pitch</u> slightly, creating a <u>rich tone</u>. This technique is also used on the <u>guitar</u> (see next page).

The **Harp** is Different...

1) The harp's <u>always plucked</u> — not bowed.

2) Most have <u>47</u> strings. Plucking each string in order on a concert harp is like playing up the <u>white notes</u> on a piano.

3) It has <u>seven pedals</u>. Pressing and releasing these lets you play <u>sharp</u> and <u>flat</u> notes.

4) You can play <u>one</u> note at a time, or play <u>chords</u> by plucking a few strings together.

EXAM TIP

Don't stop now, there are lots more instruments to come...

Make sure you learn the different string effects — you might need to identify them in the exam.

Guitars

Guitars are <u>everywhere</u> so it's best to know a bit about how they work.

An **Acoustic Guitar** has a **Hollow Body**

The <u>acoustic guitar</u> makes a sound the same way as the orchestral strings — by vibrating air in its belly.
Slightly different types are used by pop, folk and classical guitarists, but the <u>basic design</u> is similar.

HOLLOW BODY makes the string vibrations <u>resonate</u>, giving a louder sound.

STRINGS tuned to the notes E(low)-A-D-G-B-E(high). Low E is the string nearest your head as you're playing. Played with <u>fingers</u> or a <u>plectrum</u>.

FRETS (the little metal strips on the fingerboard/neck) help the player find the <u>correct finger position</u> for different notes.

acoustic guitar

There are three different kinds of acoustic guitar:
1) The <u>classical</u> or <u>Spanish</u> guitar has <u>nylon strings</u> (the thickest three are covered in <u>fine wire</u>).
2) The <u>acoustic guitar</u> has <u>steel strings</u> and is used mainly in <u>pop</u> and <u>folk music</u>.
3) The <u>12-stringed guitar</u> is often used in <u>folk music</u>. There are <u>two</u> of each string, giving a '<u>thicker</u>' sound which works well for accompanying <u>singing</u>.

Some guitar music is written in <u>tablature</u> (tab for short) — the numbers tell guitarists which frets to place their fingers at for each string.

This means play the 2nd fret on the A string, then the open D string, then both at the same time.

Electric Guitars Use an **Amplifier** and a **Loudspeaker**

electric guitar

1) An <u>electric guitar</u> has <u>six strings</u>, just like an acoustic guitar, and is <u>played</u> in a similar way.
2) The main difference is that an electric guitar has a <u>solid body</u>. The sound's made louder <u>electronically</u>, using an <u>amplifier</u> and a <u>loudspeaker</u>.
3) A <u>combo</u> (short for combination) is an <u>amplifier</u> and <u>loudspeaker</u> '<u>all in one</u>'.

The **Bass Guitar** has **Four Strings**

1) The <u>bass guitar</u> works like a guitar except it usually has <u>four strings</u>, not six.
2) They're tuned to the notes <u>E-A-D-G</u> (from lowest note to highest).
3) It's <u>lower pitched</u> than other guitars because it has <u>thicker and longer</u> strings.
4) Most bass guitars have frets, but there are some (imaginatively named <u>fretless basses</u>) that don't.

Like ordinary guitars, you can get electric or acoustic basses.

Guitar Strings are **Picked** or **Strummed**

1) Plucking <u>one string</u> at a time is called <u>picking</u>. <u>Classical</u> and <u>lead guitarists</u> pick the notes of a <u>melody</u>. <u>Bass</u> guitarists almost <u>always</u> pick out the individual notes of a bass line. They <u>hardly ever strum</u>.
2) Playing <u>two or more</u> strings at a time in a sweeping movement is called <u>strumming</u>. It's how <u>chords</u> are usually played. <u>Pop</u> and <u>folk guitarists</u> tend to play <u>accompaniments</u> rather than tunes, so they do more strumming than picking.
3) A <u>plectrum</u> is a small, flat piece of plastic that guitarists can use to pluck or strum with.
4) '<u>Hammer-on</u>' and '<u>pull-off</u>' are techniques that allow a guitarist to play notes in <u>quick succession</u> — they create a <u>smoother</u>, more <u>legato</u> sound than picking.

The guitar's a really popular instrument...

Make sure you learn the different types of guitar, and the proper words for the various <u>playing techniques</u>.

Keyboard Instruments

The actual <u>keyboard</u> looks much the same on most keyboard instruments, but the wires and mysterious levers <u>inside</u> vary quite a bit. That means the <u>sounds</u> they make vary too.

Harpsichords, Virginals and Clavichords Came First

harpsichord

1) Harpsichords were invented long before pianos. They're still played today but they were <u>most popular</u> in the <u>Baroque</u> and <u>early Classical</u> periods.
2) Harpsichords have quite a <u>tinny</u>, <u>string</u> sound. When you press a key a string inside is <u>plucked</u> by a lever. You can't vary the <u>strength</u> of the pluck, so you <u>can't</u> vary the <u>dynamics</u>.
3) A <u>virginal</u> is a <u>miniature</u> table-top version of a harpsichord. In the <u>sixteenth century</u>, virginals were really popular in England.
4) The <u>clavichord</u> is another early keyboard instrument. Clavichords are small and have a <u>soft</u> sound. The strings are <u>struck</u> with hammers (called "blades"), not plucked, so you can <u>vary</u> the dynamics a <u>little bit</u>.

The Most Popular Keyboard Instrument Now is the Piano

1) The piano was invented around <u>1700</u>. The <u>technology</u> is <u>more sophisticated</u> than it was in earlier keyboard instruments. When a key's pressed, a hammer hits the strings. The <u>harder</u> you hit the key, the <u>harder</u> the hammer hits the strings and the <u>louder</u> the note — there's a big range of <u>dynamics</u>.
2) Pianos have a wide range of <u>notes</u> — up to <u>seven and a half octaves</u>.
3) Pianos have <u>pedals</u> that let you change the sound in different ways.

The <u>soft</u> pedal on the left <u>mutes</u> the strings, making a softer sound.

The <u>sustain</u> pedal on the right <u>lifts</u> all the <u>dampers</u>. This lets the sound <u>ring on</u> until you release the pedal.

<u>Grand pianos</u> have a <u>middle pedal</u> too. This lets the player <u>choose</u> which notes to sustain. Modern pianos might have an extra mute pedal for <u>very quiet</u> practising.

For more detail on the piano, have a look at page 93.

Traditional Organs Use Pumped Air to Make Sound

1) The traditional organ (the <u>massive instrument</u> with hundreds of metal pipes that you see in churches and concert halls) is one of the most <u>complicated</u> instruments ever designed.
2) Sound is made by <u>blowing air</u> through sets of pipes called <u>ranks</u>. The air is pumped in by <u>hand</u>, <u>foot</u> or, on more recent organs, <u>electric pumps</u>.
3) The pipes are controlled by <u>keyboards</u> (called <u>manuals</u>) and lots of <u>pedals</u> which make a keyboard for the player's feet.
4) <u>Pressing</u> a key or pedal lets air pass through one of the pipes and play a note. <u>Longer</u> pipes make <u>lower</u> notes. <u>Shorter</u> pipes make <u>higher</u> notes.
5) Organs can play <u>different types of sound</u> by using differently designed pipes. Buttons called <u>stops</u> are used to select the different pipes. One stop might select pipes that make a <u>trumpet</u> sound, another might select a <u>flute</u> sound...
6) Modern <u>electronic organs</u> don't have pipes. Sound is produced <u>electronically</u> instead. These organs are much <u>smaller</u> and <u>cheaper</u> to build.

You've got to learn it all...

Listen to music played on each of these instruments so that you know how they all sound — harpsichords have a more <u>jangly</u> tone than pianos, and organs are fairly easy to spot as well.

Percussion

A percussion instrument is anything you have to <u>hit</u> or <u>shake</u> to get a sound out of it. There are <u>two</u> <u>types</u>: those that play tunes are called <u>tuned percussion</u>, and the ones you just hit are <u>untuned</u>.

Tuned Percussion Can Play **Different Notes**

<u>XYLOPHONES</u> have <u>wooden</u> bars. The sound is '<u>woody</u>'.

<u>GLOCKENSPIEL</u> — Looks a bit like a xylophone but the bars are made of <u>metal</u>. Sounds <u>tinkly</u> and <u>bell-like</u>.

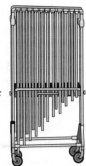

<u>CELESTA</u> — a bit like a glockenspiel except that you use a <u>keyboard</u> instead of whacking it with a hammer.

<u>TUBULAR BELLS</u> — Each of the <u>hollow steel tubes</u> plays a different note. Sounds a bit like <u>church bells</u>.

<u>TIMPANI</u> — also called <u>kettledrums</u>. The handles on the side or the foot pedal can be used to tighten or relax the skin, giving <u>different notes</u>.

<u>VIBRAPHONE</u> — This is like a <u>giant glockenspiel</u>. There are long tubes called <u>resonators</u> below the bars to make the notes <u>louder</u> and <u>richer</u>. <u>Electric fans</u> can make the notes <u>pulsate</u>, giving a warm and gentle sound.

There are **Hundreds** of **Untuned Percussion** Instruments

<u>Untuned percussion</u> includes any instrument that'll <u>make a noise</u> — but <u>can't</u> play a tune. These are the instruments that are used for <u>pure rhythm</u>. It's pretty much <u>impossible</u> to learn <u>every</u> untuned percussion instrument, but try and remember the names of these.

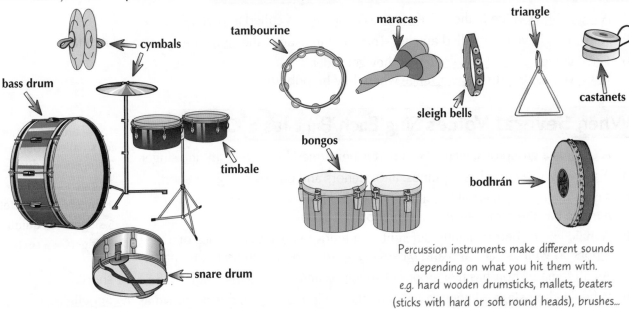

cymbals

bass drum

tambourine

maracas

triangle

sleigh bells

castanets

timbale

bongos

bodhrán

snare drum

Percussion instruments make different sounds depending on what you hit them with. e.g. hard wooden drumsticks, mallets, beaters (sticks with hard or soft round heads), brushes...

Remember — xylophones are wooden, glockenspiels are metal...

In a band, the drummer's job is to make a song sound like it's going somewhere and keep everyone in <u>time</u>. In an orchestra, percussion emphasises the <u>rhythm</u> of the piece and also adds <u>special effects</u> — you can imitate thunder with a drum roll on the timpani, or the crashing of waves with clashes of the cymbals.

The Voice

There are special names for male and female <u>voices</u> and <u>groups</u> of voices.

Female Singers are Soprano, Alto or Mezzo-Soprano

1) A singer with a particular type of voice is expected to be able to sing a certain <u>range</u> of notes.

2) The range of notes where a particular singer is most <u>comfortable</u> is called the <u>tessitura</u>. This term can also describe the <u>most commonly used</u> range of notes within a vocal or instrumental part of a piece.

3) A <u>high</u> female voice is called a <u>soprano</u>. The main female parts in operas are sung by sopranos.

4) A <u>lower</u> female voice is called an <u>alto</u> — short for <u>contralto</u>.

5) <u>Mezzo-sopranos</u> sing in the <u>top</u> part of the <u>alto</u> range and the <u>bottom</u> part of the <u>soprano</u> range.

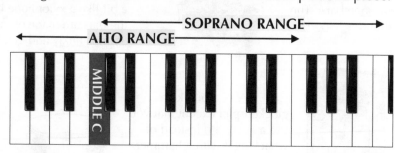

Male Voices are Tenor or Bass

1) <u>Higher</u> male voices are called <u>tenors</u>.

2) <u>Low</u> male voices are called <u>basses</u> (it's pronounced "bases").

3) <u>Baritones</u> sing the <u>top</u> part of the <u>bass</u> range and the <u>bottom</u> part of the <u>tenor</u> range.

4) Men who sing in the <u>female vocal range</u> are called <u>countertenors</u>.

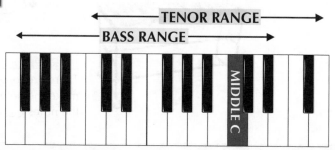

5) Some tenors, baritones and basses can push their voices <u>higher</u> to sing some of the same notes as a <u>soprano</u>. This is called <u>falsetto</u> singing.

Children's Voices are Either Treble or Alto

1) A <u>high child's</u> voice in the <u>same range</u> as a <u>soprano</u> is called a <u>treble</u>.

2) A <u>low child's</u> voice is called an <u>alto</u>. They sing in exactly the <u>same range</u> as an adult alto.

3) <u>Girls'</u> voices <u>don't change much</u> as they get older.
   <u>Boys'</u> voices <u>drop</u> to a <u>lower range</u> when they hit puberty.

When Several Voices Sing Each Part It's a Choir

1) A <u>choir</u> is a group of singers. Each part is performed by <u>more than one</u> singer.

2) A <u>mixed voice choir</u> has sopranos, altos, tenors and basses (<u>SATB</u> for short).

3) An <u>all-male choir</u> has trebles, altos, tenors and basses — a treble has the same range as a soprano, so it's basically SATB.

4) A <u>male voice choir</u> is slightly different — it tends to have two groups of <u>tenors</u>, as well as <u>baritones</u> and <u>basses</u> (<u>TTBB</u> for short), with no higher parts.

5) An <u>all-female choir</u> has <u>two groups of sopranos</u> and <u>two groups of altos</u> (<u>SSAA</u> for short).

6) When a choir sings <u>without</u> an instrumental <u>accompaniment</u>, this is known as '<u>a cappella</u>'.

7) Music written for a choir is called <u>choral music</u> — see page 101.

> These are the names for smaller groups:
> 2 singers = a **duet**
> 3 singers = a **trio**
> 4 singers = a **quartet**
> 5 singers = a **quintet**
> 6 singers = a **sextet**

No excuses — get on and learn all the voices...

The different voices don't just sound different in pitch — they've got different characters too, e.g. sopranos usually sound very clear and glassy, and basses sound more rich and booming.

Wind, Brass and Jazz Bands

In your listening exam, you'll get marks for saying what type of <u>group</u> (or <u>ensemble</u>) is playing. <u>Wind</u>, <u>jazz</u> and <u>brass</u> bands can sound quite <u>similar</u>, so make sure you know the differences.

Wind Bands have Woodwind, Brass and Percussion

1) Wind bands are <u>largish groups</u>, made up of 'wind' instruments — woodwind and brass — and percussion instruments.

2) There's <u>no string section</u>. If there was it would be an orchestra...

3) <u>Military bands</u> are wind bands. They tend to play <u>marches</u> — pieces with a <u>regular rhythm</u> (usually $\frac{4}{4}$ or $\frac{2}{4}$ time) that can be marched to.

Brass Bands have Brass and Percussion

1) A brass band is a group of <u>brass</u> and <u>percussion</u> instruments.

2) A typical brass band would have <u>cornets</u>, <u>flugelhorns</u>, <u>tenor</u> and <u>baritone horns</u>, <u>tenor</u> and <u>bass trombones</u>, <u>euphoniums</u> and <u>tubas</u>.

3) The exact <u>percussion instruments</u> depend on the piece being played.

4) Brass bands have been popular in <u>England</u> for <u>years</u>.

5) <u>Contests</u> are organised through the year to find out which bands are 'best'. There's a <u>league system</u> similar to football. The divisions are called <u>sections</u>. There are <u>five sections</u> and bands are <u>promoted</u> and <u>demoted</u> each year depending on how they do at the <u>regional</u> and <u>national</u> contests.

Jazz Bands are Quite Varied

1) Jazz bands have <u>no fixed set of instruments</u>.

2) Small jazz groups are known as <u>combos</u>. A typical combo might include a <u>trumpet</u>, <u>trombone</u>, <u>clarinet</u>, <u>saxophone</u>, <u>piano</u>, <u>banjo</u>, <u>double bass</u> and <u>drum kit</u> — but there's no fixed rule. Combos play in small venues like <u>clubs</u> and <u>bars</u>.

3) Larger jazz bands are known as <u>big bands</u> or <u>swing bands</u>. Instruments are doubled and tripled up so you get a <u>much bigger sound</u>. Big bands were really popular in the <u>1930s</u> and <u>1940s</u>. They played live at <u>dance halls</u>.

4) A large jazz band with a string section is called a <u>jazz orchestra</u> (though some jazz orchestras don't have a string section — they're just big jazz bands).

Jazz Bands have a Rhythm Section and a Front Line

In a jazz band, players are either in the <u>rhythm section</u> or the <u>front line</u>.

1) The <u>rhythm section</u> is the instruments responsible for <u>keeping the beat</u> and <u>adding the harmony parts</u>. The rhythm section's usually made up of the <u>drum kit</u> with a <u>double</u> or <u>electric bass</u>, <u>electric guitar</u> and <u>piano</u>.

2) The instruments that <u>play the melody</u> are the <u>front line</u>. This is usually <u>clarinets</u>, <u>saxophones</u> and <u>trumpets</u>, but could also be guitar or violin.

Keep at it — there are more groups to come...

You need to know the differences between wind, brass and jazz bands — if you reckon you've got it sorted, test yourself by covering up the page and writing down the instruments that play in each type of band.

Chamber Music

Chamber music is music composed for <u>small groups</u> and it's pretty formal stuff.

Chamber Music was Originally 'Home Entertainment'

1) '<u>Chamber</u>' is an old word for a room in a posh building like a palace or a mansion.

2) <u>Rich people</u> could afford to <u>pay musicians</u> to come and play in their 'chambers'. Musical families could play the music for themselves. The music written for these private performances is called <u>chamber music</u>.

3) Nowadays, you're more likely to hear chamber music in a <u>concert hall</u> or on a <u>CD</u> than live at someone's house. Let's face it — most people haven't got the cash to hire musicians for the evening, and they can download any music they want to listen to.

Chamber Music is Played by **Small Groups**

1) The rooms where musicians came to play were nice and <u>big</u> — but <u>not enormous</u>. Limited space meant that chamber music was written for a <u>small number</u> of musicians — between <u>two</u> and <u>eight</u>.

2) There's a <u>name</u> for each size of group:

> **Duet** = two players
> **Trio** = three players
> **Quartet** = four players
> **Quintet** = five players
> **Sextet** = six players
> **Septet** = seven players
> **Octet** = eight players

Have a look at the names for singing groups on p.68 — they're much the same.

These instruments make up a 'piano trio' — see below.

3) With so <u>few people</u> in chamber groups, you <u>don't</u> need a conductor. Instead, one of the players <u>leads</u>. The others have to <u>watch</u> and <u>listen</u> carefully, to make sure the <u>timing</u>, <u>dynamics</u> and <u>interpretation</u> are right.

4) Each part in the music is played by <u>just one person</u>.

Some **Chamber Groups** are **Extra-Popular** with Composers

Chamber music is written <u>more often</u> for some instrumental groups than others.
These are some of the most <u>popular</u> types of chamber group:

String trio	— violin, viola, cello
String quartet	— first violin, second violin, viola, cello
Piano trio	— piano, violin, cello (<u>not</u> three pianos)
Clarinet quintet	— clarinet, first violin, second violin, viola, cello (<u>not</u> five clarinets)
Wind quintet	— usually flute, oboe, clarinet, horn and bassoon

Chamber groups are small...

Learn the instruments that play in all the different chamber groups. Keep a special eye out for the piano trio and clarinet quintet — they're not what you'd expect. And finally, don't forget there's no conductor.

The Orchestra

If you go to a classical concert, more often than not there'll be an <u>orchestra</u> up there on stage.
Loads and loads of classical music has been written for orchestras.

A **Modern Orchestra** has **Four** Sections

If you go and see a <u>modern symphony orchestra</u>, it'll have <u>four sections</u> of instruments
— strings (p.64), woodwind (p.63), brass (p.62) and percussion (p.67).
The strings, woodwind, brass and percussion always sit in the <u>same places</u>.

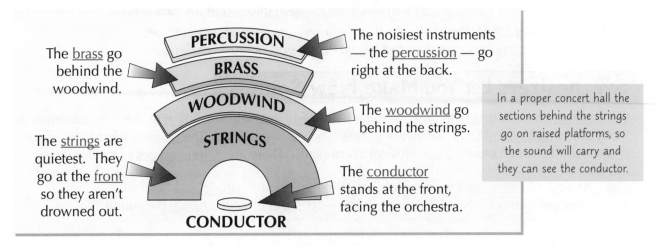

The <u>brass</u> go
behind the
woodwind.

The noisiest instruments
— the <u>percussion</u> — go
right at the back.

The <u>woodwind</u> go
behind the strings.

In a proper concert hall the
sections behind the strings
go on raised platforms, so
the sound will carry and
they can see the conductor.

The <u>strings</u> are
quietest. They
go at the <u>front</u>
so they aren't
drowned out.

The <u>conductor</u>
stands at the front,
facing the orchestra.

The **Conductor** has a **Complete Overview**

1) The conductor has a <u>score</u> — a version of the piece with <u>all the parts</u>. The <u>parts</u> are arranged in a <u>standard order</u>, one on top of the other, so that it's easy to see what any part is doing at any time. Woodwind parts are written at the <u>top</u>, followed by brass, percussion, and strings at the <u>bottom</u>.

2) The conductor <u>controls the tempo</u> by beating time with their hands, or a <u>baton</u> — a pointy white stick that's easy to see. There's a different way of beating time for each <u>time signature</u>.

3) The conductor '<u>cues in</u>' musicians — especially helpful for <u>brass</u> and <u>percussion</u>, who sometimes don't play anything for <u>hundreds of bars</u>, then suddenly have to play a <u>really loud, important bit</u>.

4) The conductor <u>interprets</u> the music. A conductor can decide whether to play one bit <u>louder</u> than another, whether to play a section in a <u>moody</u> or a <u>magical</u> way, and whether to make a piece sound very <u>smooth</u> or very <u>edgy</u>. They're a bit like a <u>film director</u> deciding the best way to <u>tell a story</u>.

An **Orchestra** is Any **Large Group with Strings**

<u>Symphony orchestras</u> (above) are the biggest type of orchestra. There are <u>other</u> smaller kinds too:

1) <u>String orchestra</u> — an orchestra with <u>stringed instruments</u> only.
2) <u>Chamber orchestra</u> — a <u>mini-orchestra</u>. It has a small string section, a wind and brass section with <u>one or two</u> of each instrument (but <u>no</u> tubas or trombones) and a small percussion section.

You have to do what the conductor tells you...

Copy out the diagram of the orchestra, but don't copy the labels. Close the book and see if you can fill in the different instrument sections in the right places. Then learn all about the conductor.

Music Technology

Modern <u>technological</u> and '<u>virtual</u>' instruments allow a huge variety of sounds to be created.

MIDI lets you Connect Electronic Musical Instruments

1) <u>MIDI</u> was invented in 1983. It stands for <u>Musical Instrument Digital Interface</u>. It's a way of <u>connecting</u> different electronic instruments.

2) MIDI equipment is connected by <u>MIDI cables</u>.

3) <u>MIDI data</u> is digital information (i.e. in <u>zeroes</u> and <u>ones</u>). It's sent down the MIDI cables. MIDI <u>instruments</u> turn MIDI <u>information</u> into <u>sound</u> (or vice versa).

4) One important <u>advantage</u> of MIDI is that it allows <u>musical equipment</u> to be <u>linked</u> with <u>computers</u>, opening up a whole <u>new world</u> of music-making.

Synthesizers Let You Make New Sounds

<u>Synthesizers</u> come in <u>different forms</u> — some have <u>keyboards</u> and some <u>don't</u>. The most common ones today are <u>virtual synthesizers</u>, which are <u>software-based</u> (see below). The <u>point</u> of them is to let you <u>create</u> sounds, which often <u>imitate</u> musical instruments. There are <u>different types</u> of synthesizers:

1) <u>Analogue synthesizers</u> were mainly made in the <u>70s</u> and <u>early 80s</u>. They've often got lots of <u>knobs</u> and <u>sliders</u> — you use these to <u>change</u> the sound.

2) <u>Digital synthesizers</u> started to be popular in the <u>80s</u>. Most modern synthesizers are digital, though some of them try to <u>mimic</u> analogue synths. Digital synths usually have <u>fewer</u> knobs and sliders than analogue ones.

3) <u>Software synths</u> started to become popular in the <u>late 90s</u>. Software synths are <u>computer programs</u> (often <u>linked</u> to a <u>sequencer</u> — see below). They often have <u>graphical sliders</u> and <u>knobs</u> that you can move with a <u>mouse</u>. Some of them try to be like analogue and early digital synthesizers. They also try to <u>recreate</u> classic <u>electric instruments</u> like the <u>Hammond organ</u>.

Sequencers Let You Record, Edit and Replay Music

1) <u>Sequencer</u> is the posh word for equipment that can <u>record</u>, <u>edit</u> (mess about with) and <u>replay</u> music stored as <u>MIDI</u> or <u>audio</u> information. A "<u>sequenced composition</u>" is a musical piece produced mainly from synthesized sounds using a sequencer.

2) Modern sequencers are usually <u>computer programs</u>, which often include <u>synthesizers</u> and <u>samplers</u>.

3) Most sequencers can record <u>audio</u> (real sounds) as well as the <u>MIDI</u> stuff, so you can create <u>synthesized</u> music and then record your own <u>voice</u> or <u>instruments</u> along with it. If you're unhappy with part of a recording, it's easy to replace that section with a <u>re-take</u>.

4) Modern sequencers are <u>multi-track recorders</u>. This allows the various lines of music, such as those played by different instruments, to be recorded on <u>separate tracks</u>. The individual tracks can then be <u>edited separately</u> to achieve the perfect <u>balance</u> of sounds.

5) One of the big <u>advantages</u> of a sequencer is that it shows your music as actual <u>notation</u> or as <u>representative boxes</u> — this makes it much easier to change and try out new ideas.

6) <u>Drum machines</u> are special sequencers that play back rhythm patterns using built-in drum sounds.

This can all be a bit confusing...

Some of this stuff is quite <u>technical</u> — but don't panic. You <u>don't</u> need to have an <u>in-depth</u> <u>understanding</u> of how the different types of technology work — as long as you know <u>what</u> they do and what people <u>use them for</u>. You can even have a go at using them in your <u>compositions</u>.

Music Technology

Sampling is a very popular way of putting different sounds into your music.
Samples can be fiddled with and looped to make long repeated sections.

Samplers let you 'Pinch' Other People's Sounds

1) A sampler is a piece of equipment that can record, process (change) and play back bits of sound.

2) These sections of sound are called samples.

3) Samplers are often used to take a bit of a piece of music that's already been recorded to use in some new music.

4) You can sample anything from instruments to birdsong — even weird things like a car horn.

5) Today, samplers are most often used to reproduce the sound of real instruments, such as strings or piano. Most pop music is sampled.

6) Pop stars often use samples of other people's music in their own music — anything from other pop songs to bits from Classical pieces. For example:

- Madonna used a sample of ABBA's 'Gimme! Gimme! Gimme! (A Man After Midnight)' in her 2005 hit 'Hung Up'.
- Take That sampled 'Dies Irae' from Verdi's Requiem in 'Never Forget' (1995).
- Fallout Boy used a sample of 'Tom's Diner' by Suzanne Vega in their song 'Centuries' in 2014.

Samples Can be Added to Other Pieces

1) You don't have to create a piece made up entirely of samples — you can just add one or two, or use a whole range to create a collage of sound. The collage can then be put over the top of a repeating drum and bass loop.

2) DJs and producers often do this when they make a dance remix of a piece.

REMIX is a term used for a different version of a piece of music.
They're often used to turn pop or rock tunes into dance music
— e.g. by speeding them up and giving them a fast drum beat.

3) Samples can be added to a piece by over-dubbing — adding tracks over the top of other tracks. You can record a drum track, then overlay the guitar part, then the vocal part, etc.

DJs Choose, Play and Alter Music

1) DJs (disc jockeys) choose which tracks (lines of music) to play, and change bits of them (e.g. by adding samples). Some DJs also rap over the top of the music.

2) DJs play music in clubs and on the radio.

3) At a live performance in a club, the DJ sometimes adds extra sounds using samples, keyboards or a drum machine to build the piece up.

4) DJs use a mixing desk to combine different tracks and add extra sounds to the music, and a set of decks to play their music.

5) The amplification is important — DJs need to make sure the right parts stand out, and that all parts can be heard. The amplification can be changed in live performances.

There's even a dance remix of Beethoven's 5th Symphony...

Again, there's lots of technical bits on this page. You might choose to use some samples in your own compositions, but even if you don't, you need to know how other people (like DJs) might use them.

Timbre

When you're listening to music, you can pick out <u>individual instruments</u> because of their <u>unique sound</u> — e.g. a trumpet sounds nothing like a violin. This is all down to a little thing called <u>timbre</u>.

Every Instrument Has its Own **Timbre**

1) <u>Timbre</u> is the <u>type of sound</u> that different instruments make. It's also known as <u>tone colour</u>.

2) <u>Musical notes</u> (and all sounds) are made by <u>vibrations</u>. Different instruments produce vibrations in <u>different ways</u>. For example, on a <u>string</u> instrument, the <u>bow</u> is drawn across the <u>string</u> to make it vibrate. On a <u>brass</u> instrument the vibrations are produced when the player '<u>buzzes</u>' their lips. The different <u>vibrations</u> make the <u>timbres</u> different.

3) The <u>size</u> and <u>material</u> of the instrument alter the timbre as well — e.g. a <u>cello</u> has a different timbre to a <u>violin</u> because it's <u>bigger</u>, and <u>wooden</u> flutes sound different from <u>metal</u> ones.

4) The same instrument can sound <u>different</u> depending on who's playing it. The <u>tone</u> (or quality) of the sound is affected by an individual's <u>playing style</u> and can be described as <u>rich</u>, <u>full</u>, <u>strong</u>, etc.

5) The overall nature of the sound produced by an instrument is called its <u>sonority</u>. <u>Timbre</u> and <u>tone</u> contribute to this, along with the <u>dynamics</u> and <u>articulation</u> of the music.

Instruments From the **Same Family** Have **Similar Timbres**

Even though each instrument has a <u>unique</u> timbre, it can still sometimes be <u>hard</u> to tell ones from the <u>same family</u> apart. Different families of instruments <u>change</u> the <u>timbre</u> in <u>different ways</u>:

STRING INSTRUMENTS

- String instruments (like the <u>violin</u>, <u>viola</u>, <u>cello</u> and <u>double bass</u>) have a <u>warm</u> sound. Notes are produced by making the <u>strings vibrate</u>, either using a <u>bow</u> or the <u>fingers</u>.
- All string instruments can be played *con arco* (with a bow), *pizzicato* (plucked), *con sordino* (muted) or *sul ponticello* (close to the bridge).
- <u>Double stopping</u> is when <u>two strings</u> are pressed at the <u>same time</u>, so <u>two notes</u> can be played at once.
- <u>Tremolo</u> sounds like <u>trembling</u> — the bow is moved <u>back and forth</u> very quickly.

PIANO

- When you press the <u>keys</u>, a <u>hammer</u> hits the strings inside the piano, making them <u>vibrate</u>.
- The timbre of the piano can be <u>changed</u> by using the <u>soft</u> or <u>sustain pedals</u>.

There's more on families of instruments and types of ensembles on pages 62-71.

WOODWIND INSTRUMENTS

- Wind instruments (e.g. <u>flute</u>, <u>clarinet</u>, <u>oboe</u> and <u>bassoon</u>) have a <u>soft</u>, <u>mellow</u> sound.
- <u>Edge-tone</u> instruments (e.g. flutes) make a <u>softer</u>, <u>breathier</u> sound than <u>reed</u> instruments (e.g. clarinets).
- Clarinets and oboes can <u>alter</u> their timbre by using a technique called '<u>bells up</u>', where the player <u>points</u> the end of the instrument <u>upwards</u>. This produces a <u>harsher</u> sound.

BRASS INSTRUMENTS

- Brass instruments (like the <u>trumpet</u>, <u>French horn</u>, <u>trombone</u> and <u>tuba</u>) have a <u>bright</u>, <u>metallic</u> sound.
- Playing <u>with a mute</u> (*con sordino*) can change the timbre.

PERCUSSION INSTRUMENTS

- Percussion instruments (e.g. <u>drums</u> and <u>xylophones</u>) make a sound when they're <u>struck</u>.
- What you hit them with can <u>change</u> the <u>timbre</u> — e.g. whether you use <u>sticks</u>, <u>brushes</u> or your <u>hands</u>.

SINGERS

- Singers produce notes when their <u>vocal cords</u> vibrate.
- The <u>speed</u> that they vibrate changes the <u>pitch</u> and the <u>timbre</u> — e.g. <u>bass</u> voices sound very <u>different</u> to <u>sopranos</u>.
- Techniques like <u>vibrato</u> (making the note <u>wobble</u>) can give a <u>richer</u> sound.
- <u>Falsetto</u> singing produces a much <u>thinner</u> sound.

I'm picking up good vibrations...

You may be asked to <u>describe</u> the timbre of different instruments that crop up in your exam.

Timbre

Electronic effects can be used to alter the timbre of an instrument or voice.

There are Lots of Different Electronic Effects

1) There are loads of different ways to change the sound of an instrument.

2) These effects are often used with electric guitars — they're really popular with rock bands, especially during guitar solos. Guitarists use pedals (e.g. a wah-wah pedal) to alter the tone or pitch.

3) The effects can also be used to change the sound of recorded music during mixing or post-processing.

4) Electronic effects (also called studio effects) include:

- **DISTORTION** distorts the sound.
- **REVERB** adds an echo to the sound.
- **CHORUS** makes it sound as if there's more than one player or singer — copies of the original sound are mixed together, with slight changes in timing and pitch.
- **PHASER** creates a 'whooshing' effect (a bit like the noise an aeroplane flying overhead makes).
- **FLANGER** similar to a phaser, but makes a more intense sound. The effect is created by combining the original sound with a copy, and varying the delay between them. It's used a lot in sci-fi programmes.
- **PITCH SHIFTING** used to bend the natural note or add another harmony.
- **OCTAVE EFFECTS** creates octaves above or below the note being played.

Synthesized Sounds have Different Timbres to Real Sounds

1) The natural sound of an instrument can be digitally reproduced to create a synthesized sound.

2) Electronic keyboards have different settings, so they can be made to sound like pretty much any instrument, from violins to percussion.

> One big difference between real and synthesized sounds is what happens to the timbre when the volume changes. When a real instrument is played louder, it has a different timbre to when it's played quietly. However, a synthesized sound has the same timbre at any volume — it's just the loudness that changes.

Sampling Uses Recordings of Real Instruments

1) The most effective way to recreate the sounds of real instruments is to use sampling (see p.73).

2) Sampling is where you record an instrument and use the recording (called a sample) in your music.

3) The samples can be altered to create different effects — there are lots of different computer programs that help you do this.

4) Samples can be looped (played over and over again), and other samples can be added over the top.

5) Most electronic music produced today uses looping, especially drum patterns.

6) It's not just instruments that can be sampled — you can take samples of anything you like, e.g. traffic noises or doorbells.

7) Lots of pop songs use samples — see if you can spot any in your favourite songs.

I'd like a sample of that cake please...

Have a listen to the 2005 hit 'Gold Digger' by Kanye West — he uses a sample of 'I Got A Woman' by Ray Charles (which was released more than 50 years earlier, in 1954).

Warm-up and Exam Questions

The questions on these pages are great for finding out what you know — don't ignore them.

Warm-up Questions

1) For each of the words below, name an instrument that links with the word:

   slide   single reed   double reed   pizzicato   wooden bars

2) Explain each of these words and phrases:

   tremolo   con sordino   tenor   falsetto

3) Name the **three** main types of guitar and briefly describe each of them.

4) In which period was the harpsichord the most popular keyboard instrument?

5) Explain the difference between a military band, a brass band and a jazz band.

6) List all the instruments that play in a piano trio and a clarinet quintet.

7) Define the following terms:

   MIDI   sampler   remix   sequencer

Exam Question

Brush up on your exam technique with this question.

This question is about two extracts, Track 30 and Track 31.

First play Track 30 **three** times, leaving a short pause for writing time between each playing.

(Track 30)

a) Name the solo woodwind instrument that plays at the beginning.

....

[1 mark]

b) What is the other instrument that plays in the extract?

....

[1 mark]

Exam Question

c)   Tick **one** box to indicate which shape best represents the opening of the melody played by the solo instrument.

Shape A   ☐

Shape B   ☐

Shape C   ☐

[1 mark]

d)   Describe the relationship of the two instruments heard here. Refer to the **texture** and any other interesting features.

....

....

[2 marks]

Two marks available means you need to make two points. Don't forget to write about <u>texture</u>.

Track 31

Now play Track 31 **three** times, leaving a short pause for writing time between each playing.

e)   Name the two solo woodwind instruments which play the melody at the beginning of this excerpt.

....

....

[2 marks]

Make sure you write about the <u>melody</u>, not the accompaniment.

Exam Question

f) Name the family of instruments playing throughout this excerpt.

....

[1 mark]

g) Ring the word that describes the scale used throughout the excerpt.

major   **minor**   **chromatic**

[1 mark]

h) Tick one of the following to represent the backing melody played by the two wind instruments.

A

B

C

[1 mark]

i) Ring **one** feature that you can hear in this excerpt.

accelerando   **crescendo**   **ritardando**

[1 mark]

Revision Summary for Section Five

This section should be easy where it's talking about your own instruments. Don't ignore the other instruments. You'll need to know enough about them to be able to describe them in the listening test. And you might need to write parts for other instruments for your composition — it'll be a big help to know what they can and can't do. Go through the questions and check you can answer them all.

1) Name three brass instruments.

2) How do you vary the pitch on a brass instrument?

3) Are all woodwind instruments made of wood?

4) Name three woodwind instruments.

5) What are the three different mouthpieces used on woodwind instruments called? How do they work?

6) What are all those little keys, springs and levers for on a woodwind instrument?

7) What's the smallest orchestral string instrument?

8) What's the biggest string instrument that you play with a bow?

9) How do you make different notes on a string instrument?

10) What makes a harp different from the other string instruments? Give three differences.

11) Where would you put a mute on a bowed string instrument and what effect would it have?

12) How many strings are there on:
    a) an acoustic guitar   b) an electric guitar   c) a bass guitar?

13) What do you call those metal bits on the fingerboard of a guitar? Do you get them on a bass?

14) What's the proper word for twanging a guitar string with a plectrum?

15) Name three different keyboard instruments.

16) What's the biggest type of keyboard instrument?

17) What's the most popular keyboard instrument?

18) How could you tell you were listening to a church organ and not a harpsichord?

19) Name three tuned percussion instruments and six untuned percussion instruments.

20) What's the highest type of singing voice?

21) What's the lowest type of singing voice?

22) What do you call a boy's voice when it's got the same range as a soprano?

23) How can you tell the difference between a wind band and a brass band?

24) How can you tell the difference between a wind band and a jazz orchestra?

25) What are the two sections of a jazz orchestra called, and what are their jobs?

26) Why's chamber music called chamber music?

27) How many people are there in: a) a trio   b) a sextet   c) a quartet   d) an octet?

28) How many clarinets are there in a clarinet quintet?

29) Sketch a plan of a standard symphony orchestra. Label the different sections and the conductor.

30) What sections are there in a string orchestra, chamber orchestra and jazz orchestra?

31) How is MIDI information stored?

32) What do sequencers do?

33) What are samples? How can they be used in tracks?

34) Explain how the sound is produced on:
    a) a string instrument b) a piano c) a brass instrument?

35) Name four different electronic effects.

The Baroque Style

You need to know all about the <u>features</u> and <u>development</u> of <u>instrumental</u> music between <u>1700</u> and <u>1820</u>. Let's start with the musical style from the start of that period — <u>Baroque music</u>.

Baroque has a **Recognisable Sound**

The <u>Baroque</u> period was from about <u>1600-1750</u>. Key composers include <u>Bach</u>, <u>Handel</u>, <u>Vivaldi</u> and <u>Purcell</u>. Baroque music's pretty <u>easy to recognise</u>. These are the <u>main things</u> to look out for:

1) The <u>melodies</u> are built up from <u>short musical ideas</u> (called <u>motifs</u>), so you get quite a bit of <u>repetition</u>.

2) The <u>harmonies</u> are simple, with a fairly narrow range of chords — mainly <u>I</u> and <u>V</u>.

3) The melody is packed with <u>ornaments</u>, added in to make it sound more <u>interesting</u> (see p.84).

4) The <u>music</u> often involves <u>counterpoint</u> — where <u>two or more different lines of melody</u> are played at the same time. This <u>texture</u> is described as <u>contrapuntal</u> (or <u>polyphonic</u> — see p.45).

5) The <u>dynamics change suddenly</u>. Each bit is either <u>loud</u> or <u>soft</u> — this is called <u>terraced</u> or <u>stepped</u> dynamics. You <u>won't</u> hear any <u>gradual changes</u> in volume (no <u>crescendos</u> or <u>diminuendos</u>). This is mainly due to the prominence of the <u>harpsichord</u> in Baroque music — harpsichords could <u>either</u> play loud or soft, but couldn't change <u>gradually</u> between the two.

6) Baroque music is <u>tonal</u>:

- From about 1600, Western composers used <u>major</u> and <u>minor keys</u> to write <u>tonal</u> music — this replaced <u>modal</u> music (see p.27).
- Composers used <u>modulation</u> to switch between keys (see p.44) — this created <u>contrast</u> in their music.
- Compositions were often made up of <u>sections</u> in <u>different keys</u>, with modulation between them. <u>New structures</u> were developed for organising pieces of music with a number of sections, e.g. <u>binary</u> and <u>ternary</u> forms (see next page).

String and **Keyboard Instruments** Played **Key Roles**

1) <u>String instruments</u> were dominant in a Baroque orchestra (just like today) — <u>violins</u>, <u>violas</u>, <u>cellos</u> and <u>double basses</u> were all used. (If you see '<u>violone</u>' in the score, it's played by a double bass today.)

2) <u>Keyboard</u> instruments such as the <u>harpsichord</u> and <u>organ</u> were also very important in Baroque music.

3) Woodwind instruments such as the <u>flute</u>, <u>recorder</u>, <u>oboe</u> and <u>bassoon</u> were also used.

4) The instruments available were much more <u>limited</u> than in the later musical periods. There were some early forms of <u>brass</u> instruments, such as <u>trumpets</u> and <u>horns</u>, but they didn't have any <u>valves</u> so could only play a <u>limited range</u> of notes.

5) <u>Orchestras</u> were generally <u>small</u> compared to modern orchestras. The size of an orchestra depended on the <u>resources</u> available, and the performance <u>space</u>. Music was often performed by <u>chamber groups</u> (see p.70) with a small number of musicians, but there were <u>larger orchestras</u> too.

Baroque Music Often Had a **Basso Continuo**

1) A <u>basso continuo</u> is a <u>continuous bass part</u> (see page 57). It's played throughout a piece, and is based on the <u>chords</u> of the piece.

2) It was often played on an <u>organ</u> or <u>harpsichord</u>, but could also feature additional instruments — e.g. <u>cellos</u>, <u>double basses</u> or <u>bassoons</u>.

 'Baroque Around the Clock' was a huge hit...
You might have to spot key features of Baroque music in the exam, so make sure you learn them.

Baroque Structures

Baroque composers used various standard structures to construct their music.

The **Concerto Grosso** was a **Popular Form** of **Orchestral Music**

1) In a concerto grosso, a small group of soloists (called the concertino) is contrasted with the rest of the orchestra (the ripieno) and the basso continuo. The ripieno is usually a string orchestra. Handel wrote several concerto grossi (plural for grosso) — in his Concerto Grosso No.5 (Op.6), the concertino is made up of two violins and a cello, the ripieno is a string orchestra, and the continuo is played on the harpsichord. J.S. Bach's Brandenburg Concertos are concerto grossi — the third movement of Brandenburg Concerto No.5 is one of your set pieces (see p.85-86 for more detail).

2) Baroque composers also wrote solo concertos. Here a single solo instrument is 'show-cased', allowing its performer to demonstrate the instrument's capabilities, accompanied by an orchestra. Vivaldi's 'Four Seasons' is a solo concerto for the violin. It was this type of concerto that was further developed by composers such as Mozart and Haydn in the Classical period — see p.90.

Binary and **Ternary Forms** are Made Up of **Different Sections**

1) Binary means something like 'in two parts' — binary form has two sections.

2) Binary form is usually used for Baroque dances, e.g. bourrée, minuet, gavotte, sarabande and gigue.

3) Each section is repeated. You play Section A twice, and then Section B twice, so it goes AABB.

4) Section B contrasts with Section A — the two bits should sound different.

5) The contrast is often made by modulating to related keys. Pieces in a minor key usually modulate to the relative major, e.g. A minor to C major. Pieces in a major key usually modulate to the dominant key (V), e.g. C major to G major.

1) Ternary form has three sections. The general structure is ABA, but the sections are often repeated, producing structures such as AABBAA.

2) Section A ends in the home key, normally with a perfect cadence (see pages 42-43). This makes it sound like a complete piece in itself.

3) In Section B the music often modulates to a related key, like the dominant or relative minor, and then goes back to the home key before it ends.

4) The last section can be exactly the same as Section A, or a slightly varied version. If it is varied, you call it A1 instead of A.

In a ritornello (see p.86), the same musical idea or theme is repeated at various points in the piece. A more formal structure of this type is a rondo, where a main theme (A) is repeated, separated by a number of different sections, creating forms such as ABACA (see p.92).

Some **Works** Have an **Introduction** Called a **Prelude**

1) In the Baroque period, a prelude was a short, relatively simple piece of music. It usually served as an introduction to a longer piece or to a number of pieces of music.

2) The first movement of a suite (a set of dances) is often a prelude.

3) A prelude was often used as an introduction to a more complex piece such as a fugue (see p.85). Bach wrote a prelude and fugue in each of the 24 keys in 'The Well-Tempered Clavier' — a collection of solo pieces for keyboard instruments.

4) In the Romantic period (see p.93), the term came to be used to describe a short, stand-alone piece.

This page is just a prelude to yet more fascinating structures...

You need to be able to spot these various structures, so make sure you learn all their features. The third movement of J.S. Bach's Brandenburg Concerto No.5 is in ternary form — there's more detail on p.86.

Baroque Structures

Variations are pieces which start with <u>one pattern</u> or tune, and then <u>change it</u> in different ways. There are <u>two</u> main structures for variations. They're called '<u>theme and variation</u>' and '<u>ground bass</u>'.

Theme and Variation Form Varies the Melody

1) In <u>theme and variation form</u>, the theme's usually a memorable <u>melody</u>.

2) The theme is played <u>first</u>. There's a short <u>pause</u> before the <u>first variation</u> is played, then another pause before the next variation. Each variation is a <u>self-contained</u> piece of music. There can be <u>as many</u> or <u>as few</u> variations as the composer wants.

3) Each variation should be a <u>recognisable</u> version of the main theme, but <u>different</u> from all the others.

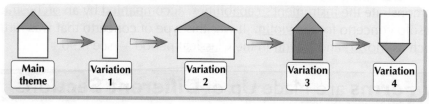

You can vary a melody in loads of simple ways:

1) Start off with a <u>basic theme</u>...

2) <u>Add notes</u> to make the melody more complex.

3) <u>Remove</u> notes to <u>simplify</u> the melody.

4) Change the <u>metre</u> — e.g. from 2 beats in a bar to 3.

5) Add a <u>countermelody</u> — an extra melody over the top of the theme.

6) You can also change the <u>tempo</u>, change the <u>key</u> (from major to minor or vice versa), change some or all of the <u>chords</u> or add a different type of <u>accompaniment</u> instead of block chords.

A <u>fantasia</u> is a composition with an <u>improvised</u> feel — the composer uses their <u>imagination</u> and <u>skill</u> to compose a piece that <u>doesn't</u> follow a <u>set structure</u>. Fantasias often involve <u>variations</u> on a <u>theme</u>.

Ground Bass Form Varies Ideas Over a Fixed Bass Part

<u>Ground bass</u> is a <u>continuous</u> set of variations — there are <u>no pauses</u>. The main theme (called the <u>ground</u>) is a <u>bass line</u> which <u>repeats</u> throughout the piece — it is also known as <u>basso ostinato</u> (see p.83). <u>Varying melodies</u> and <u>harmonies</u> which become gradually <u>more complex</u> are played <u>over</u> the ground. There are two types of Baroque dance that are in ground bass form — the <u>chaconne</u> and <u>passacaglia</u>. They're quite <u>slow</u> and <u>stately</u>.

Freshly ground bass — it goes all powdery...

Make sure you've learnt all the ins and outs of these structures. Have a listen to Purcell's 'Music for a While' and listen out for the ground bass — it's one of your set works, so there's more detail later on (p.106-107).

Baroque Melody Patterns

Composers often create a melody by starting with a <u>key phrase</u>, then <u>adapting</u> it using different <u>techniques</u>.

Melodic Inversion — Turning the Tune **Upside Down**

With <u>melodic inversion</u> you keep the <u>same intervals</u> between the notes, but they go in the <u>opposite direction</u>, i.e. down instead of up, and up instead of down. Basically you turn the tune on its head.

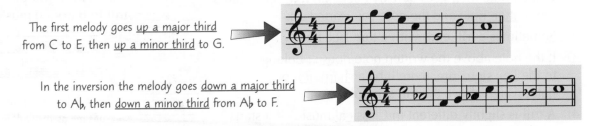

The first melody goes <u>up a major third</u> from C to E, then <u>up a minor third</u> to G.

In the inversion the melody goes <u>down a major third</u> to A♭, then <u>down a minor third</u> from A♭ to F.

Retrograde — Playing the Tune **Backwards**

Playing the notes <u>in reverse order</u> but with the same rhythm is called <u>retrograde</u>. This is the retrograde version of the first melody (above).

If you switch the notes so they're in reverse order <u>and</u> inverted, you get a <u>retrograde inversion</u>. This is the retrograde inversion of the first melody.

Sequencing — Repeat a **Pattern**, Vary the **Pitch**

1) Repeat the <u>pattern</u> of a phrase but start on a <u>different note</u>, higher or lower. This is called a <u>sequence</u>.

2) <u>Ascending</u> sequences go up in pitch. <u>Descending</u> sequences go down.

Imitation — Repeat a Phrase With **Slight Changes**

1) In <u>imitation</u>, a phrase is repeated with <u>slight changes</u> each time.

2) It works really well if one instrument or voice imitates <u>another</u> and then <u>overlaps</u>.

3) There is imitation right at the <u>start</u> of the <u>3rd Movement</u> of Brandenburg Concerto No.5 (see p.85).

original phrase

original phrase, one octave higher

imitation with modulation

overlap starts in relative minor

Ostinato — Keep **One Pattern** the **Same**, Change the Rest

1) An ostinato is a pattern that's played <u>over and over</u> again.

2) The rest of the piece <u>changes around it</u>.

3) An ostinato is usually in the <u>bass</u> line, but it can be in other parts too.

4) <u>Ground bass form</u> (p.82) features ostinato <u>phrases</u> in the bass line — the repeated phrases can be quite <u>long</u>.

Here's the repeating pattern

Ornaments in Baroque Music

Ornaments are short extra notes that liven up the main melody — Baroque composers used them a lot in their music. There are a few different types of ornament...

A **Trill** is Lots of **Tiny Quick Notes**

1) In Baroque music, the trill starts one note above the written note then goes quickly back and forth between the written note and the note you started on.

2) Sometimes a trill ends with a turn (see below).

3) If the note above the written note doesn't belong to the key signature, there'll be a sharp, flat or natural sign above the trill symbol.

4) A trill is slightly different in Classical music — it starts on the written note and goes up to the note above.

This is how you play a trill in Baroque music...

The trill lasts the same length of time as the written note.

An **Appoggiatura** is an **Extra Note** in a **Chord**

1) The appoggiatura starts on a note that clashes with the chord, then moves to a note that belongs in the chord (this is called the resolution).

2) The two notes are usually just one tone or semitone apart.

3) It normally takes half the time value of the note it 'leans' on.

Squeezing in a **Tiny Note** is Called **Acciaccatura**

"Acciaccatura" means crushing in. An acciaccatura is a note that's squeezed in before the main note and played as fast as possible.

Mordents and **Turns** are **Set Patterns** of Notes

MORDENTS

Mordents start off like trills.

The difference is they end on the written note, which is played a bit longer than the trilled notes. There are loads of different mordents but these two are the most common.

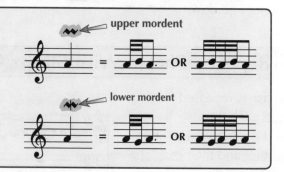

upper mordent

lower mordent

TURNS

Start on the note above the written note, then play the written note, followed by the note below the written note. End back on the written note.

For an inverted turn play the note below the written note, the written note, the note above that and finally the written note.

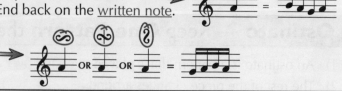

COMPOSING TIP

I've done my bit — now it's your turn...

Take a look at p.41 for more on decoration. You might even want to add some of these ornaments to your compositions to make them more exciting (don't go overboard though).

J.S. Bach — Brandenburg Concerto No.5

The 3rd Movement of J.S. Bach's Brandenburg Concerto No.5 in D Major is one of your set pieces.
This concerto is one of six written by Bach for the Margrave of Brandenburg around 1721.

J.S. Bach Came From a **Family of Musicians**

1) Johann Sebastian Bach (1685-1750) was born in the Thuringia region of Germany.
He was from a family of well-known performers and composers.

2) Bach wrote in all genres except opera. He is particularly known for instrumental
music such as the Brandenburg Concertos and sacred choral music such as masses.

3) Bach is known for long, flowing, expressive melodies. He was skilled
at writing contrapuntal music (see page 45), including fugues (see below).

4) Keyboard instruments such as the harpsichord and organ had major roles in many of Bach's works.

Brandenburg Concerto No.5 is a **Concerto Grosso**

1) Brandenburg Concerto No.5 is an example of a concerto grosso — see page 81.

2) The concertino (small group of solo instruments) consists of a solo flute, solo violin and harpsichord.

3) The ripieno (larger accompanying group of instruments) is a string orchestra.

4) The continuo is played by the harpsichord (when it's not playing a solo part), cello and double bass.

THE HARPSICHORD HAS AN IMPORTANT ROLE

- The harpsichord's prominent solo role (as well as playing the continuo) is unusual for the period.
The part is very complex at times, and is completely unaccompanied in bars 163-176.

- In some places the harpsichord player completes the harmony by realising the figured bass (see p.57).

- In Baroque music, the harpsichord player would sometimes direct the ensemble as well.

The **3rd Movement** is Both a **Fugue** and a **Gigue**

1) The 3rd Movement of the concerto is in the style of a gigue. A gigue is a 17th century dance
with a steady beat and a lively tempo. They are often written in a compound metre such as $\frac{6}{8}$.
The set piece has a time signature of $\frac{2}{4}$ but the frequent use of triplets gives it a $\frac{6}{8}$ 'feel'.

2) The music is written as a fugue — the key features of a fugue are given below. The first 7 bars
of the movement are shown at the bottom of the page to illustrate some of these features.

KEY FEATURES OF A FUGUE

- The subject (main idea) is heard first on a solo instrument — in the set piece, it's the violin.

- Other parts or instruments play the subject, one after another, in imitation — here, the flute
plays the subject next. This structure gives the music a largely polyphonic texture.

- The melodic line immediately following the subject is called the counter-subject (see below).

- Each part then continues with other contrasting melodic ideas, occasionally re-stating the subject,
or variations of it. There is no set structure for how a fugue should develop.

- Often, when one part has fast moving notes, another will have slower moving notes — see bars 3-4.

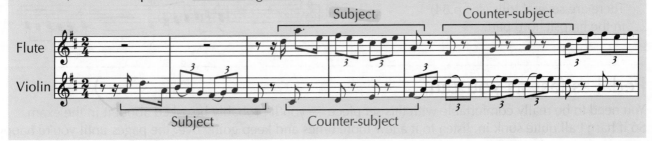

J.S. Bach — Brandenburg Concerto No.5

Listen to the music as you're reading this page — you'll need to be able to spot the features that are mentioned. You'll probably need to hear it a few times through to pick up on them all.

The 3rd Movement is in Ternary Form

1) The 3rd Movement has an ABA structure — the first section is repeated after a contrasting middle section. This is ternary form (see page 81). Section A is bars 1-78, section B is bars 79-233, and section A is then played again from bar 233 to the end.

2) Section A is in D major. The piece moves to the B minor (the relative minor) for section B, before returning to D major for the final section.

3) The main melodic section of the movement (bars 1-29) is repeated throughout the piece (in full or in part) with contrasting sections in between. This structure is known as ritornello.

4) The fugue starts in the concertino instruments and then passes to the ripieno at bar 29.

5) In some places, the harpsichord has a complex part — it plays quick semiquavers (e.g. from bar 42). The other parts are much simpler at these times, creating a light orchestral texture.

Bach Used Various Musical Devices

1) SEQUENCING

Bach uses sequences (see p.83) in this movement. This extract shows the flute and ripieno violin parts — the pattern is repeated in each bar, moving up a tone each time.

2) PEDAL POINT

A pedal point (or pedal note — see p.39) is used in bars 79-85, 90-95 and 100-106 — it's played by the viola, cello or double bass. This extract shows the flute and cello parts — the cello repeats the pedal note (B), while the melody changes in the flute, creating dissonance.

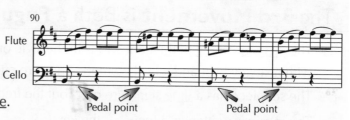

3) STRETTO

Stretto is when the fugue subject is overlapped — one instrument starts playing the subject before the previous one has finished. This builds up the intensity of the texture. It happens in the violin, viola and cello parts in bars 64-68.

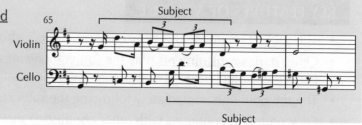

4) TRILLS

There are several trills (see p.84) in the harpsichord part.

Pedal as fast as you can...

You need to be really comfortable with this set piece — you'll probably be asked about it in the exam. So if hasn't all quite sunk in, listen to it a few more times and keep going over the pages until you're happy.

From Baroque to Classical

Classical music came from Baroque, so it's <u>similar but not the same</u>...

Tastes Moved Towards a Simpler Sound

Classical
1750–1820

1) The <u>Classical</u> period of music was from around <u>1750 to 1820</u>. <u>Mozart</u>, <u>Haydn</u> and <u>Beethoven</u> were key composers during this time.

2) The style of music <u>didn't just change overnight</u> — the Classical style <u>developed</u> from the Baroque style as <u>tastes changed</u> and <u>instruments</u> became more <u>versatile</u>.

3) Towards the <u>end</u> of the Baroque era, many composers <u>moved away</u> from the <u>polyphonic</u> sound (see p.45) that had been a key feature of the period. They began to write more <u>homophonic music</u> with a <u>clear melody line</u> and <u>fewer ornaments</u> (see p.84).

4) This development can be seen in the compositions of J.S. Bach's sons, <u>C.P.E. Bach</u> and <u>J.C. Bach</u>. They were influenced by <u>new styles</u> as well as their <u>father's compositions</u>, and they composed much more <u>homophonic</u> music than their father.

5) There was also a move towards more <u>subtle dynamics</u>. Composers began to use <u>crescendos</u> and <u>diminuendos</u> rather than sudden changes in volume — this was partly due to the invention of the <u>piano</u> (see below).

Forms and Structures Developed Too

1) Baroque forms and structures <u>changed over time</u>, and grew into popular Classical <u>structures</u>:

- The <u>solo concerto</u> became <u>more popular</u> than the <u>concerto grosso</u> (see p.81) — it became an <u>important form</u> in the <u>Classical period</u>.

- The <u>Baroque trio sonata</u> consisted of a number of movements played by <u>three instruments</u> plus a <u>harpsichord continuo</u>. This developed into the <u>Classical sonata</u>, a form consisting of three or four movements, usually composed for a <u>solo instrument</u> (see p.90).

- In the <u>Baroque</u> period, operas often began with an 'Italian overture' — an <u>orchestral</u> piece consisting of <u>three sections</u> — a <u>fast</u> section followed by a <u>slow</u> section, followed by another <u>fast</u> section. These pieces were often performed <u>independently</u> of the opera. The <u>Classical symphony</u> (see p.90) developed from this (although Classical symphonies tended to have four movements).

2) Other forms that were popular in the Baroque period continued to be used — <u>binary form</u>, <u>ternary form</u> and <u>theme and variation form</u> (see p.81-82) were still <u>important</u> in the <u>Classical era</u>. <u>New structures</u> such as <u>sonata form</u> (p.91) were also developed.

The Invention of the Piano had a Big Impact

1) The <u>piano</u> was invented in about <u>1700</u>. It became more popular than the harpsichord because it was able to create a much <u>greater variety</u> of tones — the notes could be played in a <u>legato</u> or staccato style and the <u>dynamics</u> could be <u>varied</u> depending on how hard the keys were pressed. The full name of the piano is actually '<u>pianoforte</u>', which means '<u>soft-loud</u>'.

2) <u>C.P.E. Bach</u> and <u>J.C. Bach</u> both composed for the <u>piano</u> and were <u>influential</u> in increasing its <u>popularity</u>. The piano became <u>very widely used</u> in Classical music.

3) <u>Other instruments</u> (such as the <u>clarinet</u>) were <u>developed</u>, and this led to important changes in the structure of the <u>orchestra</u> — see the next page.

Souvenir shops suffered terribly as the use of ornaments declined...

Remember, Classical music developed from Baroque music, so many of the features you've come across in Baroque music still make an appearance. But there's lots of new stuff to get to grips with too...

The Classical Orchestra

Orchestras got bigger during the Classical period as new instruments were developed.
The set-up of an orchestra (i.e. what instruments were included) became more standardised.

Orchestral Music was Written for **Wealthy Audiences**

1) At the start of the Classical period, composers worked for royalty and aristocrats.
   They were paid to write music for official events, church services and plain old entertainment.
   Composers had to write music that their patrons (employers) would approve of.

2) Later in the Classical period, society changed. Middle-class people had more money and
   wanted entertainment. Public concert halls were built, where people could go to listen to music.

3) Famous Classical composers like Haydn and Mozart worked for patrons,
   but they also put on concerts in the new concert halls.

4) By the 1800s, composers could earn quite a bit of money from ticket sales
   at concert halls. This gave them more freedom — they could write for the
   tastes of concert-goers instead of just pleasing their patrons.

Orchestras **Grew** During the **Classical Period**

1) At the start of the Classical period, composers wrote for smallish orchestras — mainly strings,
   with horns, flutes and oboes. There'd be two horns and one or two woodwind.

2) Later on, the woodwind section grew — clarinets were developed during the Classical period and
   were included in the orchestra. Mozart was the first composer to use the clarinet in a symphony.

3) Brass instruments were used more widely. Horns were developed so
   they could produce more notes and play in a greater variety of keys.

4) The percussion section grew too — timpani became a
   standard fixture, and some orchestras used bass drums,
   snare drums, triangles and cymbals as well.

5) In some early Classical music, there'd be a harpsichord (see p.66),
   but after a while composers stopped using it. The harpsichord was
   there to fill in the harmonies, but it wasn't really needed once the
   extra woodwind had been added.

6) This is a fairly typical layout for a later Classical orchestra:

PERCUSSION		
FRENCH HORNS		TRUMPETS
FLUTES		CLARINETS
	OBOES	BASSOONS
SECOND VIOLINS	VIOLAS	DOUBLE BASSES
FIRST VIOLINS		CELLOS

Classical Orchestras Mostly Use **String Instruments**

1) The most important section in a Classical orchestra is the strings.
   They're the dominant sound in most Classical music.
   The violins generally play most of the melodies.

2) The wind instruments play extra notes to fill out the harmony.
   When they do get the tune, they mostly double the string parts.

3) You do hear the occasional wind solo. Orchestral pieces called concertos (see p.90)
   feature one or two solo instruments accompanied by an orchestra.

4) In later Classical music, the woodwind section started to have a more independent role.
   They'd sometimes play the melody alone, and there'd be more solos.
   The strings were still really important though.

You need to know what instruments were used in the Classical era...

Orchestras grew in size because composers in the Classical period began to include more parts
for different instruments. This gave rise to a greater variety of music later in the Classical period.

The Classical Style

A whole <u>page</u> about the features of Classical music... enjoy.

Classical Melodies Have a **Clear, Simple Structure**

Classical music sounds <u>clearer</u> and <u>simpler</u> than music from other periods. This is partly because the melodies are structured in a very straightforward way, with <u>short</u>, <u>balanced</u> 2- or 4-bar phrases.

Here's an extract from Haydn's *Clock Symphony*:

And here's the opening of Mozart's *Piano Sonata No. 16 in C major* with two-bar phrases:

Classical **Textures** are Mainly **Melody** and **Chords**

1) Most Classical music has just <u>one melody</u> with <u>accompanying chords</u>. This makes the tune really stand out. It's called <u>homophonic texture</u> (see page 45).

2) These accompanying chords can be played in <u>different ways</u>:

These are <u>block chords</u>...

... and these are <u>broken chords</u>

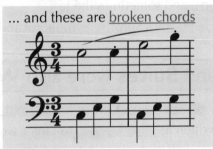

3) <u>Polyphony</u> (where <u>several tunes</u> weave in and out of each other) is used too, but not as often.

Classical Music Uses **Major** and **Minor Keys**

1) Classical music is always in either a major or minor key — the <u>tonality</u> is major or minor.
2) <u>Bright</u>, <u>cheery</u> bits are in major keys and <u>gloomy</u>, <u>sad</u> bits are in minor keys.
3) Classical harmony is what's known as <u>diatonic</u> — nearly <u>all</u> the notes belong to the <u>main key</u>.

The **Beat** is Obvious and **Easy to Follow**

1) The <u>metre</u> in Classical music is very regular. You can happily <u>tap your foot</u> in time to the music.
2) The <u>tempo</u> stays <u>constant</u> — the speed of the beat stays pretty much the same all the way through, <u>without</u> massively <u>speeding up</u> or <u>slowing down</u>.

Classical style — a wig, tailcoat and breeches...

Have a listen to Haydn's Clock Symphony and Mozart's Piano Sonata No. 16 in C Major and see if you can pick out all the features of Classical music that are described on this page.

Classical Structures

Concertos, sonatas and symphonies were very popular in the Classical period.
Take your time and make sure that you're familiar with each one of these structures.

Concertos are Played by a **Soloist** and **Orchestra**

1) A concerto is a piece for a soloist and orchestra. The soloist has most of the melody, and can really show off. The orchestra does get the melody too — they're not just an accompaniment.

2) A concerto usually has three movements — quick, slow and quick.

3) They often have a bit called a cadenza (p.57), where the orchestra stops and the soloist can show everyone how brilliant they are. A cadenza is sometimes improvised — it's often just indicated by a pause above the music.

4) Piano and violin concertos were most popular in the Classical period, though some composers wrote clarinet, horn and trumpet concertos too.

5) Famous examples of Classical concertos include Haydn's Trumpet Concerto in E♭ major (listen out for the cadenza in the first movement) and Mozart's Horn Concerto No. 4 in E♭ major.

A **Symphony** is Played by a **Full Orchestra**

1) A symphony is a massive piece. They can last more than an hour and have real impact because they use the full orchestra.

2) Symphonies usually have four movements (but some have three, and they can have more than four). The contrast between the movements is important.

3) At least one of the movements is in sonata form (see next page) — usually the first, and sometimes the last.

4) Examples include Haydn's Surprise Symphony and Beethoven's Eroica Symphony.

Overtures and **Suites** were also Written for **Orchestras**

1) An overture is a one-movement piece for orchestra.

2) Overtures are written as introductions to larger works like operas and ballets.

3) They use ideas, moods and musical themes from the main work to prepare the audience. For an example, have a listen to Mozart's overture to his opera *The Magic Flute*.

4) Classical orchestral suites are another offshoot of ballets and operas.

5) In music from this period, a 'suite' is an orchestral arrangement of the music used to accompany the action on stage. It would be put together as a separate piece of music and played at concerts.

Sonatas are for **One** or **Two** Instruments

1) Sonatas are mostly written for one instrument, but there are some sonatas for two instruments and a few for two different instruments, with each one playing a different part.

2) A sonata usually has three or four movements, with breaks in between them.

3) A sonata has a similar structure to a symphony — it has one or more movements in sonata form (see next page).

4) Piano sonatas were very popular in the Classical era — Haydn alone wrote 62. Have a listen to Mozart's Piano Sonata in C Major, Haydn's Piano Sonata in C Major and the set piece Beethoven's Sonata Pathétique.

Classical Structures

The <u>movements</u> of compositions were usually written in <u>standard forms</u> and arranged in a certain order. <u>Symphonies</u>, <u>sonatas</u> and <u>concertos</u> all follow a <u>similar pattern</u> — now there's a stroke of luck...

Symphonies, Sonatas and Concertos have a Standard Structure

1) The <u>four movements</u> of a <u>symphony</u> have the forms shown in the <u>table</u> below.

2) <u>Sonatas</u> with <u>four movements</u> also follow this structure. If the <u>sonata</u> only has <u>three movements</u>, the <u>minuet</u> (third movement in the table) is <u>left out</u>.

3) <u>Concertos</u> usually have <u>three movements</u> — they have the <u>first</u>, <u>second</u> and <u>fourth</u> movements from the table.

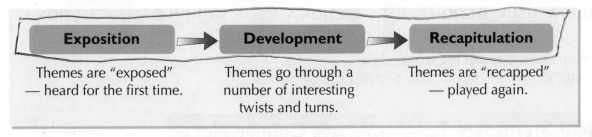

FIRST MOVEMENT	sonata form	brisk and purposeful
SECOND MOVEMENT	ternary or variation form	slower and songlike
THIRD MOVEMENT	minuet or scherzo	fairly fast and dance-like
FOURTH MOVEMENT	rondo, variation or sonata form	fast and cheerful

See page 81 for ternary form and page 82 for variation form. The other forms are explained over the next couple of pages.

Sonata Form has Three Main Sections

The <u>movements</u> of a sonata or symphony are themselves made up of a number of <u>different sections</u>. <u>Sonata form</u> has the following sections:

Exposition → **Development** → **Recapitulation**

Themes are "exposed" — heard for the first time.

Themes go through a number of interesting twists and turns.

Themes are "recapped" — played again.

1) The <u>exposition</u> has a number of <u>contrasting themes</u>. It ends in a <u>different</u> (but related) key to the one it started in.

2) The <u>development</u> keeps the piece <u>interesting</u>. It takes <u>extracts</u> from the exposition <u>themes</u>, explores <u>variations</u> on them, and presents them in <u>different keys</u> — the development often <u>modulates</u> through a number of keys. Completely <u>new</u> material might be introduced too.

3) The <u>recapitulation</u> pulls it all <u>together</u> again — the exposition themes are <u>repeated</u>, generally in the <u>same order</u> as in the exposition. They're usually <u>changed</u> a bit — the composer might add <u>ornaments</u> (see p.84) or <u>shorten</u> them. Some themes are heard in a <u>different key</u> — a theme that was in the <u>relative key</u> in the exposition usually moves to the <u>tonic key</u> in the recapitulation.

4) Composers sometimes use <u>bridge sections</u> between the themes and <u>links</u> between the main sections. They usually add a <u>coda</u> to finish off the piece <u>neatly</u> as well.

Fear not, there are more forms to come...

Make sure you're completely happy with <u>sonata form</u> — it'll come in handy for the set piece. Remember, sonata form is the structure of the <u>first movement</u> of a sonata, not the whole thing.

Classical Structures

Here's some more detail on the <u>forms</u> that make up the <u>movements</u> of a <u>sonata</u> or <u>symphony</u>.

Minuets and Scherzos are in Ternary Form

1) In a <u>sonata</u> or <u>symphony</u>, 'minuet' is short for '<u>minuet and trio</u>' and <u>scherzo</u> is short for '<u>scherzo and trio</u>'. The <u>third movement</u> of a four-movement work is either a minuet or a scherzo.

2) A minuet is a <u>French dance</u> with <u>three beats</u> in a bar.

3) The <u>trio</u> is <u>another minuet</u> in a <u>contrasting</u> but <u>related</u> key — often the <u>dominant</u> or <u>relative minor</u>. It's often written for <u>three instruments</u> (which is why it's called a trio).

4) The <u>minuet</u> is played <u>first</u>, <u>followed</u> by the <u>trio</u> section, and then the <u>minuet</u> is played <u>again</u> — this gives the movement <u>ternary form</u> (see p.81).

5) The <u>individual</u> minuet and trio sections often have their <u>own ternary form</u>. A <u>common structure</u> for a minuet and trio is shown below.

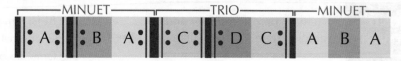

6) A <u>scherzo and trio</u> is very <u>similar</u>, but a scherzo is <u>faster</u> and more <u>light-hearted</u> than a minuet — scherzo means '<u>joke</u>' in Italian. <u>Beethoven</u> was one of the first composers to use a scherzo like this.

Rondo Form Can Have Any Number of Sections

1) The <u>fourth movement</u> of a <u>sonata or symphony</u> is often a <u>rondo</u>.

2) <u>Rondo</u> means <u>going round</u>. A rondo starts with a main idea in <u>Section A</u>, moves into a <u>new section</u>, goes round again to <u>A</u>, moves into another <u>new section</u>, goes round again to <u>A</u>, etc. etc. The <u>new section</u> after each Section A always <u>contrasts</u> with A.

3) Section A is known as the <u>main theme</u> or <u>refrain</u>. The contrasting sections are called <u>episodes</u>.

4) The main theme is always in the <u>home key</u>. Each <u>episode</u> tends to modulate to a <u>related key</u> for contrast.

Musical Signposts Tell You What's Coming Next

1) You've seen that the <u>movements</u> of a work are themselves made up of a <u>number of sections</u>. The most obvious clue that a new section is starting in Classical music is a <u>change of key</u>.

2) Classical composers were also keen on dropping <u>hints</u> that a new section was about to start. These hints are known as <u>musical signposts</u>. They're not all that easy to spot at first, but with a bit of <u>practice</u> you should get the hang of it:

- <u>Bridge passages</u> lead smoothly into the new theme and also help <u>prepare</u> the new key.
- <u>Cadences</u> (p.42-43) clearly mark the end of a phrase or section, and they come at the <u>end</u> of a piece too. When they do, the <u>chords</u> used in the <u>cadence</u> are repeated several times, to let the audience know it's all over.

ABACADAEAFAGAHA — my rondo got a bit out of hand...

Classical composers were real masters of form and structure. They liked their music to be carefully constructed and beautifully balanced, with helpful hints to what was coming next. How kind of them.

The Romantic Period

The Romantic period was about how passionate emotions can be expressed through art and music.

The **Romantic Period** Came **After** the **Classical Period**

1) The Romantic period was from about 1820-1900.

2) Romantic music was very expressive — composers used music to express contrasting emotions and ideas such as love and hate, happiness and grief, and life and death.

3) Composers were influenced by what they saw in nature, and by supernatural ideas too. They also wrote music based on poems and paintings, and used their music to tell stories.

4) Beethoven (see next page) bridged the Classical and Romantic periods. His early works were influenced by Classical composers such as Mozart and Haydn, but his work became increasingly expressive as his career progressed.

5) Tchaikovsky, Wagner and Chopin are famous Romantic composers.

Romantic Music is More **Dramatic** Than Classical

1) Romantic composers used a wide range of dynamics, with lots of sudden changes. They used a lot of sforzandos and accents as well — it made the music very dramatic.

2) To make the music more expressive, composers gave extra instructions — as well as tempo markings, they would include instructions like *dolce* (sweetly), *amoroso* (lovingly) or *agitato* (agitated).

3) There were more tempo changes — a piece might change speeds lots of times within the same section. Musicians used *rubato* too — speeding up in one phrase and then slowing down to make up for it.

4) Composers added extra notes to chords to make the harmonies more interesting — they helped create dissonance (clashing notes), which let them show emotions like pain and misery.

5) Orchestras got much bigger — extra instruments were added to all sections, especially woodwind and percussion. Brass instruments now had valves so were able to play more notes. This meant that composers could write music with a larger range of textures, timbre and dynamics.

6) There was a lot of virtuoso playing — composers wrote technically difficult music which gave performers the chance to show off. It was very exciting to watch and listen to.

7) Lots of Romantic composers were very proud of the countries they came from — they used folk tunes and dance rhythms from their homelands to show their national pride.

The **Piano Developed** in the **Romantic Period**

Beethoven composed and performed numerous works for the piano. However, the pianos available to him could not stand up to the demands of his compositions — he played his pieces so energetically that he snapped the strings and splintered the hammers. Better instruments were needed, and this led piano makers to make many developments during the 19th century. These improvements made the piano increasingly popular with Romantic composers. The main developments were:

- The piano got bigger (and louder). It had a larger number of keys, covering seven octaves, and a bigger dynamic range too.
- The sustain pedal and the soft pedal became more effective.
- A felt covering on the hammers (instead of a leather one) created a softer, more rounded tone.
- The strings inside were both thicker and longer, making a fuller tone.
- The frame was made of metal rather than wood, which made pianos easier to transport.

If music be the food of love, play on...

Now you've learnt all about the Classical and Romantic eras, it's time to have a look at your next set work...

Beethoven — Sonata Pathétique

The <u>1st Movement</u> from <u>Piano Sonata No. 8 in C minor</u> by <u>Ludwig van Beethoven</u> is one of your <u>set pieces</u>. It is known as '*Sonata Pathétique*' — this doesn't mean 'pathetic' in the modern sense of the word, but refers to the <u>emotional</u> and <u>passionate</u> nature of the music.

Beethoven was an **Influential Composer**

1) <u>Ludwig van Beethoven</u> was a <u>German</u> composer who lived from <u>1770-1827</u>.

2) He was a <u>very significant</u> composer in Western classical music — his music is famous for its <u>drama</u>, <u>intensity</u> and <u>emotion</u>.

3) He wrote music in <u>many different forms</u> — including <u>orchestral music</u> (especially <u>symphonies</u>), <u>sonatas</u> and <u>string quartets</u>.

4) Beethoven was important in <u>developing</u> musical <u>styles</u> — he moved from the <u>stricter forms</u> and <u>harmonies</u> of the <u>Classical</u> period to the <u>freer forms</u> and <u>richer harmonies</u> of the <u>Romantic</u> era.

Beethoven Wrote Many **Sonatas**

1) Beethoven wrote <u>sonatas</u> for a <u>range of solo instruments</u>, such as <u>piano</u>, <u>violin</u> and <u>cello</u>.

2) He wrote the most for the <u>piano</u> — he composed <u>32 piano sonatas</u> in total.

3) Beethoven was a <u>skilled pianist</u> himself, and his piano sonatas are considered to be some of his most <u>expressive</u> and <u>powerful</u> music.

4) <u>Piano sonatas</u> by <u>earlier composers</u> tended to follow the <u>three-movement structure</u> from p.91 — a <u>first</u> movement in <u>sonata form</u>, a <u>second slower movement</u> and a <u>faster, lively third movement</u>.

> • *Sonata Pathétique* follows this pattern of <u>three movements</u>. The <u>1st movement</u> is quite unusual because of the <u>very slow introduction</u>, which <u>returns</u> briefly <u>twice</u> during the much faster main part of the movement. The introduction is just <u>10 bars long</u>, but lasts about <u>1 minute 45 seconds</u>.
>
> • The <u>2nd movement</u> is a <u>slow</u> movement — its tempo is <u>Adagio cantabile</u>, meaning <u>slow and songlike</u>.
>
> • The <u>3rd movement</u> is in <u>rondo form</u> and is marked <u>Allegro</u> (meaning <u>quick</u>). The main theme of this movement is very <u>similar</u> to <u>theme B</u> of the <u>exposition</u> of the 1st movement (see next page).

The **Set Piece** is in **Sonata Form**

1) The <u>1st Movement</u> of *Sonata Pathétique* is in <u>sonata form</u>. The <u>table</u> below shows where the <u>three main sections</u> of the sonata form appear in the piece — the <u>exposition</u>, <u>development</u> and <u>recapitulation</u> (see p.91).

2) The <u>exposition</u> is usually <u>repeated</u> (but in some recordings it isn't).

Section	Introduction	Exposition	Transition	Development	Recapitulation	Transition	Coda
Bars	1-10	11-134	135-138	139-196	197-296	297-300	301- end

3) There are <u>variations</u> in <u>tempo</u> throughout the movement — the <u>introduction</u> is marked <u>Grave</u>, meaning <u>very slow and solemn</u> but the other sections are <u>Allegro di molto e con brio</u> which means <u>very fast</u> and played with <u>spirit</u>. The 'transitions' are short four-bar <u>references</u> to the <u>introduction</u>, played at the same <u>slow tempo</u>, providing <u>contrast</u> with the <u>main sections</u>.

4) The piece ends with a <u>coda</u> which <u>mirrors</u> the start of the <u>exposition</u>.

Beethoven — Sonata Pathétique

SET
PIECE

This sonata highlights the way in which Beethoven's career bridged the Classical and Romantic periods.

Sonata Pathétique Shows How Music Was Developing

Beethoven's music in this sonata illustrates the transition from the Classical period to the richer harmonies and more dramatic, emotional style that were characteristic of the Romantic period.
Many of these characteristics are seen in the introduction to the movement (bars 1 and 2 are shown):

- **Dissonance** — indicated with * here.
- **Variation in dynamics** — across the movement the dynamics range from pp to ff, with sudden changes such as the fp (see p.19) in bar 1, and more gradual crescendos and diminuendos.
- **Dramatic chords** — there are slow, dotted homophonic chords in the opening bars.
- **Contrast** — this is created by the faster scales in bar 4 and bars 9-10.
- **Large pitch range** — in bars 8 and 9, the melody part (the highest notes) ranges from middle C in the first chord to a high F, 2½ octaves higher. The first chord of bar 9 (G7) spans nearly 4 octaves.
- **Chromatic motion** (see p.27) — parts of the harmony are chromatic (e.g. bar 4).

The Exposition has Three Themes

The exposition (bars 11-134) is made up of three different musical ideas:

- **Theme A** — bars 11-50. This starts in the key of C minor. The theme consists of rising and falling music over a 'murky bass' — where notes an octave apart are played alternately (broken octaves).

- **Theme B** — bars 51-88. This theme starts in E♭ minor (see the G♭ accidental in bar 51). This is unusual — if a composer begins a piece in a minor key, they often move to the relative major key. With the first theme in C minor, the obvious key to move to would be E♭ major (the relative major) — but Beethoven chose E♭ minor instead.

- **Theme C** — bars 89-134. Beethoven now uses the relative major, starting this theme in E♭ major. A lot of the music is made up of broken chords. The bass part makes use of Alberti bass (see p.39) where chords are played as separate notes (e.g. in bars 105-109).

The Themes are Used Throughout the Movement

The **DEVELOPMENT** (bars 139-196) is a variation on theme A of the exposition — this can be heard most clearly in the staccato parts. The murky bass continues to be used, and broken octaves are also used in the right-hand part (see bars 151-168). There are also references to the introduction — e.g. the melody in bars 142-143 mirrors the first phrase of bar 5. There are a number of modulations within the section.

In the **RECAPITULATION** (bars 197-296), each of the three exposition themes appears in turn. Theme A is in the same key as in the exposition (C minor). Themes B and C are in different keys — theme C is now also in C minor, which leads into a final reference to theme A at the end of the section. Theme A returns once more in the **CODA**, after which the piece concludes with ff chords and a perfect cadence.

I'm feeling suddenly dynamic...

To see how Beethoven's sonata is 'modern' for the period, compare it with the 1st movement from an earlier Classical sonata such as Mozart's Piano Sonata in C major or Haydn's Piano Sonata in C major.

Warm-up and Exam Questions

Use the warm-up questions to get your brain in gear before attempting the exam questions.

Warm-up Questions

1) Describe how dynamics were used in the Baroque period.
   There were only terraced dynamics — loud and soft

2) In a concerto grosso, what is:
   a) the concertino? *The soloists*
   b) the ripieno? *The accompaniment instruments*

3) What is an appoggiatura?
   An additional grace note

4) Name an instrument that was included in the Classical orchestra but was not used in orchestras of the Baroque period.
   Piano

5) What is the standard structure of a Classical concerto?
   First movement, second movement, third movement & 4th movement.

6) What are the three main sections of a piece in sonata form?
   Exposition, development & recapitulation

7) Name two Classical composers.
   Mozart and Chopin

Exam Questions

Have a go at these exam-style questions.

Track 32 is an extract from the 3rd Movement of J.S. Bach's Brandenburg Concerto No.5.
Play the extract **three** times. Leave a short pause between each playing.

a) Write down two solo instruments that are heard in this extract.

   The flute and the violin

   [2 marks]

b) Write down two instruments that play an accompanying role in the extract.

   harpsichord and cello

   [2 marks]

Exam Questions

c) i) Which musical device is frequently heard in the extract?
Tick the correct answer.

Ostinato ☐

Drone ☐

Imitation ☐

Ornamentation ☑

[1 mark]

ii) What musical form is this composition written in?

.... Fugue ....
[1 mark]

d) i) Which period of Western musical history was this piece of music composed in?

.... Baroque ....
[1 mark]

ii) Describe some of the aspects that make this extract typical of the period.
Comment on the instrumental groupings and texture.

....

....

....

....

....

....
[3 marks]

Exam Questions

Track 33 is an extract from the 1st Movement of Beethoven's Sonata Pathétique.
Play the extract **three** times. Leave a short pause between each playing.

a)   Name two musical elements that change considerably during this extract.

......Dynamics....and....tempo...

....

[2 marks]

b)   Describe the texture of the opening three bars of the extract.

......Melody-dominated......homophonic. Both..moving..in..Sync.....
......Right...hand....playing....melody...with...left...hand...playig.....
......accompanying....chords...

[2 marks]

c)   Beethoven is known as a composer who bridged the Classical and Romantic
     musical periods. Describe the features of this extract that illustrate how music
     was developing as it moved towards the Romantic era.

......There...is...a....dramatic....contrast...which...shows...the......
......development...of....the...era. He...uses...a....range..of...dynamics....
......and....tempo....changes...to...demonstrate...this...effectively......
......He....also....explicitly....uses...the....full...potential..of......
......the....piano..which..was..a.....new...instrument...at...the......
......time...before...there....was...only...a..harpsichord.......
......He..does..this..by.....using...a.....wide...tessitura...and.....
......a...certain....sonority..

[4 marks]

Exam Questions

d) i) Which of the following is used frequently in the right-hand part
        during the second half of this extract?
        Tick the correct answer.

Mordent ☐

Staccato ☑

Triplets ☐

Acciaccatura ☐

[1 mark]

ii) Which of these devices is used in the bass part
    during the second half of this extract?
    Tick the correct answer.

Ground bass ☐

Ostinato ☐

Sequence ☐

Murky bass ☑

[1 mark]

Revision Summary for Section Six

What you need to take away from this section are the facts about Baroque, Classical and Romantic music — it's really important that you know how they were different from each other. Have a go at these questions to check that you're up to speed. You know what to do — keep going through them until you can answer them all without needing to look back through the section.

1) Give the approximate dates of the Baroque period.
2) What is a basso continuo and what instruments would normally play it?
3) What is a concerto grosso?
4) Which Baroque structure can be described as ABA?
5) What was the function of a prelude in the Baroque period?
6) In theme and variation form, what is the theme?
7) What is the main difference between theme and variation form and ground bass form?
8) Explain what each of these terms means:
   a) melodic inversion   b) retrograde   c) ostinato.
9) Name three different ornaments used by Baroque composers and explain what they are.
10) What is the key signature of Brandenburg Concerto No.5?
11) What type of dance is the 3rd Movement of Brandenburg Concerto No.5 based on?
12) In a fugue what is: a) the subject   b) the counter-subject?
13) What melodic device is used throughout a fugue?
14) Which instruments play the continuo in the 3rd Movement of Brandenburg Concerto No.5?
15) Is the 3rd Movement of Brandenburg Concerto No.5 homophonic, monophonic or polyphonic?
16) Is the 3rd Movement of Brandenburg Concerto No.5 in binary or ternary form?
17) What is: a) sequencing   b) pedal point   c) stretto?
18) Give the approximate dates of the Classical period.
19) Why did the piano become increasingly popular in the Classical period?
20) What was the most important section in a Classical orchestra?
21) Classical music usually has a homophonic texture. What does this mean?
22) What is a symphony?
23) How many instruments are sonatas usually composed for?
24) What is the structure of a sonata with 4 movements?
    Which movement is omitted if the sonata only has 3 movements?
25) Which two musical periods were bridged by Beethoven's career?
26) Name three techniques that Romantic composers used to show drama and emotion in their work.
27) What is the full name of Beethoven's Sonata Pathétique?
28) In what form did Beethoven write the 1st Movement of Sonata Pathétique?
29) At which points in the movement does Beethoven reference the introduction?
30) What key does the exposition section of Sonata Pathétique begin in?
31) a) What is the relative major of the key at the start of the exposition?
    b) When is this key first heard?
32) What is the meaning of: a) Grave   b) Allegro   c) *fp*?
33) Name two types of bass pattern that are used in the exposition
    of the 1st Movement of Sonata Pathétique.

Choral Music

Choirs have been around for ages. They vary in size from just a few singers to hundreds, and perform anywhere from school halls and churches to concert halls, theatres and cathedrals.

Choral Music has Been Around for Over 600 Years

1) The first choral pieces were sung in churches in the 14th century.
   Before that, monks used to sing plainsong (a unison chant).

2) Most choral music in Renaissance and Baroque times was sacred (church music).

3) Masses were sung in Catholic churches. They were part of the church service.
   A requiem was a mass for the dead. There's more about masses on p.104.

4) Oratorios are Bible stories set to music (see p.103). Masses, requiems and oratorios
   are all sacred music. They're made up of choir sections and solo sections.

5) Secular (non-religious) choral music is mainly made up of choruses in operas (see p.102).
   Operas often tell love stories and are performed on stage. The chorus emphasises important bits.

Choirs Were Originally All Male

There's more on the different types of voice on p.68.

1) Baroque choirs were fairly small — they'd sometimes have just one singer on each part.
   All parts were sung by men (women were banned from singing in church).

2) Most choir music was written for 4 different voices: treble (a boy soprano), countertenor or alto
   (a high-pitched voice known as falsetto), tenor (a high male voice) and bass (a low male voice).

3) By the Victorian era, choirs were huge — they'd often have over 100 members (it was a popular
   Victorian hobby). The Huddersfield Choral Society was started in 1836 and still exists today.

4) Some choirs are mixed-sex, with music arranged for SATB voices: soprano (a high female voice),
   alto (a lower female voice), tenor (a high male voice) and bass (a low male voice).

5) All-female choirs are usually SSAA (2 soprano parts and 2 alto parts) or SSA (2 soprano parts and
   1 alto part). Male voice choirs are often TTBB (2 tenor parts, 1 baritone part and 1 bass part).

Choral Singing is Still Popular Today

1) 20th and 21st century choirs are generally smaller than the large Victorian choirs —
   they'll often have around 80 members though. Some can have as many as 130 members.

2) Lots of 20th century choral works are written for chamber choir and chamber orchestra. These are
   just small versions of choirs and orchestras (they're called 'chamber' because they used to perform
   in rooms or chambers, rather than a concert hall). Chamber choirs normally have 20-25 members.

3) Chamber choir pieces may have been a reaction against 19th century composers,
   who often composed pieces for massive choirs.

Choirs Have Soloists Too

There are sometimes solo sections in choral works — the soloist might be accompanied
by the rest of the choir, or just sing on their own. The main solo voices are:

- Soprano, alto, tenor or bass (as described above).
- Mezzo-sopranos (a female voice that's lower than a soprano but higher than an alto),
  baritones (a male voice that's lower than a tenor but higher than a bass) or contralto
  (the lowest female voice that has a similar range to a countertenor).

Requiems, oratorios — there's Masses of stuff on this page...

Masses and requiems aren't just written by pre-20th century composers. Benjamin Britten (1913-1976) wrote
a War Requiem in 1961-62 using Latin words from the Requiem Mass and war poems by Wilfred Owen.

Opera

Operas are large vocal works, made up of both solo and chorus sections.

Operas are Like **Plays** Set to **Music**

1) An opera is a story set to music with singing and acting.
   Most operas are divided up into three parts (or 'Acts').

2) Operas are secular (non-religious).

3) The main characters are played by solo singers.

4) The main characters are supported by a chorus and an orchestra.

5) The story is acted out — usually with lavish sets, costumes and special effects.

6) In some operas every single word is sung (this is known as sung-through)
   — in others there's a bit of talking from time to time.

7) Some operas have really serious, tragic themes. Others are more light-hearted and comic.
   These are the names for the main types:

Grand opera	serious, set entirely to music (sung-through)
Opera seria	formal, serious opera, often mythological themes
Opera buffa	comic opera with lighter, more everyday themes
Opéra comique	like opera buffa but with some spoken dialogue
Operetta	shorter than a full opera, lighter themes

8) The words of an opera are called the 'libretto'.
   This is often written by a 'librettist' working alongside the composer.

In Opera There are **Three Types** of **Song**

ARIA

1) An aria is a solo vocal piece, backed by the orchestra.

2) Arias are used to show the thoughts and emotions of the main characters.

3) The arias have the memorable, exciting tunes. They're challenging for the performers and let them show their vocal tone and agility.

In England and France, arias are sometimes known as 'airs'.

RECITATIVE

1) A recitative is a song for a soloist which tells the story and moves it along. The rhythm of the words tends to imitate the rhythm of normal speech.

2) A recitative is performed in a half-spoken, half-singing style used for some conversations.

3) A recitativo secco is a recitative that's unaccompanied or backed by simple chords.

4) A recitativo stromentato or accompagnato is a recitative with orchestral backing. The accompaniment's used to increase the dramatic tension of the words.

CHORUS — A bit where the whole chorus (or choir) sings together. Choruses are usually written for SATB choirs (see previous page), but in Baroque operas, the soprano parts would be sung by trebles (boy sopranos).

Anyone for a sing-song then...

Don't worry, I'm not going to suggest you listen to a whole opera for your revision tonight. But it's worth listening to bits of different operas, and trying to spot the different types of song. Good examples of arias include Puccini's 'O Mio Babbino Caro' and Mozart's 'Non So Più'.

Oratorios

Oratorio is another important type of vocal music. If you write a whole oratorio for your composition, the examiners will be so impressed they'll probably fall down in a <u>faint</u>. Very undignified.

Oratorios are **Religious** Versions of **Operas**

1) Oratorios often tell <u>Bible stories</u>, or tales with a <u>religious</u> or <u>moral</u> theme
   — they're a type of <u>sacred music</u>.

2) They're <u>not</u> usually <u>acted out</u> with <u>scenery</u> and <u>costumes</u> (like operas are).

3) They normally have an <u>instrumental accompaniment</u>.

4) They can be performed in <u>concert halls</u> as well as <u>churches</u>.

5) Oratorios have <u>arias</u>, <u>recitatives</u> and <u>choruses</u> (see previous page) just like operas.

6) The table below gives some <u>composers</u> and their most famous oratorios. Have a listen to them and try to spot the different types of <u>song</u>, as well as listening out for the different <u>musical styles</u>.

COMPOSER	LIVED	FAMOUS ORATORIO
Carissimi	1605-1674	Jephte
Handel	1685-1759	Messiah
Haydn	1732-1809	The Creation
Berlioz	1803-1869	L'Enfance du Christ
Mendelssohn	1809-1847	Elijah
Elgar	1857-1934	The Dream of Gerontius
Tippett	1905-1998	A Child of Our Time

Messiah is a Famous **Oratorio** by **Handel**

1) <u>Messiah</u> tells the story of <u>Jesus' life</u>.

2) It's written for <u>SATB soloists</u>, <u>SATB choir</u> and a <u>full orchestra</u>.
   At the time Handel wrote it, all the parts would have been sung by <u>men</u>.

3) Handel wrote it for a <u>small choir</u>, but in <u>Victorian</u> times,
   Messiah would have been performed by <u>hundreds</u> of singers.

4) Much of the Messiah is <u>melismatic</u> (a <u>single syllable</u> of text is sung over a <u>succession</u> of notes). In the chorus '<u>For Unto Us a Child is Born</u>', the <u>soprano</u> part has a run of <u>57 notes</u> for the word '<u>born</u>'.

The opposite of melismatic is <u>syllabic</u>, where every <u>syllable</u> is sung to a <u>single note</u>.

Tenor

Crook - ed

5) Handel also uses <u>word-painting</u> — where the music <u>matches</u> the words. E.g. the word '<u>crooked</u>' is <u>split</u> over four notes each time it is sung, making it <u>sound</u> crooked.

6) The most famous bit of the Messiah is probably the '<u>Hallelujah Chorus</u>', but there are lots of other <u>choruses</u> and <u>recitatives</u>.

7) There are <u>solos</u> (or <u>arias</u>) for different voices.
   Here are some good <u>examples</u> to listen out for:

   - '<u>The Trumpet Shall Sound</u>' (bass solo)
   - '<u>Rejoice Greatly</u>' (soprano solo)
   - '<u>Every Valley Shall Be Exalted</u>' (tenor solo)

Hallelujah — it's the end of the page...

Listen out for the accompaniment in the solo sections — Messiah was written in the Baroque period, so the orchestra would have included a basso continuo, often a harpsichord (see p.57). 'The Trumpet Shall Sound' features a prominent trumpet part in the accompaniment.

Smaller Vocal Pieces

These songs are shorter than operas, but you still need to know their <u>forms</u>.

Lots of Music Was Written to be **Sung** in **Church**

CANTATA

1) A <u>cantata</u> is a piece made up of a number of <u>arias</u>, separated by <u>recitatives</u> (see p.102).

2) Some things in a <u>cantata</u> are similar to an <u>oratorio</u>. They are performed by <u>solo singers</u>, a <u>chorus</u> and an <u>orchestra</u>. There's <u>no scenery</u> and <u>no acting</u> and they were written to be performed in a <u>church</u> or <u>concert hall</u>.

3) The <u>difference</u> is that the <u>words</u> are taken from books or poems — they're not specially written. Most cantatas have a religious theme — but <u>not all</u> of them.

In J.S. Bach's secular Wedding Cantata, the first aria talks about the snow of winter giving way to spring.

CHORALE

<u>Chorales</u> are hymns. They have <u>simple language</u> and a melody that's <u>easy to sing</u>. <u>J.S. Bach</u> wrote lots of them. Here's a bit from a chorale he put in St. Matthew's Passion.

O Lord, who dares to smite Thee?

MOTET & ANTHEM

A <u>motet</u> is a short piece written to be performed by the <u>choir</u> in church. Motets are written for <u>Roman Catholic</u> churches and the words are often in <u>Latin</u>. They are <u>polyphonic</u> — see p.45. <u>Anthems</u> are very similar to a motet except they're written for <u>Protestant</u> churches, so the words aren't in Latin.

MASS

The <u>mass</u> is the name of a Roman Catholic church service — these parts of the mass are sung by the choir, or the choir and soloists:

Musical settings of the Mass were originally written to be <u>used in church</u>, but nowadays they're played in concerts, too. The text is usually in <u>Latin</u>.

- Kyrie — *Lord have mercy...*
- Gloria — *Glory be to God on high...*
- Credo — *I believe in one God...*
- Sanctus — *Holy, holy, holy...*
- Benedictus — *Blessed is He...*
- Agnus Dei — *O Lamb of God...*

(Some of them are quite long, so I've only given you the starting bits.)

Madrigals are Non-Religious

Most madrigals were written in the <u>1500s</u> and <u>1600s</u>. They're about <u>love</u> or the <u>countryside</u> — or both. Most have <u>no accompaniment</u>. They're usually written for between <u>2</u> and <u>8</u> people, and each person sings a <u>different part</u>. Madrigals are <u>polyphonic</u> (see p.45) and often use <u>imitation</u> (see p.83).

Now is the month of May-ing, When mer-ry lads are play-ing; Fa la la la la la la la la la, Fa la la la la la la.

They don't seem to have mentioned karaoke...

Even though this page is called 'smaller vocal pieces', a mass can still be quite long — it's just small in comparison to an opera or oratorio. Remember, non-religious music is known as secular music.

Romantic Songs — Lieder

'Lied' is the German word for 'song'. It's pronounced <u>LEED</u>.
If you're talking about <u>more than one</u> Lied you say <u>Lieder</u> (not 'Lieds').

Lieder are Romantic Songs

1) A <u>Lied</u> is a <u>song</u> for <u>one singer</u> and a <u>piano</u>. The piano part's <u>not</u> just a background accompaniment — it adds a lot to the <u>story-telling</u> of the piece. Lieder were really popular in Europe during the <u>Romantic</u> period — a bit like the pop songs of today.

Romantic music was very <u>expressive</u> and <u>dramatic</u> — there's more about it on p.93.

2) The <u>words</u> of a Lied are really important. They're usually based on <u>German poems</u> from the 18th and 19th centuries. Lieder usually tell a <u>story</u> — they're often <u>dramatic</u> and full of <u>emotion</u>. The music <u>illustrates</u> the words, so you can tell when it gets sad or scary (like music in a film).

3) Some Lieder are <u>through-composed</u> (see p.56). This means that the music is <u>different</u> in each verse. Others have a <u>strophic</u> structure (p.56), where the verses all have the <u>same</u> melody. There are lots of <u>motifs</u> — little bits of music that <u>represent</u> an <u>idea</u>, <u>character</u> or <u>place</u>. The motifs are <u>repeated</u> throughout the songs so you can follow what's happening. Sometimes the motifs match the words — in <u>Schubert's</u> 'Gretchen at the Spinning Wheel', the piano <u>mimics</u> the sound of the spinning wheel.

4) <u>Schubert</u> is one of the best known composers of Lieder. Other composers include <u>Schumann</u>, <u>Beethoven</u> and <u>Brahms</u>. Most well-known Lieder composers were German or Austrian.

Lieder Can be Put Together in Song Cycles

1) Sometimes a <u>collection</u> of Lieder would be put together in <u>song cycles</u> by the composer. These are just groups of songs on the same <u>theme</u>.

2) Schubert's most famous song cycles are '<u>Winter Journey</u>' and '<u>The Fair Maid of the Mill</u>'.

3) Both cycles are collections of songs based on the poems of a German poet called <u>Müller</u>. They tell stories of <u>lost love</u> and <u>rejection</u>.

'The Erl King' is a Good Example of a Lied

1) '<u>The Erl King</u>' is a Lied by Schubert, based on a poem by <u>Goethe</u>, a German poet.

2) It tells the story of a father carrying his dying child on horseback. The child can see the <u>Erl King</u>, a spirit of death.

3) It's a very <u>tragic</u> song — the boy dies at the end.

4) There are 4 <u>characters</u> in the story: the father, his son, the Erl King and the narrator.

5) Schubert uses the music to create different characters. Each character sings at a different <u>pitch</u> so that you can tell them apart when one <u>tenor</u> sings all 4 parts.

6) The piano part's very <u>dramatic</u> — the <u>repeated triplets</u> sound like the horse's galloping hooves.

Franz Schubert — Lieder of the pack...

Don't forget, in Lieder, the piano part's <u>more</u> than just an accompaniment. The <u>words</u> are often (but not always) in <u>German</u>, so if you hear German with a piano accompaniment, it's probably a Lied.

Purcell — Music for a While

SET PIECE

Now it's time for the <u>first set work</u> for this area of study — I bet you've been waiting for this music for a while (sorry, I couldn't resist). Anyway, here it is...

Music for a While was Written for the Theatre

See p.80-84 for more on Baroque music.

1) <u>Henry Purcell</u> (1659-1695) was one of the most famous English composers of the <u>Baroque</u> period.

2) He wrote a wide range of music, including <u>sacred choral music</u>, <u>chamber music</u>, <u>orchestral music</u> and music for the <u>theatre</u>. His music for the theatre included both <u>opera</u> and <u>incidental music</u> (songs and instrumental pieces to be performed as part of a <u>play</u>).

3) *Oedipus* was a play by the English dramatist <u>John Dryden</u> — it was based on a story by the Greek writer <u>Sophocles</u>. Purcell wrote the incidental music for *Oedipus*.

4) '<u>Music for a While</u>' is the second of four movements that Purcell wrote for *Oedipus*. It is sung by a <u>priest</u> who is attempting to summon the <u>ghost</u> of a <u>dead king</u>.

Music for a While has a Ground Bass

1) This song is written for a <u>singer</u> with <u>continuo</u>. The song was originally written for a <u>high male voice</u> (a <u>tenor</u> or <u>countertenor</u>), but some later arrangements are written for a <u>soprano</u>.

2) The <u>continuo</u> is usually made up of <u>two instruments</u> — often the <u>cello</u> and the <u>harpsichord</u>, which read from the <u>same</u> bass part. The <u>use</u> and <u>sound</u> of the continuo is a key feature of <u>Baroque music</u>.

3) In this song, Purcell uses a <u>ground bass</u> (see p.57).

> • Ground bass is a <u>repeating melodic phrase</u> in the <u>bass part</u>.
> • In 'Music for a While', the ground bass is <u>three bars long</u>. This is a bit <u>unusual</u> (especially for a piece in $\frac{4}{4}$) — you'd usually expect the ground bass to be <u>2</u>, <u>4</u>, or even <u>8 bars long</u>.
> • Purcell used ground bass many times in his compositions. One of his most well-known can be heard in the song '<u>When I am Laid in Earth</u>' from his opera <u>*Dido and Aeneas*</u>.
> • Here is the ground bass from 'Music for a While':

4) The ground bass is frequently <u>chromatic</u> — there is often a <u>rise</u> of a <u>semitone</u> between <u>two consecutive notes</u> (e.g. F♯ to G in the first bar, then G♯ to A a couple of notes later). The shape of the melody is generally <u>ascending</u>.

5) The <u>ascending shape</u> of the <u>ground bass</u> is <u>contrasted</u> with the <u>descending shape</u> of the <u>voice</u> part — this is known as <u>contrary motion</u>. There's more about the vocal part on the next page.

6) The ground bass <u>changes</u> in <u>bar 14</u> — it no longer follows the pattern shown above. It <u>resumes</u> in <u>bar 29</u>, and then lasts till the <u>end</u> of the piece.

7) The <u>quavers</u> in the ground bass continue throughout the song — this is an example of a <u>walking bass</u> in <u>Baroque</u> music.

I think that's given you a thorough grounding in the bass part...

Have a look back at pages 85-86 on Bach's *Brandenburg Concerto No.5* (and listen to the piece as well) — it also uses a continuo. Don't get confused by the fact that the ground bass is described as a walking bass — in jazz music, a walking bass is usually crotchets, but in Baroque music it was often quavers.

Purcell — Music for a While

We've dealt with the 'accompaniment' part of this piece, now let's move onto the vocal part.
I'll talk about the harmony and structure as well, but I know you're most excited about the voice.

Purcell uses **Word Painting** and **Melisma** in the Vocal Part

Purcell uses a number of <u>musical devices</u> to convey the <u>meaning</u> of the <u>lyrics</u>.

1) There are a number of examples of <u>word-painting</u> (see p.103) in 'Music for a While':

   - In <u>bars 23-25</u>, the <u>short notes</u> (quavers with quaver rests in between)
     sound like <u>raindrops</u> as the singer repeats the word '<u>drop</u>'.
     These notes are also generally <u>descending</u>, like <u>falling raindrops</u>.

   - In <u>bar 12</u>, there is a <u>discord</u> between the continuo and the singer to illustrate the
     word '<u>pains</u>'. This then <u>resolves</u> (see p.41) as the lyrics move to the word '<u>eas'd</u>'.

   - The word '<u>eternal</u>' in <u>bars 20-21</u> is <u>held</u> over a number of notes to make it <u>longer</u>.

2) The word 'eternal' is also <u>melismatic</u> — there are <u>many notes</u> to <u>one syllable</u>. A lot of the rest
   of the music is <u>syllabic</u> (<u>one note</u> to <u>one syllable</u>), which makes it easier to <u>hear</u> the words.

3) In <u>bars 17</u> and <u>18</u>, the music <u>stops</u> (apart from the continuo) for a quaver to <u>emphasise</u> the word '<u>dead</u>'.

4) Most of the words and phrases are <u>repeated</u>, which makes them <u>stand out</u>.
   Purcell also places <u>key words</u> or <u>syllables</u> on the <u>main beats</u> to <u>highlight</u> them further.

Music for a While is in a **Minor Key**

1) The <u>structure</u> of the music is <u>ternary form</u>, or <u>ABA</u>. <u>Section A</u> lasts from <u>bars 1</u> to <u>10</u> and <u>section B</u>
   lasts from <u>bars 11</u> to <u>28</u> (where the <u>ground bass</u> changes). Section A is then <u>repeated</u> from <u>bar 29</u>
   and <u>extended</u> with another repetition of the phrase '<u>shall all your cares beguile</u>'.

2) The main <u>tonality</u> of the piece is <u>minor</u> — the version you're studying is in <u>A minor</u> (although the
   <u>original</u> piece was written in <u>C minor</u>). The minor key reinforces the <u>sombre</u> nature of the <u>lyrics</u>.

3) It might be a bit hard to <u>identify</u> the <u>key signature</u> because the ground bass is very <u>chromatic</u>
   (see previous page), with lots of <u>accidentals</u>. However, there's a <u>perfect cadence</u> (see p.43)
   in A minor in bars 3-4 that <u>establishes</u> the key signature early on.

4) The middle section passes through several <u>closely related keys</u>:

   - <u>E minor</u> in bar 15 (the <u>dominant minor</u>), and E major in bar 28 (the <u>dominant major</u>)
   - <u>G major</u> in the middle of bar 18
   - <u>C major</u> (the <u>relative major</u>) in bar 22
   - <u>A major</u> (the <u>tonic major</u>) in the middle of bar 23
   - A final return to <u>A minor</u> (the <u>tonic</u> key) in bar 29 when the <u>ground bass</u> returns

5) There are quite a few <u>suspensions</u> in this piece. This is where a note is <u>held</u> over a change of
   chord in order to create <u>dissonance</u> (see p.41). For example, in bar 17, a <u>D</u> in the <u>vocal part</u>
   (on the word '<u>Alecto</u>') is <u>tied</u> over the bar line and creates a <u>discord</u> against the <u>C</u> in the <u>continuo</u>.

Have a go at word painting...

Remember — the focus of this area of study is music for solo voice with accompaniment. So make sure
you know the key features of both the vocal part and the accompanying parts (especially the continuo).

Pop Music

Time to jump forward about 300 years and have a look at pop music.

Pop Ballads Tell Stories

1) Ballads have been around since at least the fifteenth century. Back then a ballad was a long song with lots of verses that told a story. It's the type of thing that was sung by wandering minstrels.

2) Modern pop and rock ballads still tell stories. Often they're slow and sad and tell some kind of love story. Songwriters like to put a romantic or spooky twist right at the end to keep people listening.

3) Each verse has the same rhythm and melody but different lyrics. You'll hear ballads sung in many different styles — a rock ballad accompanied by heavy drums and amplified guitars sounds pretty different to a folk ballad played on an acoustic guitar.

4) Emotional, slow ballads sung by boy and girl bands such as Take That and The Spice Girls were huge in 1990s pop — ballads were the perfect song type to get teenage fans to fall in love with the band.

Singer-Songwriters Write Lots of Ballads

Singer-songwriters are artists who write and sing their own stuff. They tend to accompany themselves on either the guitar or piano and write a fair few ballads. The style of the music depends on the singer's own personal style. Here are a few performers who write their own songs — they all sound very different:

1) Bob Dylan's most famous ballad, released in 1963, is an anti-war song called 'Blowin' in the Wind'. Bob sings a simple diatonic tune in a major key and accompanies himself on an acoustic guitar with simple strummed chords giving the song a folky feel. All the verses have the same music and the same last line — 'The answer my friend is blowing in the wind, the answer is blowing in the wind'. The repeated line works like a mini-chorus.

2) Sting just about always writes his own songs. He accompanies himself on bass guitar, but he's also backed by his band. Sting's music takes a lot from soul and jazz. 'Seven Days' is a particularly jazzy ballad — it's in $\frac{5}{4}$ and uses major seventh chords, as well as notes from the blues scale (see p.110).

3) Kate Bush bases the story of her ballad 'Wuthering Heights' on the book with the same name. No one else in pop sounds quite like Kate Bush — she sings in a wailing, ghostly manner.

Alicia Keys

- Alicia Keys is an R&B singer-songwriter. She accompanies herself on the piano.
- Her songs are influenced by Classical music, hip-hop, soul, gospel and jazz.
- Her debut single 'Fallin'' was a huge success. It combines elements of R&B, gospel and soul, and talks about falling in and out of love. The accompaniment is fairly simple — Keys plays the piano, and there is also a light drum track and strings.
- 'If I Ain't Got You' is a song from her second album, *The Diary of Alicia Keys*. The piano is the main feature of the accompaniment, but there are also guitars, drums, saxophones and trumpets. The song has a bluesy feel. The lyrics are about how nothing is important without love.
- 'Dragon Days' from the same album has a heavier instrumental accompaniment, with more prominent drums and electric guitars, but the piano is still a constant feature. The lyrics have a fairytale theme, with ideas such as a damsel in distress, a castle, a knight and a prince.

The Accompaniment Complements the Voice

VOICE The story is the most important part of a ballad — e.g. Snow Patrol's 'Set the Fire to the Third Bar', and The Script's 'Man Who Can't Be Moved'. Vocals are clear and unhidden by the accompaniment.

ACCOMPANIMENT The accompaniment generally reflects the themes of the vocals. There's usually a lot of repetition or inversion of motifs that are sung in the main melody. The texture of the accompaniment often varies to make the dynamics (crescendos and diminuendos) more dramatic. Sometimes there's an instrumental section where an instrument (e.g. saxophone or electric guitar) does a variation on the tune.

Pop Music

There's a bit more you need to know about pop music — including structures and vocal techniques.

Most Pop Songs Have a **Verse-Chorus Structure**

After the intro, the structure of a pop song basically goes verse-chorus-verse-chorus...
- All the verses usually have the same tune, but the lyrics change for each verse.
- The chorus has a different tune from the verses, usually quite a catchy one. The lyrics and tune of the chorus don't change.
- In a lot of songs the verse and chorus are both 8 or 16 bars long.

Songs usually finish with a coda or outro — a bit that finishes it off nicely.

The old verse-chorus thing can get repetitive. To avoid this, most songs have a bridge section that sounds different. A middle 8 is a type of bridge — it's an 8-bar section in the middle of the song with new chords, new lyrics and a whole new feel. Some pop ballads have an uplifting modulation (key change) towards the end as well.

Sometimes the bridge is an instrumental section (e.g. a guitar solo).

Singers Can Do All Sorts of **Fancy Stuff**

There's more than one way to sing a song.
Make sure you can describe exactly what you're hearing. Listen out for...

1) *A CAPPELLA* — singing with no instrumental backing.
2) *VIBRATO* — when singers quiver up and down slightly in pitch. It makes the voice sound warmer and more expressive.
3) *FALSETTO* — when men (or occasionally women) make their voices go really high, like Sam Smith or the Bee Gees.
4) *PORTAMENTO* — when a singer slides from one note to another.
5) *RIFFING* — when singers decorate and add bits to the tune. They often go up and down a scale before coming to rest on one note. Riffing usually comes at the end of a phrase, between sections or to finish the song. Whitney Houston, Mariah Carey and Celine Dion are famous for riffing.

The **Lead Singer** Sings the **Main Melody**

The lead singer (or vocalist) sings the main melody of a song. They're the soloist, and often the most famous member of the band. If you get a pop song in the Listening Test, say something about the lead vocalist's style. It's even worth mentioning dead obvious stuff like whether the singer's male or female.

Backing Singers Sing the **Harmonies**

The backing vocalists are the ones who sing the harmonies. These are the main ways backing singers do their thing:

Listen out for the backing vocals in 'God Only Knows' by The Beach Boys — they sing in unison, in harmony and also in canon (see p.46).

IN HARMONY	**IN UNISON**	**DESCANT**	**CALL AND RESPONSE**
all singing different notes	all singing the same notes	singing a higher part in time with the main tune	repeating whatever the lead vocalist sings or answering the lead with another tune

I'm singing in the shower, just singing in the shower...

I'm guessing you're familiar with pop songs from life outside of the classroom — but now you can try and pick out the different features mentioned above the next time you listen to them.

The Blues

The blues style has been around for years. It first became really popular in the 1920s, and <u>still</u> has a big influence on pop music today.

African Slaves in America Started Off the Blues

1) In the <u>1600s</u> and <u>1700s</u>, millions of Africans were captured and sold as <u>slaves</u>. Many were taken to work on plantations in <u>North America</u>.

2) To pass the time and take their minds off their work, which was often brutally hard, they sang <u>work songs</u>, using their tools to give the music a <u>beat</u>. The lyrics were often about the <u>hardship</u> and <u>misery</u> of living as a slave.

3) Over the years, <u>African musical styles</u> like <u>call and response</u> singing (p.55) blended with features of <u>European music</u>, especially <u>chords</u>. This combination was the beginning of the <u>blues</u>.

4) Even after slavery was finally <u>abolished</u> in the <u>1860s</u>, ex-slaves living in the <u>southern states</u> were poor and powerless. The <u>lyrics</u> and <u>tone</u> of their songs carried on being <u>sad</u> and '<u>blue</u>'.

5) The traditional blues instruments are <u>harmonica</u>, <u>guitar</u>, <u>banjo</u>, <u>violin</u> (or <u>fiddle</u>), <u>piano</u>, <u>double bass</u> and the <u>voice</u>. They're all <u>acoustic</u> — electric instruments hadn't been invented when blues began.

6) In the <u>early twentieth century</u> black Americans started playing the blues in bars and clubs <u>beyond</u> the southern states. By the <u>1920s</u> blues was massively popular all over America with both white and black audiences.

7) In the <u>1940s</u> and <u>1950s</u> a style called <u>rhythm & blues</u> (R&B) was developed. It's a <u>speeded-up</u> version of blues played on <u>electric guitar</u> and <u>bass</u>.

Blues has its Own Scale

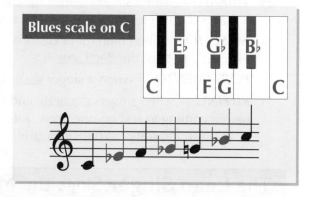

Blues scale on C

1) You get a blues scale by <u>flattening</u> the <u>3rd</u>, <u>5th</u> and <u>7th</u> of any major scale. The unflattened <u>5th</u> is played too.

2) The flattened notes are called <u>blue notes</u>. They're not always lowered by a <u>full semitone</u> — sometimes they're flattened by a <u>smaller</u> interval called a <u>microtone</u>.

3) Singers and players often <u>slide</u> up or down to blue notes — this is known as <u>pitch bend</u>. This feature comes from the '<u>bent</u>' notes used in African singing.

4) The <u>2nd</u> and <u>6th</u> notes are often left out.

Blues Melodies have Swinging, Offbeat Rhythms

1) In normal '<u>straight</u>' rhythm the beats split up into <u>equal halves</u>.

I want chips and egg

I want <u>chips</u> and <u>egg</u>

2) In the blues, the first half of the beat <u>steals</u> some time from the second half. The first bit ends up <u>longer</u> and with more <u>oomph</u>. This gives the music a <u>swinging</u> feel.

3) The blues uses lots of <u>syncopation</u>. You get a <u>lively offbeat sound</u> by avoiding the <u>strong beats</u> — it puts the <u>oomph</u> in <u>unexpected places</u>.

Please don't make me beg

The blues has influenced almost all forms of popular music...

The blues doesn't have to be mournful, sad and depressing — it just sounds better that way...

The Blues

There are lots of different types of blues, but the most popular song structure is the <u>12-bar blues</u>.

Twelve-bar Blues has a **Repeated 12-Bar Structure**

12-bar blues uses a set <u>chord pattern</u>, <u>12 bars long</u>. Singers like <u>Bessie Smith</u> and <u>Robert Johnson</u> made the 12-bar blues structure really popular in the 1920s — it's been around ever since and is still one of the most popular styles.

Bar 1	Bar 2	Bar 3	Bar 4
Chord I	Chord I	Chord I	Chord I

Bar 5	Bar 6	Bar 7	Bar 8
Chord IV	Chord IV	Chord I	Chord I

Bar 9	Bar 10	Bar 11	Bar 12
Chord V	Chord IV	Chord I	Chord I (V)

1) The only chords are <u>I</u>, <u>IV</u> and <u>V</u>.
2) The 12-bar pattern is <u>repeated</u> right through the song.
3) You can make the chords even more <u>bluesy</u> by adding the <u>minor 7ths</u> (see p.29).

When the 12-bar structure is going to be repeated, <u>chord V</u> is played in bar 12 instead of chord I. This leads back smoothly to Bar 1.

12-bar blues has had a huge influence on other musical styles including <u>ragtime</u>, <u>jazz</u>, <u>rock and roll</u> and <u>R&B</u>. Loads of <u>pop songs</u> today still use the standard 12-bar structure.

Twelve Bars Break Nicely into **Three Lines**

The 12-bar chord pattern of 12-bar blues breaks up nicely into <u>three lines</u>, each with <u>four bars</u>. The <u>lyrics</u> of a 12-bar blues song usually stick to <u>three lines for each verse</u> of the song.

Lines 1 and 2 are usually the same.
→ *Woke up this morning feeling blue.*
→ *Woke up this morning feeling blue.*

Line 3 is different, but rhymes with lines 1 and 2.
→ *Feeling sad and lonesome without you.*

The words are usually pretty <u>gloomy</u>.

Each line takes up 4 bars, but the words don't always fill up the whole line.
The singer's bit (the <u>call</u>) is followed by an instrument playing an answer (the <u>response</u>) in the gap before the next line.

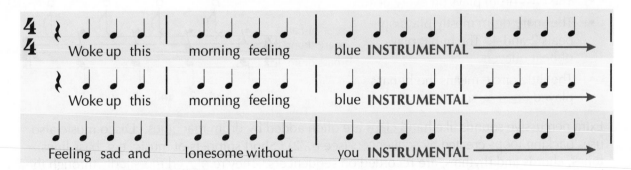

 ## Woke up this morning feeling like I wanted some more sleep...
You might want to use 12-bar blues for your composition. So make sure you know the <u>blues scale</u>, <u>rhythms</u> and <u>chords</u> used in the 12-bar structure, and everything else on these two pages.

Disco

The dancing was embarrassing. The clothes were awful. The make-up was unspeakable. Disco was ace.

Disco was the Dance Music of the 1970s

Disco first reared its groovy head in nightclubs in <u>New York</u>. The roots of disco were in <u>soul</u>, <u>jazz</u> and <u>funk</u>. Disco was played in clubs and it <u>totally changed them</u>...

1) Until about the 1960s <u>audio equipment</u> was pretty ropey — you couldn't play a recording loud enough to dance to, so most clubs had live bands.

2) In the 1970s, <u>amplifiers</u>, <u>turntables</u> and <u>loudspeakers</u> got loads better. Suddenly you could play records loud enough to fill a club with sound. <u>DJs</u> took over from band leaders as the important people in a club.

3) <u>Lighting technology</u> got more exciting too — <u>flashing lights</u> and <u>effects</u> became part and parcel of the experience of a night out in a club.

The Strong Beat and Catchy Tunes Made Disco Easy to Like

1) Disco tunes are almost always in $\frac{4}{4}$. They're played at around <u>120 beats per minute</u>.

2) The simple beat makes disco tunes really <u>easy to dance</u> to because just about any dance move will fit. People loved this because it gave them the freedom to make up their <u>own moves</u>.

3) People also liked the <u>catchy tunes</u>. Every disco tune has a <u>hook</u> — a short stab of <u>tune</u>, a <u>word</u> or a <u>phrase</u> that sticks in people's minds so they remember (and buy) the record.

4) Disco songs almost always follow a <u>verse-chorus structure</u> (see p.109). The <u>coda</u> (or <u>outro</u>) usually <u>fades out gradually</u> so the DJ can <u>mix</u> the end of one song with the beginning of another — this means that people can <u>keep dancing</u>, and don't have to <u>stop</u> in between songs.

5) The <u>vocal line</u> is often in a fairly <u>high register</u> (like in the Bee Gees' '<u>Stayin' Alive</u>') to soar above the <u>driving rhythm</u> (see below). The <u>lyrics</u> can be quite <u>powerful</u> (e.g. Gloria Gaynor's '<u>I Will Survive</u>', which is about coping with a <u>break-up</u>).

Disco Music Usually Has Guitars, Brass, Strings and a Drum Kit

1) <u>Electric guitars</u> play the <u>lead</u> and <u>rhythm</u> parts — the lead guitar plays the <u>tune</u> and the rhythm guitar strums the <u>beats</u>. The <u>bass guitar</u> plays <u>short, rhythmic riffs</u> (see p.58). <u>Synthesizers</u> were used as well.

2) <u>Strings</u> fill the <u>gaps</u> between the other sounds. The <u>brass instruments</u> play '<u>stabs</u>' on the <u>off-beats</u>.

3) <u>Acoustic</u> and <u>electronic drum kits</u> play the <u>rhythm</u>. Sometimes <u>drum machines</u> are used as well. The <u>basic rhythm</u> would be played <u>all the way through</u> the song and is usually something like this:

- The <u>bass drum</u> plays on every beat.
- The <u>snare drum</u> mostly plays on beats <u>2</u> and <u>4</u>. The <u>hi-hat</u> plays <u>offbeat quavers</u>.
- The little circle means the hi-hat's played <u>open</u> — so it <u>rings on</u>.

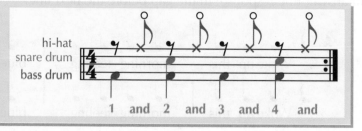

Extra percussive sounds like <u>hand claps</u> are often added by <u>drum machines</u>. Disco music also uses backing <u>loops</u> created by <u>sequencers</u> (see p.72). Short snippets of music, e.g. bass lines, tunes, chords and rhythms, are recorded on sequencers. They're <u>played repeatedly</u> through the recording. Loops are usually made so they'll <u>fit together</u> in different combinations.

At first I was afraid, I was petrified of the listening exam...

There were loads of famous disco artists in the 1970s — Donna Summer ('Love to Love You Baby'), The BeeGees and Gloria Gaynor (see above) are all great examples. Give them a listen.

Rock

Rock stars must have a pretty nice life, what with the posh hotels, adoring fans and truckloads of money. But it's their music that made them famous, and that's what this page is about.

Rock Music is Based on the 12-Bar Blues

1) Rock music started off in the 1950s. The chord structure's based on the 12-bar blues (see p.111).

2) A rock band was originally made up of a lead electric guitar, a rhythm electric guitar, a lead singer, a bass guitar and a drummer.

3) As rock developed, more instruments were added. Some bands introduced a string section (with violins and cellos), some had brass sections (trumpets and trombones) and some had wind sections (flutes, clarinets, saxophones and oboes). They also brought in keyboards and synthesizers.

4) Musicians used the effects on electric guitars to produce new sounds — like distortion, feedback (the noise you get when you stand too close to a speaker with a guitar or microphone) and reverberation (echo, see p.75).

5) Rock bands use lots of other techniques to get unusual sounds — the band Led Zeppelin used a pounding beat turned up really loud as their main rhythm. They sometimes used violin bows on their guitar strings to get a sustained note.

In the 1970s, Rock Songs Started to Develop

Bands in the 1970s started to develop the basic rock formula to make their songs last longer. Their songs had themes and some even told stories.

- Queen's 'Bohemian Rhapsody' lasts for a whopping 6 minutes. It doesn't have a chorus — it's made up of unrelated sections, including a slow ballad, a guitar solo, an operatic section and a heavy rock section.

- Pink Floyd's 1973 album 'The Dark Side of the Moon' is a concept album — there's a theme that links all the tracks.

'Bohemian Rhapsody' is through-composed (see p.56).

Rock Songs Became a Way of Expressing Yourself

1) Lots of rock bands write their own lyrics to songs (as well as the music). They use things like religious themes, protest songs and personal experiences of love.

2) Led Zeppelin, David Bowie and Bob Dylan all use the influences of folk music — they've written whole albums in a folky style.

3) Bob Dylan is also famous for his protest songs — his folky 'Blowin' In The Wind' is used as an anti-war song.

4) The more rock developed, the fewer rules it followed. Songs could be any length, and follow any chord pattern (or none at all). Bands could have any instruments, and the lyrics could be about whatever the band wanted.

5) Costumes were used to help the music along — David Bowie's jumpsuits and make-up (such as his famous lightning bolt make-up) really helped to set the scene for the characters that appeared in Bowie's songs (e.g. Major Tom and Ziggy Stardust).

Powerful Guitars Were Important in 1990s Rock

1) A lot of rock bands in the 1990s were guitar-based — they used guitars to create a really powerful sound. Power chords (made up of the tonic and fifth of a chord) were used a lot.

2) Bands like Nirvana, Blink-182 and Pearl Jam were really popular. They wrote songs about controversial topics (like drugs and mental illness) and often swore a lot.

3) 1990s rock music was fused with other types of music — like grunge, punk and funk.

Queen — Killer Queen

Now it's time for your second set work on vocal music — and it's very different to 'Music for a While'. However, it is still a piece for a solo vocal part with accompaniment — but in a different style.

Queen are a British Rock Band

1) The band Queen was formed in <u>1970</u>. They are a <u>rock band</u> (sometimes described as <u>glam rock</u>).

2) Queen had <u>four members</u>, who usually played the following roles:

- <u>Freddie Mercury</u> — lead vocals, piano, backing vocals
- <u>Brian May</u> — lead guitar, backing vocals
- <u>Roger Taylor</u> — drums, backing vocals
- <u>John Deacon</u> — bass guitar

After Freddie Mercury's death in 1991, the other members of the band have continued to perform with guest singers doing the lead vocals.

3) The song 'Killer Queen' was written by <u>Freddie Mercury</u>. It comes from Queen's <u>third</u> album *Sheer Heart Attack*, which was released in <u>1974</u>.

4) This album is <u>different</u> from Queen's previous two albums. The first two albums have more of the <u>traditional rock band</u> sound. *Sheer Heart Attack* is the album that uses the <u>recording techniques</u> of <u>layering</u> vocals and instruments — the band used these techniques regularly to achieve the distinctive Queen "<u>sound</u>".

5) Queen are hugely <u>successful</u> — they have sold <u>millions</u> of albums, had many <u>Number 1 singles</u> and performed in <u>massive arenas</u>. Their most famous hits include '<u>Bohemian Rhapsody</u>', '<u>We Will Rock You</u>' and '<u>Don't Stop Me Now</u>' (as well as loads more).

Killer Queen has a Verse-Chorus Structure

The <u>structure</u> of 'Killer Queen' is quite <u>straightforward</u> — it basically follows a <u>verse-chorus structure</u>, with a couple of <u>variations</u> (there are a couple of <u>bridge sections</u>, and a little <u>guitar interlude</u> before the second verse). The verses <u>aren't</u> exactly the <u>same</u> either. The structure looks like this:

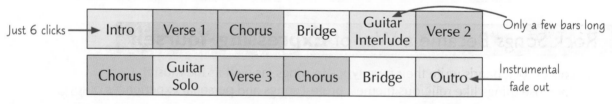

Just 6 clicks → Intro | Verse 1 | Chorus | Bridge | Guitar Interlude | Verse 2 — Only a few bars long

Chorus | Guitar Solo | Verse 3 | Chorus | Bridge | Outro ← Instrumental fade out

The <u>guitar solo</u> is performed by <u>Brian May</u>. It was actually recorded <u>after</u> the rest of the piece, as May was <u>ill</u> when the song was recorded. The solo uses <u>layering</u> (see next page), so couldn't have been performed <u>live</u> in exactly the same way.

The Song has Unusual Lyrics

1) The <u>lyrics</u> of 'Killer Queen' are a <u>key feature</u> of the song. They were written <u>before</u> the music and are very <u>wordy</u>, with lots of <u>syllables</u>. This means they dictate the <u>rhythm</u> of the melody — the <u>note lengths</u> are usually quite <u>short</u> in order to fit all the words in. Most of the song is <u>syllabic</u>.

2) The <u>words</u> themselves are quite <u>unusual</u>. The song mentions <u>Marie Antoinette</u>, <u>Khrushchev</u> and <u>Kennedy</u> (all famous historical figures). The subject of the song enjoys '<u>Moët et Chandon</u>' (champagne) and '<u>caviar</u>' and talks like a '<u>baroness</u>', which creates an image of an <u>upper-class</u>, <u>well-connected woman</u>.

3) The chorus uses lots of <u>explosive imagery</u> — e.g. '<u>gunpowder</u>', '<u>dynamite</u>' and '<u>laser beam</u>'.

Another page bites the dust...

In case you're wondering, Khrushchev was the leader of the Soviet Union and Kennedy was President of the United States at the time of the Cuban Missile Crisis in 1962. Nice little history lesson for you there.

Queen — Killer Queen

'Killer Queen' has some interesting <u>musical features</u> that you need to know about.

The **Accompaniment** Changes Throughout the Song

1) Unusually for a rock song, 'Killer Queen' <u>doesn't</u> start with an <u>instrumental introduction</u> — it starts with <u>six clicks</u>. The <u>solo vocalist</u> comes in <u>alone</u> on the last click, then the instrumentation <u>builds up</u>. The <u>piano</u> comes in first, followed by the <u>guitar</u>, <u>drums</u> and <u>bass guitar</u>, then finally the <u>backing vocals</u>.

2) The instrumentation <u>varies</u> a little in different verses — e.g. there's a <u>bell</u> and a more <u>prominent</u> guitar part in verse 2. For the first part of each chorus, the vocals are in <u>four-part harmony</u> with <u>no</u> solo line.

3) The <u>backing vocals</u> are in <u>four-part harmony</u> (another reason why the song <u>couldn't</u> be performed like this <u>live</u> — there's four-part harmony <u>and</u> a soloist, and there are only <u>four</u> members in Queen).

4) The <u>backing vocals</u> are a <u>key feature</u> of Queen songs, and help create their <u>recognisable sound</u>.

> In 'Killer Queen', the backing vocals are <u>different</u> in each verse — they mainly sing 'oooh' and 'aaah', but sometimes <u>echo</u> the solo line (e.g. '<u>naturally</u>' in verse 2) or <u>complete</u> it (e.g. '<u>drive you wild</u>' in verse 3). In the choruses, they start by singing the <u>main lyrics</u> in <u>harmony</u>, but also add <u>punctuating chords</u> (the '<u>ba</u>'s under the solo vocal line). They sing in <u>call and response</u> with the soloist as well (e.g. '<u>anytime</u>').

The Song is in a **Major Key**

1) 'Killer Queen' is in E♭ <u>major</u> — but verses 1 and 2 actually start on a <u>C minor</u> chord (the <u>relative minor</u>).

2) There is a <u>mix</u> of <u>major</u> and <u>minor tonality</u> throughout the piece because of a number of <u>modulations</u>.

3) The song is in $\frac{12}{8}$ (<u>compound quadruple time</u>), but it changes to $\frac{6}{8}$ (<u>compound duple time</u>) for <u>one bar</u> in each verse. The use of compound time gives it a <u>swung</u> feel.

4) It has a <u>steady</u>, <u>rhythmic pulse</u>, set up from the start by the <u>opening clicks</u> and continued by the <u>rhythmic piano chords</u> (playing a <u>quaver</u> on <u>every beat</u> of the bar at the start of the first two verses).

Killer Queen Uses Different **Effects**

Layering has to be done in the <u>studio</u> — it couldn't be done in a <u>live</u> performance.

1) The song contains a lot of <u>layering</u> of both <u>instruments</u> and <u>voices</u>.

> Layering means that <u>one part</u> is recorded <u>onto another</u>. If necessary, a <u>third</u> is recorded onto that, and so on until every part is recorded. This recording technique is called <u>multi-tracking</u>. Each part is recorded onto a <u>different track</u> and then played <u>together</u>. The <u>separate</u> tracks can then be <u>altered</u> in different ways to achieve the required sound.

2) Layering is used in the <u>guitar solo</u> — you can hear <u>separate parts</u> being played at the <u>same time</u>. This creates a '<u>bell effect</u>' — notes are played <u>one by one</u>, and <u>sustained</u> to create a <u>chord</u>.

3) Layering is also used in the <u>vocal parts</u> (see above). Queen also famously used this technique in the vocal parts of '<u>Bohemian Rhapsody</u>'.

4) Queen also use a <u>flanger</u> effect (see p.75) on the <u>guitar</u> and in the <u>vocals</u> (listen out for it when they sing '<u>laser beam</u>' in the second chorus and '<u>wanna try</u>' in the final bridge).

5) They also use the vocal technique of <u>portamento</u> (or <u>glissando</u>) — e.g. every time they sing '<u>Killer Queen</u>'.

6) <u>String-bending</u> is used in the <u>guitar solo</u> — the <u>pitch</u> is changed by <u>pushing</u> the string <u>across</u> the fingerboard. <u>Sliding</u> is also used — the player moves between <u>notes</u> by sliding <u>up or down</u> the neck.

GCSE Music — it'll absolutely drive you wild...

'Killer Queen' is a song (and a character) in the musical *WE WILL ROCK YOU*, based on the songs of Queen. There's more about musicals in Section 8 — including your study piece ('Defying Gravity' from *Wicked*).

Warm-up and Exam Questions

Before you get stuck into the exam-style questions, have a go at these warm-up questions first.

Warm-up Questions

1) Give two examples of sacred choral music.
2) What were the four different voices in a Baroque choir?
3) Name the five main types of opera.
4) What is an aria?
5) Describe the texture of a madrigal.
6) How does Schubert make the characters in 'The Erl King' sound different?
7) What play is 'Music for a While' from?
8) What is a suspension?
9) Describe the typical structure of a pop song.
10) Describe four different ways backing singers can sing.
11) Who first created blues music?
12) Write out the chord pattern used for 12-bar blues.
13) Give two features that made disco music so popular.
14) What is a power chord?
15) What is layering?

Exam Questions

To make sure you really know your stuff, here's an exam question on each of the set pieces.

Track 34 is an extract from 'Music for a While' by Henry Purcell.
Play the extract **three** times. Leave a short pause between each playing.

Track 34

a) During which period of Western classical music history was this piece composed?

.... Baroque ....

[1 mark]

b) What is the musical device Purcell uses in this extract?
Circle the correct answer.

imitation   drone   ground bass   pedal note

[1 mark]

Exam Questions

c) Explain how Purcell uses word-painting on the word 'eas'd'.

......At the start of the word 'eas'd' there is suspense,......
......which is resolved which gives a sense of the music......
......being eased.

[2 marks]

d) The music is composed for a solo voice and continuo.
Name the two instruments that make up the continuo.

......Harpsichord and ~~double bass~~ cello......

......

[2 marks]

e) i) What musical device does Purcell use on the word 'eternal' each time it is sung?
Circle the correct answer.

imitation   **melisma**   **ornamentation**   **syllabic**

[1 mark]

ii) Why do you think Purcell uses this device on this word?

......Used for word painting, to make the word......
......really show the eternality and extent.......

[1 mark]

f) Describe some of the musical features of this song. Comment on some of the
following features: how the text is set to music, tonality, pitch and rhythm.

......

......

......

......

......

......

[4 marks]

Exam Questions

Track 35 is an extract from 'Killer Queen' by Queen.
Play the extract **three** times. Leave a short pause between each playing.

(Track 35)

a) i) What chord accompanies the line 'To avoid complications',
        heard at the start of the extract? Circle the correct answer.

   Eb major   Eb minor   Bb minor   C minor   Bb minor

   [1 mark]

   ii) What is the relationship between this chord and the key signature?

   ....

   [1 mark]

b) What vocal effect is heard on the word 'Queen' in the chorus?
    Circle the correct answer.

   vibrato   riffing   improvisation   portamento

   [1 mark]

c) Describe the accompaniment during the verse and chorus.

   ....

   ....

   ....

   ....

   ....

   ....

   [4 marks]

d) What instrument is playing the solo?

   ....

   [1 mark]

Revision Summary for Section Seven

That section certainly covered a lot of ground — from Baroque to pop and rock in the blink of an eye. Just have a go at these revision questions, then you can stop to catch your breath and work out which decade you're in. You know the drill — try and answer them without looking back at the section, then go back over any bits you're not sure about.

1) What is a falsetto voice?

2) What are the four different voices in an SATB choir?

3) Describe two common structures of all-female choirs.

4) What is a baritone voice?

5) What is an opera?

6) What is a libretto?

7) Name the three types of song in an opera.

8) What is a recitativo secco?

9) What is an oratorio?

10) Name a famous oratorio by Handel.

11) Give a brief definition of word-painting.

12) Describe a cantata and a chorale.

13) What is a motet?

14) What is a Lied?

15) Name a famous composer of Lieder.

16) Who wrote 'Music for a While'?

17) What sort of voice is 'Music for a While' written for?

18) What is a continuo, and what are the typical instruments in a continuo?

19) What is a ground bass?

20) Explain the terms melismatic and syllabic.

21) What is the structure of 'Music for a While'?

22) Is 'Music for a While' in a major or minor key?

23) What is a ballad?

24) Name three singer-songwriters.

25) Name three different vocal techniques that singers use.

26) What is the blues scale?

27) Explain the difference between straight and swung rhythms.

28) What is syncopation?

29) Name three genres that use a 12-bar blues structure.

30) When did disco music first become popular?

31) What are the typical instruments used in disco music?

32) Name three rock bands.

33) What is a concept album?

34) Name three famous Queen songs.

35) Describe the structure of 'Killer Queen'.

36) Describe the backing vocals in 'Killer Queen'.

37) What time signature is 'Killer Queen' in?

38) Name three different effects used in 'Killer Queen'.

Musicals

Musical theatre is a lighter, more modern version of opera. It's been developing since the 19th century.

Musicals Have **Songs, Dialogue** and **Dances**

1) Musicals came from less serious versions of opera, like opéra comique and operetta (see p.102).
   Towards the end of the 19th century, Gilbert and Sullivan wrote lots of popular comic operas.

2) The type of musicals that are around today started in the 1920s, and developed
   throughout the rest of the 20th and into the 21st century. They started out on Broadway,
   a famous theatre street in New York. Some started in London's West End.

3) Musicals use singing, dancing and talking to tell stories.

4) They usually have an orchestra to accompany the singers and play incidental (background) music.

5) Some musicals that started out on the stage have been made into really popular films —
   like *Grease*, *West Side Story* and *Sweeney Todd*. Sometimes, a musical that started
   life as a film is adapted into a musical performed on stage — like *Billy Elliot*.
   Both these things have happened to *Hairspray* — it was originally a (non-musical) film
   which was adapted into a Broadway musical, then the musical was made into a (musical) film.

6) Some musicals are based on novels — like *Wicked*, *Oliver!* and *Matilda The Musical*.

Musical Styles are Always **Changing**

Musicals are generally written in the style of the popular music that's around at the time — so musicals
from different times sound very different. Earlier musicals were influenced by jazz and swing music
(see p.142-143), while lots of musicals from the 1970s onwards used rock music (see p.113).
Have a listen to some of these musicals to hear the different styles they use:

1920s-1950s	*COLE PORTER*: Paris, Anything Goes, Kiss Me, Kate, Silk Stockings
1940s-1950s	*RODGERS & HAMMERSTEIN*: Oklahoma!, South Pacific, The King and I, The Sound of Music
1950s-2010s	*STEPHEN SONDHEIM*: Follies, Sweeney Todd and lyrics for West Side Story
1960s-1990s	*KANDER & EBB*: Cabaret, Chicago, Kiss of the Spider Woman
1970s-2010s	*ANDREW LLOYD WEBBER*: Joseph and the Amazing Technicolour Dreamcoat, Jesus Christ Superstar, Evita, Cats, Phantom of the Opera, School of Rock
1970s-2000s	*SCHÖNBERG & BOUBLIL*: Les Misérables, Miss Saigon

Some **Pop Songs** Start Life in **Musicals**...

Songs from musicals sometimes hit the charts.
In the UK, musicals by Andrew Lloyd Webber and Tim Rice have spawned a few chart hits:

- 'Don't Cry For Me Argentina' from *Evita*.
- 'Memory' from *Cats*.
- 'No Matter What' from *Whistle Down the Wind* (sung by Boyzone).

...While Some **Musicals** are Made Up of **Pop Songs**

On the other hand, sometimes chart hits find their way into musicals — *Mamma Mia!* was
written around a collection of ABBA hits, and *WE WILL ROCK YOU* is based on the songs
of Queen (including 'Killer Queen' — see p.114-115). The plots of these musicals often
have nothing to do with the band, but use their songs to tell the story.

Musicals

Here's how to create that Broadway sound...

Most Musical Songs are **Easy on the Ear**

Musicals are meant to be <u>entertaining</u> and <u>easy to listen to</u>. This is how they do it...

1) The tunes are easy to <u>sing</u> — audiences tend to prefer songs they can sing along to.
2) The harmony is <u>diatonic</u> — it'll be in either a major or a minor key.
3) The song <u>structure</u> is often <u>simple</u>, with alternating verses and choruses and a middle eight (similar to the structure of a <u>pop song</u>).

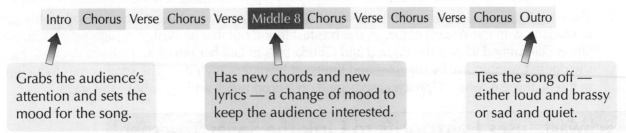

| Intro | Chorus | Verse | Chorus | Verse | Middle 8 | Chorus | Verse | Chorus | Verse | Chorus | Outro |

Grabs the audience's attention and sets the mood for the song.

Has new chords and new lyrics — a change of mood to keep the audience interested.

Ties the song off — either loud and brassy or sad and quiet.

4) The chorus is often in <u>32-bar song</u> form. The 32 bars break down into 4 sections of 8 bars each. Sections 1, 2 and 4 use the <u>main theme</u> (sometimes with slight variations). Section 3 has a <u>contrasting theme</u> (middle eight).
5) The chorus has a <u>hook</u> — a catchy bit of lyrics and tune that makes the song memorable, e.g. '<u>I like to be in America</u>' (*West Side Story*), '<u>Supercalifragilisticexpialidocious</u>' (*Mary Poppins*) or '<u>And all that jazz</u>' (*Chicago*). The hook is the bit that gets stuck in the audience's head (so they want to order a CD when they get home) and often becomes the title of the song.

There are **Four Basic Types** of Musical Song

When you hear a musical song you should be able to identify what <u>type</u> of song it is:

1) **SOLO CHARACTER SONG** — a character sings about how they're <u>feeling</u> — in <u>love</u>, full of <u>hate</u>, over the moon with <u>happiness</u>, etc. '<u>Naughty</u>' from *Matilda The Musical* and '<u>Whistle Down the Wind</u>' from the musical of the same name are both solo character songs.

2) **DUET** — duets are basically the same as solo character songs, except there are <u>two people</u> singing so you get <u>two different reactions</u> to a situation. '<u>I Know Him So Well</u>' from *Chess* is a great example.

3) **ACTION SONG** — the words of the song tell you what's going on in the <u>plot</u> — they lead you into the next bit of the story.

4) **CHORUS NUMBER** — the whole <u>ensemble</u> get together and have a <u>big old sing-song</u>. Like at the end of *Grease* — 'We go together like ramma lamma lamma ka dingedy ding de dong...' and '<u>You Can't Stop the Beat</u>' at the end of *Hairspray*.

You can also get trios, quartets etc. (i.e. more than one character singing, but not a chorus number).

All these styles of song developed from opera — solo songs are like <u>arias</u>, action songs are like <u>recitatives</u>. The lyrics in a musical song tell part of the story. They're usually <u>written first</u>, so the composer has to fit the music around them.

It's showtime — let's see those jazz hands...

Have a listen to 'Mama I'm A Big Girl Now' from *Hairspray* — it's a really good example of a trio. In the song, three different characters have the same argument with their mothers.

Wicked — Defying Gravity

The musical *Wicked* tells the alternative story of the good and wicked witches from *The Wizard of Oz*.

The Musical Was Written by **Stephen Schwartz**

1) The novel <u>Wicked: The Life and Times of the Wicked Witch of the West</u> was written by <u>Gregory Maguire</u> and published in 1995. <u>Stephen Schwartz</u> wrote the <u>music</u> and <u>lyrics</u> to adapt it into a musical, which premiered in 2003.

2) *Wicked* focuses on <u>Elphaba</u> (the Wicked Witch of the West) and <u>Glinda</u> (the Good). Despite their <u>differences</u> (and contrary to what you expect from *The Wizard of Oz*), they actually become <u>friends</u>. *Wicked* explores their <u>relationship</u> against the backdrop of the <u>politics</u> and <u>corruption</u> of Oz.

3) The song '<u>Defying Gravity</u>' is the <u>finale</u> of the <u>first act</u>. Elphaba no longer wants to follow her <u>dream</u> of working with the Wizard of Oz, as she has just found out that he is <u>plotting</u> against his citizens. She is determined to <u>fight</u> the Wizard and Glinda tries to talk her out of it. Elphaba decides that she doesn't want to live by the <u>rules</u> and <u>limits</u> set by others anymore. The song comes to a <u>climax</u> in the <u>final verse</u>, where Elphaba <u>casts a spell</u> on a broomstick and <u>flies</u> above the stage.

Schwartz uses **Leitmotifs** to **Link** the Songs Together

1) A <u>leitmotif</u> is a phrase or piece of music that <u>represents</u> a particular <u>character</u>, <u>place</u> or <u>emotion</u>. They're used a lot in <u>film music</u> (see p.124) but Schwartz uses them throughout *Wicked* — bits from <u>other songs</u> pop up in different places to <u>link</u> back to that part of the story (see below).

2) 'Defying Gravity' follows a general <u>verse-chorus structure</u>, but the use of <u>leitmotifs</u> means there are a few <u>differences</u>:

Echoes the song 'The Wizard and I'.

The choruses are the 'Defying Gravity' bits.

Intro	Interlude 1	Verse 1	Chorus 1	Verse 2	Chorus 2

Interlude 2	Chorus 3	Repeat of intro	Verse 3	Chorus 4	Coda

Echoes the song 'The Wizard and I' and is repeated in 'For Good' — see below.

Echoes the opening song 'No One Mourns the Wicked'.

3) The <u>accompaniment</u> changes throughout the piece. Sometimes the <u>same section</u> is <u>repeated</u> with a <u>different accompaniment</u> — e.g. the <u>intro section</u> is repeated in the <u>middle</u> of the piece and again in the <u>coda</u>, but it has a completely <u>different mood</u> each time.

The Song is **Influenced** by **'Somewhere Over the Rainbow'**

1) In 'Defying Gravity', the '<u>Unlimited</u>' theme (<u>Interlude 2</u>) uses the <u>first seven notes</u> of the melody of '<u>Somewhere Over The Rainbow</u>', a song written for the film *The Wizard of Oz*.

2) However, the two melodies sound <u>completely different</u> as they use <u>different rhythms</u> — 'Defying Gravity' uses some <u>syncopation</u> and a <u>triplet</u>, whereas 'Somewhere Over The Rainbow' uses <u>on-beat</u> rhythms. They can be in <u>different keys</u>, but the <u>intervals</u> between the notes in each melody are the <u>same</u> (an <u>octave leap</u> between the <u>first two notes</u>, followed by a note <u>one semitone down</u>, and so on).

3) The theme appears as an <u>interlude</u> in several of the musical numbers — in '<u>The Wizard and I</u>', Elphaba sings about her <u>future</u> being 'unlimited'. It is then used in '<u>Defying Gravity</u>', and then again at the beginning of '<u>For Good</u>' when Elphaba <u>changes</u> the lyric to 'I'm <u>limited</u>...'.

4) According to Schwartz, he included this as both a <u>tribute</u> to *The Wizard of Oz* and as an <u>inside joke</u> about copyright law — by using only 7 notes, he should be safe from any accusations of <u>copying</u>.

Do some revision and you can be unlimited...

It's well worth having a listen to the whole *Wicked* soundtrack — it'll help you spot the leitmotifs used in 'Defying Gravity' and give you a better idea of how they're used. Plus, it's an excellent musical.

Wicked — Defying Gravity

Now it's time to have a look at some of the other musical elements of 'Defying Gravity'.

The **Music** Helps Convey the **Meaning** of the **Lyrics**

1) At the beginning of the piece, the lyrics are punctuated by chords.
   This emphasises Glinda's and Elphaba's frustration with each other.

2) In Elphaba's first verse, the metre is quite unclear — the orchestra will follow the singer at this point.
   This verse is accompanied by tremolo strings (see p.64). This reinforces the fact that Elphaba
   is feeling shaken — she has realised that the things she used to believe in are no longer true.
   Tremolo strings are also used at the end of the piece to add tension and drama.

3) As Elphaba sings 'close my eyes and leap', the melody also leaps (by a perfect fifth), reflecting the text.
   This is an example of word painting (see p.103). Another example of the music mimicking the lyrics
   is when the orchestra play ascending phrases as she sings 'look to the western sky'.

4) Almost all of the song is syllabic (one syllable per note — see p.103), and some parts of the
   choruses are disjunct (there are big jumps between notes). This makes the music feel more urgent.

5) As the song progresses, Elphaba holds the notes of the chorus for longer as she gains confidence in
   her actions. In verse 3 and chorus 4, the song reaches its climax and she sings in the higher register
   of her vocal range — this reflects the fact that she is flying (both literally and metaphorically).

6) The lyrics end as they start, with Glinda singing 'I hope you're happy'. However, these words
   are accompanied by dark minor chords, dramatic percussion and an echo of the song 'No One
   Mourns the Wicked' from the beginning of the show. This gives the audience an idea of what is to
   come — there are bad things on the horizon, and Elphaba probably won't be 'happy'.

The Music is Very **Dramatic**

HARMONY AND TONALITY: The majority of the music is in D♭ major with modulations to
G♭ major (the subdominant key) and unrelated keys including E major, B major and G major.
This major tonality reinforces the fact that Elphaba is the heroine of the musical, even though she
has been denounced as 'wicked'. The harmony uses suspended chords (chords with a second or
fourth instead of a third) — the dissonance adds to the drama and hints that bad things are about
to happen. Some chords only have the tonic and fifth (i.e. no thirds), which means that you can't
tell if the chord is major or minor. This ambiguity reflects the fact that nothing is as it seems in Oz.

RHYTHM AND METRE: At the beginning, the time signature changes between $\frac{3}{2}$ and $\frac{2}{2}$ before
settling into $\frac{4}{4}$ (although it goes back into $\frac{2}{2}$ when they sing 'I hope you're happy' for the second
time). There are a variety of syncopated rhythms, and triplets are used in Glinda's part when she
tells Elphaba she's having 'delusions of grandeur', which highlight their conflicting emotions.
Ostinato patterns (see p.83) are used in the accompaniment in the choruses to add drama.

TEXTURE: The texture of the piece is mostly homophonic (see p.45) — the singers are accompanied
by chords from the orchestra. Towards the end of the piece, there is polyphony between the
lines sung by Elphaba, Glinda and the ensemble as the song reaches its dramatic conclusion.

INSTRUMENTATION: *Wicked* is written for a large pit orchestra. The music uses synthesizers,
piano/keyboard, harp, guitar, bass guitar, brass (trumpets, trombones and French horns), strings
(violins, viola and cello), woodwind (flute, oboe, clarinet, saxophone and bassoon) and percussion.
There is a big dramatic crescendo in the orchestra to lead into the final verse and chorus.

Defying Gravity — don't try this at home...

Remember to always think about the effect of each musical feature you spot. It's good to be able to identify
the different elements, but you'll get even more marks if you can say why the composer chose to use them.

Film Music

SPOILER ALERT: the next six pages may contain spoilers. Consider yourself warned.
Composers who write film music have to write music to fit with the action already set by the film makers.

Look Out for **Leitmotifs** in Most Film Music

'Leitmotif' can also
be spelt 'leitmotiv'.

1) A leitmotif is a tune that returns throughout the film (there's often more than one).

2) It represents a particular object, idea or character in the story,
and often returns in the background or in an altered form.

3) Leitmotifs are used throughout the *Lord of the Rings* films (see p.126). 'Hedwig's Theme'
is the main leitmotif in the *Harry Potter* films — it's repeated in all the films and played by
different instruments. It's associated with the world of magic and wizards.

4) Sometimes the leitmotifs give you a hint as to what will happen later in the film — if a character turns
out to be a bad guy, their theme might have menacing chords being played in the background.

> In the final few bars of 'Anakin's Theme' from *Star Wars: Episode I — The Phantom Menace*
> (1999), you can hear echoes of 'Darth Vader's Theme' from *Episode V* (also by John Williams).
> This is a subtle hint that Anakin (who's good in this film) will become Darth Vader.

Composers Use Lots of **Repetition** in Film Music

1) Repeated sections of music can be used to link different parts of the film together
— it can remind you of something that happened earlier in the film.

2) A leitmotif can be repeated throughout the film, but might be transformed to reflect
what's going on. The instrumentation can be changed, or it can be repeated in a
different key. Sometimes just the rhythm of the leitmotif is played in the background
— it might be so quiet it's hardly noticeable, but it all adds to the drama.

3) Often at the end of the film there's a triumphant modulation of the main theme (as long as the film
has a happy ending). It ends in a happy, uplifting key with a drawn-out cadence (see p.42-43),
to show that the story of the film has been resolved.

4) Of course, if the film doesn't have a happy ending (or if there's going to be a sequel),
the theme may be left unresolved, giving the film a more open or darker ending.

5) Repetition can be used to create tension and suspense — a repeated sequence that's getting
louder and louder can really have you on the edge of your seat.

Some Films Use **Pop Songs** to Get **Publicity**

1) Lots of films have pop songs as part of their soundtrack — they're usually released
in the charts to generate publicity. They're often performed by famous pop stars
— like Pharrell Williams' song 'Happy' for the film *Despicable Me 2* (2013).

2) Some films have pop songs over the opening or closing credits. These songs aren't always in the
same style of music as the rest of the film, and often don't appear anywhere else in the film
(e.g. Take That's 'Rule The World' is only heard over the closing credits of the 2007 film *Stardust*).

3) A song used as the title track might return in the background later. For example, the song
'My Heart Will Go On' by Celine Dion pops up many times in the film *Titanic* (1997).

A good excuse to watch some films...

If you decide to compose a piece of film music, think about the atmosphere you want to create.
The composition brief might tell you to set a scene, create a mood or describe a character.

Film Music

Film composers use music to <u>set the scene</u> — it helps you believe it's in a <u>different country</u> or <u>time</u>.

Traditional Instruments Give You a Feel for Time and Place

1) Music can be used to create the mood of a different <u>time</u> or <u>place</u>.

2) <u>Westerns</u> are set in 19th century North America. They generally tell a simple story and they can often be very <u>dramatic</u> and <u>violent</u>.

3) Westerns use music <u>from the time</u> to <u>set the scene</u>. For example, guitarist <u>Ry Cooder</u> composed music for *The Long Riders* (1980). He used <u>traditional music</u> and <u>instruments</u> like the Spanish guitar, banjo, honky-tonk piano, tin flute, trombone and percussion.

4) Films set in the <u>70s</u> or <u>80s</u> might use <u>pop songs</u> from the time to set the scene. People will <u>recognise</u> the songs and it'll <u>remind</u> them of that decade.

5) <u>John Barry's</u> score for *Out of Africa* (1985) combines <u>original compositions</u> with <u>traditional African music</u> to help the audience imagine the film's setting — the track 'Karen's Journey' is based on 'Siyawe', a traditional African song.

6) <u>Deborah Lurie's</u> music for the film *Dear John* (2010) uses <u>traditional bluegrass instruments</u> (such as the fiddle/violin and acoustic guitar) for the scenes set in <u>South Carolina</u>.

The Music in War Films Creates the Atmosphere

1) The music in war films needs to create an <u>atmosphere</u> for the <u>time</u> and <u>place</u> of the war, as well as showing the <u>action</u> and <u>emotion</u> of the plot. For example, the battle scenes of *Gladiator* (2000) are accompanied by <u>threatening music</u> (by <u>Hans Zimmer</u>) which creates tension.

2) <u>Sound effects</u> (like <u>explosions</u> and <u>gunfire</u>) can be incorporated into the music to suggest <u>war</u>.

3) *633 Squadron* (1964) is set in the <u>Second World War</u>. The theme music (by <u>Ron Goodwin</u>) is very <u>heroic</u>. It's <u>fast</u> with <u>strong accents</u> — it matches the <u>action</u> of the <u>battle scenes</u>. The <u>soaring brass melodies</u> represent the <u>soaring planes</u>.

Unnatural Sounds Make Strange Places Seem Even Stranger

<u>Horror</u>, <u>science fiction</u> or <u>fantasy</u> films are often set in <u>strange places</u> or other <u>planets</u>. Composers need to <u>transport</u> the audience to a <u>weird reality</u>, where nothing is quite what you'd expect.

1) <u>Unusual harmonies</u> and <u>time signatures</u> are used when things are a bit <u>weird</u> — they're not what you're expecting, so they sound odd.

2) <u>Synthesizers</u> and <u>samples</u> of bizarre <u>sounds</u> often have no relation to what's happening on-screen, but make the audience wonder what's going on and set their imagination racing.

3) <u>Instruments</u> or <u>voices</u> can be <u>distorted</u> using <u>computers</u>.

4) There's often no clear <u>structure</u> so it's hard to predict what's going to happen.

5) <u>Discords</u> and <u>diminished</u> chords make it difficult to listen to.

6) <u>Rapid scalic patterns</u> (going up and down scales) and <u>interrupted cadences</u> (see p.43) can make <u>pulse-raising</u> scenes feel more frantic.

7) In the famous <u>shower scene</u> in *Psycho* (1960), the <u>stabbing</u> of the <u>knife</u> is accompanied by (and emphasised by) the <u>violins</u> also <u>stabbing</u> out a <u>high-pitched tritone</u> (p.29). Each chord goes right through you, and makes what you're seeing on-screen feel much more <u>real</u>.

8) *Planet of the Apes* (1968) uses <u>unusual instruments</u> (such as <u>metal bowls</u> as <u>percussion</u>), <u>alternative ways</u> of playing instruments (such as playing horns <u>without mouthpieces</u>), <u>irregular rhythms</u> and <u>dissonance</u> to create a <u>weird</u>, <u>unearthly</u> feeling.

Music revision can be used to put you in a mood...

There are loads of little tricks that film composers can use to help set the scene and create an atmosphere.

Film Music

Sometimes, film music helps you understand what's happening. It's used to help communicate what's going on, instead of just relying on the action and dialogue on-screen.

The **Style** of Music **Changes** With the **Mood** of the Scene

1) The soundtracks for the three _Lord of the Rings_ films (2001-2003) were written by Howard Shore.

2) Shore created different leitmotifs (see p.124) to represent the different places and characters in the films. For example, the one that represents the group of characters who make up the Fellowship of the Ring is heroic — it appears less frequently after the Fellowship falls apart.

3) The Shire (the home of the Hobbits) is represented by a happy melody in a major key — the theme first appears in the piece 'Concerning Hobbits'. It's first played on a solo Irish tin whistle then solo violin. It's light and playful, and reflects the comfort and safety of the Shire.

4) During fight scenes, the mood is tense and dramatic — the music is played by low brass instruments. There are lots of crescendos to accompany the escalating action.

5) Shore uses a large choir throughout the films to create a sense of mystery and drama. The choir often sings in the (made-up) languages of Middle Earth.

The Music **Shows** What's **Not On Screen**

It's often the composer's job to create a feeling of something being there that's not seen.

1) Minor and more dissonant chords make you feel uneasy.

2) Low pitches in brass and strings sound dark as if you're underground.

3) Percussive, metallic sounds with reverb effects make you imagine someone lurking about or lying in wait.

4) Suspensions that don't resolve (see p.41) build tension and make you think danger is near.

5) Dynamics swell from quiet to loud and then drop back to quiet, as if someone's coming in and out of the shadows.

Music Has to be **Structured** and **Timed** to **Fit** the Film

1) Film directors need music to be synchronised with the action to the split second.

2) Different sections of a film show different moods. The music can easily be chopped up and moved around using samplers and computer programs such as Cubase and Pro Tools®.

3) Music is used during action scenes to imitate the movements of the actors — like in the fight scenes in _Pirates of the Caribbean_ (which had music composed by Klaus Badelt).

Diegetic Music is Music the Characters Can **Hear**

1) In most films, the music is extra-diegetic — it's not actually part of the story. It's put 'over the top' of the action to increase the effect of the film. It's for the audience's benefit only.

2) Sometimes film-makers want to include music in the story for the characters (as well as the audience) to hear — this is diegetic music.

- In _The Hunger Games: Mockingjay — Part 1_ (2014), Katniss sings a song for one of her companions. It is recorded and turned into a propaganda video by the rebels, and used as their battle song.

- Throughout _Brief Encounter_ (1945), Rachmaninov's _Second Piano Concerto_ is used extra-diegetically. It represents the main character's changing emotions as she has an affair. At one point in the film, she turns on the radio, and Rachmaninov's _Second Piano Concerto_ is playing. The music has become diegetic. Her husband later asks her to turn the music down — this could be seen as him suppressing his wife's emotional needs.

Film Music

Music for fantasy or horror often makes you feel like you're in <u>another world</u> or a kind of <u>nightmare reality</u>. The music can also help to <u>build tension</u> and to <u>make you jump</u>.

You Are **Lulled** Into a **False Sense of Security**

1) When music's in a calm <u>major key</u>, you don't feel like anything bad's going to happen. For example, in *Gladiator*, the music that plays when Maximus thinks of his home is a <u>simple</u>, gentle melody composed by Hans Zimmer and Lisa Gerrard.

2) <u>Beware</u> — sometimes the same <u>theme</u> comes back in an <u>altered form</u> — like in a <u>minor key</u> — to show that things have started to <u>go wrong</u>.

Composers Can Keep You on the **Edge** of Your Seat

1) <u>Ostinati</u> keep the <u>audience</u> on <u>edge</u> for a long time. For example, in *Halloween* (1978), there's an ostinato played in a <u>minor key</u> — it's then played on a <u>different note</u> to keep the audience wondering where the scary person is going next.

2) In some sci-fi films there's background music with just drums and bass, generated on <u>computers</u>, that's played under the <u>dialogue</u> throughout the film. This lets the audience know that the danger is always there.

3) A good example of this is in *Tron: Legacy* (2010), which has music written by <u>Daft Punk</u>. They use <u>computer-generated noises</u> to mimic the sound of high-intensity <u>computer games</u> from the '80s, which helps create the <u>virtual-reality setting</u>.

4) <u>Sustained</u> notes create <u>suspense</u> (e.g. tremolo strings).

5) Composers know how to build the <u>tension</u> and make you feel like <u>something bad</u> is going to happen:

- <u>Dynamics</u> get <u>louder</u>.
- <u>Tempo</u> gets <u>faster</u> — like the <u>two-note motif</u> in *Jaws* (1975), which <u>speeds up</u> (and gets <u>louder</u>) as the shark gets closer.
- <u>Pitch</u> gets <u>higher</u>.
- A <u>tune</u> played earlier in a <u>scary bit</u> sometimes <u>comes back</u> to remind you.
- Sometimes they use <u>silence</u> before a <u>loud</u> bit just to make you <u>jump</u>.

Thrillers Have Lots of **Tension** and **Action**

1) Thrillers and spy movies are often <u>serious</u> and <u>tense</u> — the music has to create the right atmosphere. It has to set the scene for <u>conspiracies</u> and people dealing with <u>shadowy figures</u> and <u>underground organisations</u>.

2) There are often lots of <u>layers</u> to the story. A composer uses lots of <u>techniques</u> to show that there's more than one thing going on. E.g. in *The Usual Suspects* (1995), the composer <u>John Ottman</u> creates <u>tension</u> and <u>drama</u> by using:

- <u>Long notes</u> in the <u>foreground</u> with <u>ostinato</u> patterns in the <u>background</u>.
- A <u>repeated pattern</u> on the <u>woodblock</u> sounds like someone's <u>on the move</u> while <u>percussive bursts</u> and <u>brass motifs</u> played on top suggest someone's trying to catch them.

Silence — something bad's about to happen...

Next time you're watching a film, pay attention to the music and try to work out what effect it has. You could even watch the scene without the music to see how important the music is.

Star Wars: Episode IV — Main Title

OK, so the actual piece you have to study is the Main Title/Rebel Blockade Runner from Star Wars: Episode IV — A New Hope by John Williams. However, that was far too long to fit in the title box sorry.

John Williams Has Written Lots of Film Music

1) John Williams (born in 1932) is an American composer who has written music for a number of films. His film scores are some of the most recognisable ever written, and he has been nominated for (and won) many Academy Awards, Golden Globe Awards and Grammy Awards for his music.

2) He frequently writes music for films directed by Steven Spielberg — including *Jaws*, *Close Encounters of the Third Kind*, the *Indiana Jones* films, *E.T. the Extra-Terrestrial*, *Jurassic Park*, *Schindler's List* and *Saving Private Ryan*.

3) He also wrote music for all the *Star Wars* films (so far), *Superman* and the first three *Harry Potter* films (including the most famous bit, 'Hedwig's Theme').

4) The wide variety of films he writes for shows his versatility as a composer. He can write for dramatic action films (e.g. *Indiana Jones*), tense thrillers (*Jaws*), sci-fi films (*E.T.*), war films (*Saving Private Ryan*) and many more. The main theme for *Schindler's List* is beautiful and sad, and suits the film perfectly.

5) Williams is well-known for his use of leitmotifs (see p.124) — he uses them throughout his film scores to great effect. His music is frequently written for a large orchestra.

Star Wars: Episode IV Was Released in 1977

1) Episode IV was actually the first *Star Wars* film to be made (although it wasn't called Episode IV until later). Episodes IV-VI were released between 1977 and 1983, followed by a prequel trilogy (episodes I-III) from 1999-2005. There's a third trilogy being made — Episode VII was released at the end of 2015.

2) The epic saga is a combination of sci-fi and fantasy (it's sometimes described as a 'space opera'). The films tell the story of the Rebel Alliance's battle against the evil Galactic Empire. In Episode IV, you meet Luke Skywalker and follow his journey as he learns about 'the Force' and becomes part of the Rebel Alliance.

3) Your set piece (Main Title/Rebel Blockade Runner) is played over the opening credits of the film. The music accompanies scrolling text that sets the scene and explains what's happening. The rebel blockade runner is Princess Leia's spaceship, which you see after the credits have finished.

Williams Uses Leitmotifs

Remember from p.124 that a leitmotif is a phrase of music that represents a particular character or place. It's a compositional technique that was used a lot in the Romantic period (see p.93) — Richard Wagner used it in his operas and Richard Strauss used it in many of his compositions, such as the opera *Salome*. A strong leitmotif for a character is important so that the listener can recognise it straight away.

1) The music of *Star Wars* uses many different leitmotifs throughout the whole soundtrack.

2) Characters such as Darth Vader and Princess Leia have their own leitmotifs, and 'the Force' has a leitmotif too.

3) This main theme represents the heroic, adventurous nature of the film. This is reflected by leaps of perfect 4ths, perfect 5ths and minor 7ths as well as soaring high notes.

Form your own Rebel Alliance to protest about younger siblings...

If you've got some free time, sit down and watch some of the *Star Wars* films (I know there are a lot — you don't have to watch them all). Listen out for the leitmotifs and think about what effect they have. You could even pick a leitmotif and try and work out why it's appropriate for the character or place it represents.

Star Wars: Episode IV — Main Title

Now you know all about *Star Wars* (what, you need more than a 2-sentence plot summary?),
it's time to have a look at some of the musical features of the piece in a bit more detail.

Main Title/Rebel Blockade Runner Starts With a Fanfare

1) The piece starts in a steady $\frac{4}{4}$ (marked '<u>maestoso</u>', which means '<u>majestically</u>') with a <u>fanfare</u> played by the <u>brass</u> and <u>percussion</u>. This grabs the audience's <u>attention</u> and establishes an <u>optimistic</u>, <u>ceremonial</u> feel — perfect for a film called '<u>A New Hope</u>'. It is used to build <u>excitement</u> before the main theme begins and accompanies the words '<u>Star Wars</u>' as they appear on screen.

2) The fanfare is <u>loud</u> — the first note is marked *sfz* (<u>sforzando</u> — <u>strongly accented</u>) and the rest of the fanfare is <u>marcato</u> ('<u>marked</u>', or <u>accented</u>). This makes it sound <u>strong</u> and <u>powerful</u>.

3) The <u>rhythm</u> of the fanfare is mainly <u>triplets</u> — they make the music sound <u>energetic</u>, even though the <u>tempo</u> is quite <u>stately</u>. It often moves in steps of <u>perfect 4ths</u> and <u>5ths</u>, which sound <u>heroic</u>.

4) The <u>trombones</u> and <u>trumpets</u> play in <u>canon</u> for some of the fanfare (see p.46) — the trombones <u>start</u>, then the trumpets <u>echo</u> them <u>one beat later</u>. This gives the opening a polyphonic <u>texture</u> — it <u>contrasts</u> with the <u>main theme</u>, which is <u>homophonic</u>. In the <u>final beat</u> of the fanfare, the music <u>slows down</u> slightly and the <u>brass</u> play in <u>unison</u> to emphasise the start of the main theme.

The Main Theme is a March

1) After the opening fanfare, the <u>time signature</u> changes to $\frac{2}{2}$ but the <u>beat</u> stays the <u>same</u> — it just changes from <u>4 beats</u> in a bar to <u>2 beats</u> in a bar. It has a <u>regular pulse</u> and the <u>accents</u> are usually on the <u>first beat</u> of the bar, which are key features of a <u>march</u>.

2) This section is in <u>ternary form</u> (see p.81) — there's the <u>main theme</u> dominated by the <u>brass instruments</u>, a <u>gentler string section</u>, then the main theme <u>returns</u> again.

3) The <u>trumpets</u> play the <u>main theme</u>, accompanied by <u>driving triplets</u> in the <u>lower brass</u>, <u>strings</u> and <u>percussion</u> (although <u>most</u> of the <u>orchestra</u> plays the <u>same rhythm</u> in <u>rich chords</u> at the end of the first phrase). The <u>woodwind</u> and <u>violins</u> play <u>soaring high notes</u> which give the impression of <u>flying through space</u>. Later in the theme, they play <u>rapid semiquavers</u>, which gives the piece <u>momentum</u>.

4) In the <u>middle section</u>, the <u>strings</u> play the <u>melody</u> in <u>unison</u>, accompanied by <u>woodwind triplets</u>. In <u>contrast</u> to the brass melody, the <u>strings</u> play a mainly <u>conjunct</u> tune (though there are some <u>leaps</u> too).

5) The overall <u>texture</u> is <u>homophonic</u> — the main trumpet/string melody is <u>accompanied</u> by the rest of the orchestra. The <u>size</u> of the orchestra means that the texture is very <u>thick</u>, and the music is <u>loud</u>.

6) The music is in a <u>major key</u>, which is common for a march (though you can get some marches in minor keys). This sounds <u>bright</u> and <u>optimistic</u>, which emphasises the '<u>hope</u>' of the title of the film.

7) This section of the music accompanies the <u>scrolling text</u> (see previous page).

There's a Slower, Quieter Bit Then a Final Climax

1) As the <u>scrolling text</u> disappears, the music <u>slows down</u> and <u>diminuendos</u> as the screen goes black.

2) However, this moment of <u>peace</u> only lasts for a <u>few seconds</u> — as a pair of moons above a planet come into view, the music <u>builds up</u> again with a <u>dramatic crescendo</u> and <u>booming percussion</u>.

3) <u>Low</u>, <u>minor chords</u> with a <u>driving triplet rhythm</u> accompany two spaceships that come on screen, locked in <u>battle</u>. The music is <u>tense</u> — it <u>slows down</u> considerably and builds in <u>intensity</u> as the huge Imperial spaceship fills the screen. You then hear the <u>leitmotif</u> that represents the <u>Empire in pursuit</u>.

4) As the piece finishes, there are <u>long</u>, <u>low</u>, <u>ominous-sounding notes</u> — a sign of things to come.

I hope this page has given you A New Hope for your exam...

The title music is actually used in <u>all</u> of the *Star Wars* films, which makes it even more recognisable. However, in the other films, the second part of the music (the 'Rebel Blockade Runner' bit) is different.

Warm-up and Exam Questions

Here are some nice straightforward questions to test you on Music for Stage and Screen.

Warm-up Questions

1) What is a musical?
2) Describe 32-bar song form.
3) Name the **four** main types of songs found in musicals.
4) Who wrote the music and lyrics for *Wicked*?
5) Which characters sing 'Defying Gravity'?
6) What is a leitmotif?
7) How is repetition used in film music?
8) Why are instruments from a particular time or place sometimes used in film music?
9) Name **three** films that John Williams composed music for.
10) What is happening on screen during the main theme of *Star Wars: Episode IV*?

Exam Questions

Here are a couple of exam-style questions to test you on the set pieces.

These questions are about 'Defying Gravity', from the original Broadway cast recording (2003) of *Wicked* by Stephen Schwartz. This song is sung by Idina Menzel and Kristin Chenoweth.

Unfortunately, we were unable to get permission to include this track on our audio CD.

However, it's readily available to listen to online —
you just need to listen to 2:34 – 3:45 of the recording.

Play the extract **three** times. Leave a short pause between each playing.

a) i) What is the string technique used during the chorus
('I'd sooner buy defying gravity...')?
Circle the correct answer.

con sordino   **pizzicato**   **double stopping**   **col legno**

[1 mark]

ii) What is the string technique used during the spoken lyrics
('Come with me...')?
Circle the correct answer.

con sordino   **pizzicato**   **tremolo**   **col legno**

[1 mark]

Exam Questions

b) What is the interval between 'un' and 'li' in the word 'unlimited'?

....

[1 mark]

c) Each chorus is in a major key. What is the tonality of the 'unlimited' section?
Put a tick in the correct box.

☐ chromatic

☐ minor

☐ major

☐ modal

[1 mark]

d) Describe two similarities and two differences between each version of the chorus
in this extract.

....

....

....

....

....

....

[4 marks]

e) Describe the rhythm of the chords in the closing seconds of the extract.

....

[1 mark]

Exam Questions

Track 41 is an extract from 'Main Title/Rebel Blockade Runner'
from *Star Wars: Episode IV — A New Hope* by John Williams.
Play the extract **three** times. Leave a short pause between each playing.

Track 41

a) What is the main rhythmic feature throughout this music?
Circle the correct answer.

dotted rhythms   syncopation   triplets   cross-rhythms

[1 mark]

b) i) Which instrument plays the main theme the first time it is heard?

....

[1 mark]

ii) Why do you think John Williams has chosen that instrument?
Give one reason.

....

[1 mark]

c) Circle two words that describe the string melody.

staccato   legato   conjunct   disjunct   sforzando

[2 marks]

d) Describe two similarities and two differences between the opening fanfare
and the main theme.

....

....

....

....

....

....

[4 marks]

Revision Summary for Section Eight

Well, that's the end of what I personally think is the most interesting section of the book — I mean, where else are you going to get away with watching a load of musicals and films in the name of revision? Anyway, to make sure everything has really sunk in, have a go at these questions. You should be able to answer them without looking back — if there are any you're not sure of, look over that page again.

1) Give one example of a musical that was based on a book.
2) Name four different composers who wrote musicals.
3) Name one song from a musical that became a chart hit.
4) In musical terms, what is a hook?
5) What does an action song in a musical do?
6) Briefly describe the structure of 'Defying Gravity'.
7) Explain how Stephen Schwartz uses leitmotifs in 'Defying Gravity'.
8) What key is most of 'Defying Gravity' in?
9) Describe the texture of 'Defying Gravity'.
10) What's a leitmotif (in film music)?
11) How do composers use repetition in film music?
12) Why do some films use pop songs?
13) Name three traditional instruments used in film music for Westerns.
14) How does John Barry create the African setting of *Out of Africa*?
15) Describe how Ron Goodwin's music in *633 Squadron* represents the battle scenes.
16) What type of films might use unusual harmonies or weird time signatures?
17) Describe how the music in *The Lord of the Rings* films illustrates the different places and characters.
18) Give three techniques that composers use to create a feeling of something that isn't on screen.
19) Name two computer programs that are used to synchronise the music to the action.
20) What is diegetic music?
21) Describe how Rachmaninov's *Second Piano Concerto* is used both extra-diegetically and diegetically in the film *Brief Encounter*.
22) How can a composer show that things have started to go wrong?
23) How are ostinati used in film music?
24) How do composers create suspense?
25) Give three ways composers build tension.
26) Describe two ways John Ottman creates tension and drama in *The Usual Suspects*.
27) Who wrote the music for *Star Wars*?
28) What genre are the *Star Wars* films?
29) How are leitmotifs used in the music for *Star Wars*?
30) How does the composer create a fanfare at the start of the Main Title/Rebel Blockade Runner?
31) Identify two features that show this piece is a march.
32) What happens towards the end of the piece?

World Music

In this final section, you'll look at music from other parts of the world and how they can be combined in fusions. Some of the different types of music are covered in more detail later in the section.

Music is Part of **Culture** and **Tradition** Around the World

1) World music is a broad term that includes things like folk music, tribal music and traditional music from different places.

2) The music is often an important part of the culture of a region — for example, Brazilian music plays a key role in its carnivals, which are a celebration of the culture and religion of the country.

3) Music is used for ceremonies of celebration and mourning, and can also be used for communication — for example, the talking drums used in African music (see p.136-137).

4) Instruments vary depending on the materials available — e.g. bamboo is used to make a number of instruments for Indian and Gamelan music (see below).

5) Singing is used a lot in music all over the world — sometimes a cappella (without accompaniment).

Here are Some **Examples** of Different Types of **World Music**

INDIAN MUSIC

The sitar

* Indian classical music is based on a raga (a set of notes, usually between 5 and 8). Ragas are meant to create different moods for times of the day and seasons.

* Raga performances are improvised (see p.144) but based on traditional tunes and rhythms. The melody is played over a drone (a simple rhythmic pattern of 2 notes).

* Traditional Indian instruments are the sitar (a large, long-necked string instrument, often with 7 strings), the tambura (similar to a sitar but usually has 4 strings) and the tabla (a pair of drums) — but there are many other instruments too. The melody is improvised on the sitar, the tambura plays the drone (which creates harmony) and the tabla play the rhythm.

GAMELAN MUSIC

* Gamelan music comes from the Indonesian islands of Java and Bali. It's played at celebrations, religious events and for entertainment. It's a big honour to play gamelan music.

* It's played by a percussion orchestra (also called a gamelan) that's made up of gongs (e.g. the gong ageng or the bonang), metallophones (e.g. the saron and the gender) and drums (e.g. the kendang gending and the ketipung). There are also a few string instruments (e.g. the celempung) and wind instruments (the suling). The gamelan is considered to be a single instrument.

* Gamelan music is based on a five-note scale (called a slendro) or a seven-note scale (a pelog). All the parts work around a core melody played on the saron, which is repeated over and over again to create a rhythmic cycle. The gongs mark the rhythm and the drummers keep the tempo and cue in the other players. The other instruments decorate the melody.

* Gamelan music is heterophonic (see p.45).

* It isn't written down — people learn the music.

AFRICAN MUSIC

African music varies widely throughout the continent. Sub-Saharan African music (from the area south of the Sahara desert) uses drums and a cappella singing — see p.136-137.

Oh now what's its name... it'll come... wait... no... no... it's gong ageng...

Spirituality is an important part of both Indian and gamelan music. Balinese and Javanese people believe that the instruments have a connection to heaven, and won't step over them in case they break the link.

World Music and Fusion

There are so many different types of music from the Americas that I thought they deserved their own little section. And then I decided I'd better mention fusion as well, as that's what this Area of Study is about.

Music **Varies** Throughout **America**

A lot of the music from the <u>Americas</u> has been shaped by its <u>history</u> — a lot of America was <u>colonised</u> (e.g. by the <u>British</u>, <u>French</u>, <u>Spanish</u> and <u>Portuguese</u>), bringing different musical styles. The <u>slave trade</u> brought enslaved <u>Africans</u> and their music to America as well. This led to a <u>wide variety</u> of music:

1) <u>North American</u> music (e.g. from the <u>USA</u>) includes the <u>blues</u> (see p.110-111), <u>jazz</u> (see p.142-143), <u>ragtime</u>, <u>rhythm and blues</u> (R&B), <u>country</u>, <u>hip hop</u> and <u>rock and roll</u>.

2) <u>Calypso</u> music is from the island of <u>Trinidad</u>, and has <u>French</u> and <u>West African</u> origins.

3) The most popular <u>Jamaican</u> music is <u>reggae</u>, which came about in the 1960s — it's a <u>development</u> of the styles <u>ska</u> and <u>rocksteady</u>, and was influenced by traditional <u>calypso</u> music.

4) <u>Son</u> is traditional <u>Cuban</u> music (see p.148). It's a <u>combination</u> of music from the <u>Spanish</u> and <u>French colonists</u> and the <u>African slaves</u> they brought with them.

> Son is played on <u>percussion instruments</u> (such as <u>claves</u>, <u>maracas</u> and <u>bongos</u>), <u>brass instruments</u> (such as <u>trumpets</u>) and <u>string instruments</u> (such as <u>guitars</u>, a <u>string bass</u> and the <u>tres</u> — which looks like a guitar but has <u>three sets</u> of <u>two strings</u>). There's a <u>lead singer</u> (the <u>sonero</u>) and a <u>chorus</u> (the <u>choro</u>) who sing in <u>call and response</u>. Son has <u>complicated rhythms</u> (<u>syncopation</u>, <u>cross-rhythms</u> and <u>polyrhythms</u>) and is meant to be <u>danced</u> to.

5) <u>Latin American</u> music has <u>Spanish</u> and <u>Portuguese</u> influences from its <u>colonial history</u>. It includes dance music such as <u>samba</u> (see p.145), <u>salsa</u> (see p.148), <u>merengue</u>, <u>bossa nova</u> and <u>tango</u>:

> Tango comes from <u>Argentina</u> and <u>Uruguay</u>. It <u>evolved</u> from a <u>traditional</u> form of music called <u>milonga</u>, combined with <u>Italian melodies</u> and <u>African rhythms</u>. Tango music is often quite <u>slow</u> and <u>deliberate</u>, with <u>dotted rhythms</u> in the <u>bass</u>. Other features include <u>staccato notes</u>, <u>syncopation</u>, <u>triplets</u> and <u>simple harmonies</u> (often in a <u>minor key</u>).

Styles Can Be **Combined** to Create **Fusions**

1) <u>Fusion</u> is when two or more <u>different styles</u> of music are <u>merged</u> to create a new style.

2) It can happen <u>gradually</u> and <u>naturally</u> over time as two cultures become <u>mingled</u>, or it can be done <u>deliberately</u> when musicians <u>experiment</u> with different styles.

3) There are <u>different ways</u> of combining styles — e.g. you can mix the <u>rhythms</u> of one with the <u>melodies</u> of another, or use the <u>instruments</u> of one culture to play the <u>melodies</u> of another.

4) As mentioned above, a lot of <u>American</u> music came about as a <u>fusion</u> of two or more cultures — the <u>traditions</u> of the <u>original country</u>, the effect of being <u>colonised</u> and the added influence of the <u>slaves</u>.

5) Some of these styles have since been fused <u>again</u> to create even more new types of music.

> For example, <u>tango</u> was combined with <u>classical</u> and <u>jazz</u> music to create <u>Tango Nuevo</u> — a type of music with more <u>complex rhythms</u> and <u>harmonies</u> than traditional tango. <u>Tango-rokéro</u> (tango rock) replaces some tango <u>instruments</u> (e.g. the <u>bandoneon</u> and <u>double bass</u>) with the <u>rhythm section</u> from a <u>rock band</u> (e.g. <u>electric guitars</u> and <u>keyboards</u>).

6) Some <u>pop music</u> deliberately fuses different styles of music. <u>Paul Simon's</u> album *Graceland* features <u>Ladysmith Black Mambazo</u>, an <u>all-male choir</u> from <u>South Africa</u> — the songs are a fusion of <u>pop</u>, <u>rock</u> and <u>folk music</u> with <u>African a cappella</u> singing (see p.137).

Create a delicious fusion of merengues and raspberries...

If there are any unfamiliar instruments or styles mentioned in this section, find a recording of them so that you know what they sound like — it might come in handy in the exam.

African Music

The next two pages are called 'African Music', but they don't cover every type of African music. Instead they focus on the <u>sub-Saharan bits</u>. That means the massive area <u>south of the Sahara</u> — the rainforest and savannah bits.

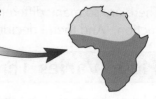

Drums Play a Big Part in African Culture

1) Drums are probably the <u>most widely played instrument</u> in Africa. In African tribal society, drums get a lot of <u>respect</u> — they're thought of as one of the best instruments.

2) Drums are used to play an <u>accompaniment</u> for <u>singing</u>, <u>dancing</u> and even <u>working</u>.

3) Drums are also used to <u>call people together</u> for important <u>community events</u> like weddings and funerals — a bit like church bells in Europe. There are <u>different drumbeats</u> for different events, so people from <u>neighbouring villages</u> can tell what's going on just by listening out for the drumbeats.

4) Most African drum music is passed on through <u>oral tradition</u> — it's not written down.

These are the Main Types of Drum

The names of the different drums can vary from country to country.

1) The <u>djembe</u> is played in Guinea and Mali in West Africa. It has a <u>single head</u> and is shaped a bit like a <u>goblet</u>. It's played with the <u>hands</u>. The overall <u>size</u> of the drum affects its <u>pitch</u> — <u>smaller</u> drums are <u>higher-pitched</u>.

2) The <u>dundun</u> is also played in Guinea and Mali. Dunduns are <u>cylindrical drums</u> played with <u>sticks</u>. There's a drum skin at each end, so they're played <u>horizontally</u>. There are three types: the <u>kenkeni</u> (a high-pitched drum that keeps the pulse going), the <u>sangban</u> (a mid-pitched drum) and the <u>dundunba</u> (a large, low-pitched drum).

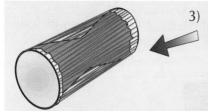

3) The <u>donno</u> from Ghana is also known as the <u>hourglass</u> or <u>talking</u> drum. The player holds it under one arm, and with the other arm hits the drumhead with a thin curved stick. The <u>strings</u> round the sides attach to the drumhead. The player can <u>squeeze</u> and <u>release</u> the strings as they play to change the pitch of the drum.

4) The <u>kagan</u> and the <u>kidi</u> (small and medium barrel-shaped drums) are both from Ghana.

Talking Drums are Used to Send Messages

1) Skilled drummers can make drums '<u>talk</u>'. They <u>change the pitch</u> to imitate changing pitch levels in ordinary <u>speech</u>. The drum sounds carry over long distances, so they can be used to <u>send messages</u>.

2) There are literally <u>thousands</u> of different <u>languages</u> and <u>dialects</u> in Africa. Each drummer imitates his own language to send messages. Drummers like to play on instruments made with <u>local materials</u>. Some believe that this <u>helps</u> the instrument 'speak' the local language.

3) The variety of local languages and materials means you get very <u>different instruments</u> and <u>different playing styles</u> from area to area.

4) There's a big variety of <u>playing techniques</u> — as well as hitting the drum with a <u>stick</u>, a lot of African drummers also play using their <u>hands</u>. There are three basic strokes: <u>slap</u> (hit the <u>edge</u> of the drum with the fingers <u>splayed open</u>), <u>tone</u> (hit the <u>edge</u> of the drum with the fingers <u>held together</u>), <u>bass</u> (hit the <u>centre</u> of the main drum skin with a <u>flat hand</u>). Striking the <u>wood</u> instead of the <u>skin</u> gives a <u>different sound</u>, and drummers can change the <u>pitch</u> by <u>tightening</u> the skin.

Drums are very important in African music...

All this drumming's starting to give me a headache — I'm off to have a lie down. Whilst I'm doing that, please can you learn all the stuff on the next few pages? That would be great, thanks — you're the best.

African Music

Drums have a special place in African music but the <u>voice</u> and <u>other instruments</u> are important too.

The **Master Drummer** Leads the Group

1) A lot of African drummers play in <u>ensembles</u>. In most drum ensembles, there is a <u>master drummer</u>.

2) A system of <u>call</u> and <u>response</u> is used to <u>structure</u> the music:

> The master drummer plays a <u>rhythmic signal</u> which sets the <u>tempo</u> and <u>rhythm</u> for the other players. After this call the other players join in with the response. This call and response pattern is usually repeated <u>many times</u> during a performance.

3) The master drummer also <u>controls</u> the build-up and release of <u>tension</u>, and leads the other players in changes of <u>dynamics</u>, <u>tempo</u>, <u>pitch</u> and <u>rhythm</u>. These <u>changes</u> are what keep the audience hooked.

The Rhythms are **Complex**

1) African music is based on <u>rhythmic cycles</u> of varying lengths, with <u>accents</u> on particular beats.

2) Rhythmic cycles with <u>accents</u> in <u>different places</u> are often played at the <u>same time</u> — this creates <u>polyrhythm</u> and <u>cross-rhythm</u> (see p.14), and adds <u>tension</u> to the music.

3) Notes that don't fall on a strong beat can be emphasised, giving a <u>syncopated</u> effect.

4) Although the music is based on repeated cycles, individual players introduce <u>small variations</u>. These gradually <u>develop</u> the basic patterns throughout the performance.

This means 'repeat the previous bar'.

The **Thumb Piano, Balafon** and **Kora** are Popular

These are some of the most popular instruments apart from drums.

A <u>balafon</u> is a wooden xylophone. The lumpy things hanging under the keys are dried <u>gourds</u>. They create a <u>warm</u>, <u>mellow</u> sound.

The <u>kora</u> is made and played by the Mandingo people. It's got <u>21 strings</u> and you play it by <u>plucking</u> — a bit like a harp.

The <u>mbira</u> or <u>thumb piano</u> is really popular — partly because it's pocket-sized. It makes a <u>liquid</u>, <u>twangy</u> sound.

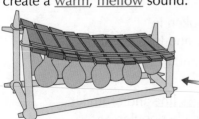

← These two are mostly → played in <u>West Africa</u>.

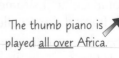

The thumb piano is played <u>all over</u> Africa.

<u>A cappella singing</u> is also important in African music. <u>South African</u> all-male choirs (such as <u>Ladysmith Black Mambazo</u>) sing a cappella. There are two main types of African a cappella singing — <u>mbube</u> (<u>loud</u> and <u>powerful</u> singing, with <u>high-pitched lead vocals</u> over a <u>four-part harmony bass line</u>) and <u>isicathamiya</u> (<u>softer</u> and <u>gentler</u>, with <u>four-part harmonies</u> singing <u>call and response</u>). Isicathamiya also has <u>dance moves</u> such as <u>stamps</u> and <u>tip-toeing</u>.

Celtic Music

Every country in the world has its own type of <u>folk music</u>. The music uses <u>local languages</u>, <u>dialects</u> and <u>instruments</u>, so it's different in different places — sometimes even from village to village.

Folk Music was Played by **Ordinary People**

1) Folk music's still around nowadays but it used to be <u>much more popular</u>. In olden times, before radios and record players, the <u>only</u> music ordinary people had was music they played themselves.

2) The tunes tend to be quite <u>simple</u> and work with just a <u>few</u> instruments or voices. This made them <u>easier</u> for people in the <u>pub</u>, or <u>field</u>, or <u>factory</u>, to learn and play.

3) Folk music was hardly ever <u>written down</u>. It survived through the <u>oral tradition</u> — people <u>heard</u> a song or tune they liked and <u>memorised</u> it.

4) Folk music changes over time as people add <u>new ideas</u>. Sometimes they're being deliberately <u>creative</u>, sometimes they <u>can't remember</u> exactly what they've heard and make up a new bit.

5) The <u>instruments</u> used to play along with folk songs and dances tend to be <u>small</u> and <u>easy to carry</u>. The most popular ones are the <u>pipe and tabor</u> (a three-holed recorder and a drum, played together for a one-man band effect), the <u>fiddle</u>, the <u>hurdy-gurdy</u>, the <u>bagpipes</u>, the <u>accordion</u> and the <u>concertina</u>.

6) The main types of folk music are <u>work songs</u> (sung by <u>labourers</u> to help them to work as a <u>team</u> and take their <u>minds</u> off their work), <u>ballads</u> (they tell <u>stories</u> of <u>love</u>, <u>real-life events</u> or <u>legends</u>) and <u>dance</u> music (see next page).

Folk Tunes are Fairly **Simple**

1) A lot of folk melodies are based on <u>pentatonic scales</u> (see p.27). They've only got five notes, which makes writing tunes with them a lot easier.

2) A <u>major pentatonic</u> scale uses notes <u>1</u>, <u>2</u>, <u>3</u>, <u>5</u> and <u>6</u> of an ordinary <u>major scale</u>.

3) A <u>minor pentatonic</u> scale uses notes <u>1</u>, <u>3</u>, <u>4</u>, <u>5</u> and <u>7</u> of a <u>natural minor scale</u>.

4) There are <u>no semitone intervals</u> in pentatonic scales. It makes it much easier to add a <u>harmony</u> because the notes don't clash. It also makes them <u>easy to sing</u>.

> The <u>structure</u> in folk tunes tends to be pretty simple too. <u>Songs</u> are often <u>strophic</u> — the tune stays the same for each verse. Strophic songs can either be a number of <u>musically identical</u> verses (with different words), or can have a <u>chorus</u> that's just a <u>slight variation</u> on the verse (so the structure is A A' A A' A...). Phrases have even numbers of bars — usually <u>four</u>. Often each phrase begins with an <u>anacrusis</u> (upbeat).

Lots of **Celtic Folk Music** Comes From **Scotland** and **Ireland**

1) Lots of places in <u>Western Europe</u> have traditional Celtic folk music — like <u>Wales</u>, <u>Cornwall</u> and <u>Brittany</u> in France.

2) Celtic folk music also includes <u>traditional Scottish</u> and <u>Irish</u> music.

3) The songs are often sung in <u>Gaelic</u> — traditional Celtic languages spoken in Scotland and Ireland. The two most common forms are <u>Scots Gaelic</u> and <u>Irish Gaelic</u>.

4) Traditional Celtic instruments include <u>fiddles</u>, <u>bagpipes</u>, <u>tin whistles</u> and <u>accordions</u>. An Irish framed drum called the <u>bodhrán</u> is also used.

5) Some bands turn folk music into a more <u>modern</u> style by adding a <u>bass line</u> and <u>drum kit</u> — bands like <u>Capercaillie</u> and <u>Runrig</u> have made Celtic folk music really popular.

Folk songs were often just passed from person to person...

Capercaillie's album *Beautiful Wasteland* is a good example of Celtic folk rock. The set work 'Release' incorporates some elements of Celtic music, so make sure you know the instruments.

Celtic Music

Dance music is an important part of folk music — it's performed at events like weddings and parties and provides a sense of community. You still see Morris dancing and Irish and Scots dancing today.

Irish Dance Music Has a **Strong, Regular Beat**

1) Traditional Irish music is played on instruments like a violin (fiddle), Irish open-holed wooden flute, tin whistle, concertina or accordion, guitar, Uilleann pipes (the Irish version of bagpipes) and percussion such as the bodhrán (a framed drum) and the spoons. The tune is usually played in unison.

2) It has a strong regular beat with the emphasis on the first beat, so it's easy to dance to. It's quite fast.

3) The melody has clear phrases in a question and answer pattern. Melodies are often made up of two 8-bar sections, each played twice (once for the left foot and once for the right) to make a 32-bar melody. The regular phrases make it easy to fit steps to and to keep in time with.

4) The music has simple harmonies. Some are in a major key, often D major or G major, and some use modes (see p.27).

5) Traditional Irish music wasn't written down — it was passed down over hundreds of years.

Irish Dances Can be **Social Dances** or **Performance Dances**

1) Social dances are ones where everyone joins in — they're either ceilidh (or céilí) dances or set dances. A ceilidh involves couples dancing in a square, circle or line. In a set dance, four couples dance in a square.

2) Social dances take place at celebrations like fairs and weddings.

3) Performance dances are watched by the audience, rather than them joining in.

4) Most performance dances are a form of step dancing. In step dancing, the complicated footwork is the most important part of the dance — dancers often keep the top half of their body still.

Reels, Jigs and **Hornpipes** are all **Performance Dances**

REELS
- Reels were first taught by travelling dance teachers in the 1700s.
- Reels are in $\frac{4}{4}$ (sometimes $\frac{2}{4}$ or $\frac{2}{2}$), with accents on the first and third beats of the bar.
- The tunes are often made up of straight (not dotted) quavers. They're quite quick.

HORNPIPES
- The hornpipe was originally an English dance — it spread to Ireland in the 18th century. It comes from the music of sailors.
- Hornpipes are in $\frac{4}{4}$.
- They often have dotted rhythms, though the musicians can choose to play them straight.
- They're a bit slower than a reel.

JIGS
- Some people think jigs started out as the marches of ancient Irish clans.
- Jigs are lively and fast. They often start on an anacrusis (upbeat).
- Single, double, light and heavy jigs (also called a hard jig or triple jig) are in $\frac{6}{8}$.
- Slip jigs are in $\frac{9}{8}$, and are graceful with hops and skips.

Some Irish **Pop** has Dance **Influences**

1) Modern Irish dance music combines folk rhythms with contemporary beats. It uses both live instruments and MIDI sequencers. A good example of this is the music from Riverdance.

2) Irish pop artists like The Corrs, Westlife and Van Morrison sometimes use elements of Irish music — for example, The Corrs use traditional Irish instruments in some of their songs.

Afro Celt Sound System — Release

'Release' is from the album *Volume 2: Release* by Afro Celt Sound System. There are a couple of recordings of this song — I'm going to talk about the album version, which is over 7 minutes long.

Afro Celt Sound System Fuse African and Irish Music

1) Afro Celt Sound System was formed in 1995 by three producers (Simon Emmerson, James McNally and Martin Russell) and vocalist Iarla O'Lionaird. The band also has a number of African and Irish musicians, as well as guest musicians (such as Sinéad O'Connor, who helped write 'Release').

2) They wanted to explore the connections between African and Irish music after Emmerson noticed similarities between traditional music from each place.

3) To create their unique sound, the band combines the following elements:

- traditional Irish and African musical styles (e.g. an Irish air with an African drumbeat)
- a mixture of Irish and African instruments (e.g. a tin whistle and a djembe drum)
- an electronic dance beat to tie the music together

There are more details on these elements below.

4) The song 'Release' was written to help the band cope with the tragic death of their keyboard player, Jo Bruce, who died in 1997. The lyrics (written by Sinéad O'Connor) reflect this.

5) 'Release' has a simple, mournful melody sung above a driving rhythm played on a combination of African and Irish percussion.

The Band Use African, Irish and Electric Instruments

'Release' uses a combination of the following instruments:

IRISH/CELTIC INSTRUMENTS
- Celtic harp
- Uilleann pipes (Irish bagpipes)
- Hurdy-gurdy (a string instrument with a keyboard)
- Bodhrán (a framed drum)
- Tin whistle and flute

AFRICAN INSTRUMENTS
- Djembe (a type of drum)
- Talking drum
- Kora (a string instrument)
- Balafon (a wooden xylophone)

See p.136-137 for more on these instruments.

ELECTRIC INSTRUMENTS
- Electric guitar
- Bass guitar
- Keyboard

VOCALISTS
- Female vocalist (Sinéad O'Connor, who sings in English)
- Male vocalist (Iarla O'Lionaird, who sings in Gaelic)
- African chanting

The Song Has a Strophic Structure

1) 'Release' is strophic, so each verse uses the same melody (although there are some slight variations in later verses, such as extending the length of the notes — see next page). There are no choruses.

2) There is a long introduction before the verses start, and short instrumental links between the verses. There are also two instrumental solos, which provide contrast and variation. The song ends with an instrumental outro that fades out. There's more detail on this on the next page.

My sound system consists of a cassette player and some tapes...

The term 'sound system' originated in 1950s Jamaica. DJs would load their sound equipment on the back of a truck and host street parties. The performance was a combination of live and recorded music.

Afro Celt Sound System — Release

'Release' uses elements from traditional Irish and African music, and fuses them together to create a new sound. This page looks at these elements in a bit more detail.

The **Rhythm** of 'Release' is **Syncopated**

The <u>key features</u> of 'Release' are:

1) **MELODY** The melody is based on a <u>C minor pentatonic scale</u> (see p.27). The <u>vocal melody</u> is quite <u>simple</u> — most of the tune <u>repeats</u> the same <u>2-bar phrase</u>, which is <u>conjunct</u> and has a fairly <u>small range</u> (from the <u>G</u> above middle C to the <u>B♭</u> below).

2) **RHYTHM** The underlying pulse uses <u>djembe drums</u> and a <u>bodhrán</u>, and plays the <u>same repeated rhythm</u> throughout most of the piece. The other percussion instruments add to the rhythmic texture. Most of the drum parts are <u>syncopated</u>.

3) **TEXTURE** The texture is mostly <u>homophonic</u>, with instruments <u>accompanying</u> the simple sung melody. There is also a <u>drone</u> that is played through most of the piece. As it progresses, <u>more instruments</u> are added to the accompaniment. Some <u>countermelodies</u> come in during the <u>instrumentals</u>, making the texture <u>richer</u> and more <u>polyphonic</u>.

4) **TIMBRE** A <u>variety</u> of different timbres are used in the piece, created by <u>instruments</u> from the <u>Celtic</u> and <u>African</u> musical traditions, as well as some <u>electronic instruments</u>. The background <u>drone</u> also changes the timbre. *See p.74 for more on timbre.*

5) **TIME SIGNATURE & TEMPO** 'Release' is in a steady $\frac{4}{4}$ all the way through. Although it is <u>dance music</u>, the piece moves at a fairly <u>moderate</u> speed of about <u>100 beats per minute</u>.

6) **DYNAMICS** The piece begins <u>quietly</u> with a long introduction featuring just a <u>few instruments</u>. When the <u>female vocalist</u> comes in, she sings <u>softly</u>. Gradually <u>more instruments</u> are added (creating a <u>natural crescendo</u>) and the vocals get <u>louder</u>.

Different Things Happen in **Each Section**

1) **INTRODUCTION** — there is a <u>drone</u> on the <u>synthesiser</u>, <u>ad lib drum sounds</u> and African chanting. The <u>main drum rhythm</u> enters and plays the <u>riff</u> above before the vocals begin. The intro is quite <u>long</u>.

2) **VERSE** — the <u>female vocalist</u> sings the main melody based on the <u>opening phrase</u>. The <u>bass guitar</u> begins to play a riff, and a <u>flourish</u> on the <u>flute</u> is heard. The music gets a bit <u>louder</u>.

3) **LINK** — <u>instrumental</u> link with another <u>flute flourish</u>.

4) **VERSE** — the <u>male vocalist</u> sings a similar melody in <u>Gaelic</u>. He <u>repeats</u> the final line <u>three times</u>, <u>extending</u> the notes.

5) **INSTRUMENTAL** — the <u>Uilleann pipes</u> improvise around the melody, and the <u>tin whistle</u> and <u>flute</u> are added. The <u>djembe</u> and <u>bodhrán</u> accompany, and the <u>male vocalist</u> comes back in.

6) **VERSE** — the <u>female vocalist</u> sings the last part of her verse in <u>English</u>, above the <u>Uilleann pipes</u> (this creates <u>polyphony</u>). The <u>male vocalist</u> repeats the last line <u>three times</u> in <u>Gaelic</u>, as he did before.

7) **LINK** — there is another <u>instrumental link</u>, with an <u>ostinato</u> played on the <u>Celtic harp</u> and <u>balafon</u>.

8) **INSTRUMENTAL** — the melody is played on the <u>hurdy-gurdy</u> with the <u>female vocalist</u> singing <u>open vowel sounds</u> above it.

9) **VERSE** — the <u>female vocalist</u> sings the <u>last four lines</u> of the verse again.

10) **OUTRO** — the <u>ostinato pattern</u> is played on the <u>Celtic harp</u> and <u>balafon</u> as the music <u>fades out</u>.

Please release me from GCSE Music...

Make sure you can identify the elements that come from the different styles of music that have been fused together — you'll probably be asked about them in the exam (the Area of Study is called 'fusions' after all).

Jazz

Jazz is a pretty massive subject, so I've tried to cram the important bits into these pages.
You'll probably have heard lots of jazz — it's a word used to cover quite a few types of music.

Jazz has its **Roots** in **African American Blues** and **Ragtime**

1) Jazz is a type of music that developed in the USA in the early 20th century. It's a fusion of African and European influences that came from the music of the newly-freed slaves.

2) It started off as Dixieland jazz in New Orleans in the early 1900s. Dixieland jazz is a mix of brass band marches, ragtime (music with lots of syncopated melodies that was often played on the piano) and blues (see p.110-111). Dixieland jazz is polyphonic (different parts move at different times).

3) It was played in bars — the only places black musicians were allowed to perform because of segregation (black people weren't allowed to use the same places as white people, like schools and bars).

4) In 1920, jazz moved to Chicago. This was the era of the Prohibition (from 1920-1933, alcohol was banned in the United States). Illegal bars (called speakeasies) often had jazz bands playing. Jazz started to get a bad reputation. Some people thought it was immoral.

5) The 1920s were known as 'the Jazz Age' or the 'Roaring Twenties'.

Swing Music was Popular in the **1930s** and **40s**

1) Swing music is a type of jazz that can be danced to. It's more structured than Dixieland jazz.

2) It's usually quite fast, and rhythms are swung (see p.110). Most pieces are in $\frac{4}{4}$. It was meant to be danced to, so it had regular phrases and emphasis on the first and third beats of the bar.

3) Swing is played by a big band (see p.143).

4) It was popular because it was played on the radio — it was a lot more accessible and acceptable than going to the illegal bars.

5) During the Second World War, swing became less popular because lots of the men who played in the big bands had gone off to war.

6) After the war, bebop (or just bop) developed from swing music. Bebop was fast with lots of improvisation. It had complex harmonies, exciting syncopated rhythms, and irregular phrase lengths. Bebop was much less structured than swing.

Free Jazz Broke all the **Rules**

1) Free jazz is a type of jazz that developed in the 1950s and 60s. It was a reaction against the limits of swing and bebop.

2) It didn't follow the normal rules of tempo and rhythm — players within the same band would play at different speeds to each other. There wasn't a regular rhythm.

3) There was lots of improvisation (see p.144) — the soloist didn't follow the chords or structure of the rest of the band.

Jazz didn't stop developing in the 60s. Some jazz musicians came up with even more experimental forms of jazz, such as avant-garde jazz. The avant-garde movement was big in music, art and literature — it involved pushing boundaries of what's considered "normal".

Mmmmmm Jaaazz...

There are loads of different types of jazz out there — the best thing you can do to get a feel for it is to listen to as much as you can get your hands on, so you're familiar with how jazz sounds.

Jazz

Jazz has lots of features that mean you'll <u>recognise</u> it when you hear it — for example, it has a <u>swing</u> to it.

Trumpets, Trombones and Clarinets are Jazz Instruments

1) A typical <u>jazz band</u> would have a <u>trumpet</u>, a <u>trombone</u> and a <u>clarinet</u> on the <u>front row</u>. Later, <u>saxophones</u> were included too. The <u>front row instruments</u> play <u>improvised solos</u>.

2) There'd be a <u>rhythm section</u> with <u>piano</u>, <u>guitar</u>, <u>drums</u> and a <u>double bass</u>.

3) Big bands are made up of <u>saxophones</u>, <u>trumpets</u>, <u>trombones</u> and a <u>rhythm section</u>. The sax section has <u>alto</u>, <u>tenor</u> and <u>baritone saxophones</u> and sometimes <u>clarinets</u>. Some big bands have a <u>singer</u> too.

4) A typical big band would have <u>5 saxophones</u> (2 altos, 2 tenors and a baritone), <u>4 trumpets</u>, <u>4 trombones</u> and a <u>4-piece rhythm section</u> (piano, bass, guitar and drums).

Jazz is Swung and Syncopated

1) Early jazz music was based on a <u>12-bar blues</u> (see p.111).

2) The <u>chords</u> were played by the <u>rhythm section</u> and the <u>front row</u> instruments would <u>improvise</u> over them.

3) Jazz musicians use <u>call and response</u> and <u>blue notes</u> — key features of jazz and blues. Blue notes are <u>flattened 3rds</u>, <u>7ths</u> and sometimes <u>5ths</u> of a <u>major scale</u>.

4) <u>Syncopated rhythms</u> move the strong beat <u>away</u> from the <u>first</u> and <u>third beats</u> of the bar. <u>Swung rhythms</u> (see p.110) are also used.

Jazz Music Wasn't Written Down

1) In early jazz (and in some today), the music <u>wasn't written down</u>.

2) There was lots of <u>interaction</u> between the soloist and the band, like <u>call and response</u> — the soloist would play a phrase (the <u>call</u>) and the band would answer it (the <u>response</u>) or the other way around. Sometimes the soloist would <u>repeat</u> ideas heard earlier in the piece and <u>develop</u> them in the solo.

3) The band would follow the <u>band leader</u>. Sometimes the band leader would also be the <u>soloist</u> or the <u>composer</u> — like <u>Louis Armstrong</u>, <u>Duke Ellington</u> and <u>Glenn Miller</u>.

4) Popular jazz pieces are called <u>jazz standards</u>. They're pieces that are part of a band's <u>repertoire</u>. Some jazz standards are '<u>I Got Rhythm</u>', '<u>My Funny Valentine</u>' and '<u>Take The "A" Train</u>'.

Jazz is Used in Lots of Fusion Genres

1) Fusions with jazz can take <u>any element</u> of jazz and add it to elements of other genres that are often quite <u>different</u>.

2) The elements of jazz often used are the <u>instruments</u>, <u>free rhythms</u>, <u>chords</u> and <u>chord patterns</u>, <u>improvisation</u> and <u>call and response</u>. The more successful fusions were made up of jazz mixed with the <u>popular</u> genres of the time:

- <u>Jazz rock</u> is a fusion of jazz and <u>rock</u> that began in the 1960s. Jazz rock usually features <u>jazz instruments</u> playing with <u>electric</u> and <u>bass guitars</u> and <u>keyboards</u>. It often has a <u>powerful rhythm</u> from the <u>amplified instruments</u>, with more complex, jazzy <u>improvisations</u>, <u>melody</u> and <u>accompaniment</u>.

- <u>Nu jazz</u> is jazz mixed with <u>electronic dance</u>, <u>funk</u> and <u>soul</u>. It started in the <u>1990s</u>, when electronic dance music was very popular. Nu jazz tracks often include <u>turntables</u> and <u>synths</u>, and have <u>free</u> and <u>changing rhythms</u>.

Improvisation

Improvisation is used in lots of different genres, including jazz.
It's not just playing notes at random though — there's quite a bit more to it.

Lots of Jazz is Improvised

1) Improvisation is where a performer makes up music on the spot. There are often improvised solo sections in jazz pieces. This means the same piece can be played in radically different ways — even if a piece is played twice by the same people, it won't sound the same.

2) The improvisations aren't totally random though — the soloist will know which chords to improvise over. This is often a 12-bar blues chord pattern (see p.111). Some improvisations use a mode (see page 27) instead of a chord pattern.

3) The soloist will know which notes are in each chord, but sometimes they'll play clashing notes to keep the solo interesting. If they're using a mode, they'll use the notes of the mode in their solo.

4) They might also use bits of the main melody of the piece as a starting point, then develop it into a much more complex phrase.

5) Jazz songs are a bit different — the singer has less chance to improvise, but they can use scat (a type of improvised singing with nonsense words and syllables).

6) Swing music has less improvisation — people wanted tunes they could recognise. There are still some sections for a soloist to improvise over, but they're shorter.

Improvisation Uses Lots of Different Techniques

Performers use lots of different musical ideas and techniques in their solos — it gives them a chance to show off, and to keep the melody exciting and interesting:

- Syncopation makes a tune feel 'jazzy' — triplets and dotted rhythms help the tune flow (see p.110).
- Blue notes (see p.110) are often used in jazz improvisations.
- Ornaments (like passing notes and appoggiaturas) make the melodies more lively (see p.41).
- Dynamics (see p.19) and accents (see p.20) also bring variety to a solo.
- Some performers pinch bits of other melodies in their solos — it keeps the audience entertained when they spot them.

Indian Music Uses Improvisation Too

1) Improvisation isn't just used in Western music — it's a big part of Indian music as well.
2) The improvisations are based on a raga (see p.134). There are hundreds of different ragas.
3) Raga performances are improvised, but based on traditional melodies and rhythms.
4) These are never written down — they are passed on from generation to generation aurally (by ear).
5) The improvised melody is often played on a sitar, or sung. They only use the notes of the raga.
6) The melody is played over a drone — a long held-on note that provides the harmony.

These are the notes of the rag desh, a night-time raga for the rainy season. The melody would be improvised using these notes over a drone.

I'll improvise my way through the listening exam...

In 'Dancing Men', a number of instruments have improvised solos (often the saxophone, trombone and drums). Have a listen to recordings of this piece by Buddy Rich, Simon Phillips and Dennis Chambers — you'll notice that the solos are completely different each time.

Samba

Samba is one of the most popular forms of dance music in South America, and around the world.

Samba Comes from **Brazil**

1) Samba is a Brazilian street carnival dance. Some of the famous Brazilian carnivals, such as the Rio Carnival, have made samba popular all over the world.

2) It's usually in either $\frac{2}{4}$ or $\frac{4}{4}$. It sounds cheery and is played at a fast tempo in a major key.

3) Samba instruments include a big variety of percussion, Portuguese guitar (a bright-sounding guitar with 12 strings), keyboards, whistles and, in larger street bands, saxophones and trumpets.

4) Samba is played by huge bands at carnivals, and by smaller bands for dancing samba-salao in ballrooms, or to accompany samba-cancao (samba songs).

The **Samba Beat** Sounds like **Footsteps**

1) The main samba beat is played by a pair of loud, resonant bass drums called surdo drums.

2) The basic surdo rhythm sounds like steady marching footsteps. The surdo players alternately hit the drum with a stick then damp it with the hand. This muting and unmuting gives the effect of offbeat springy notes in between the main beats.

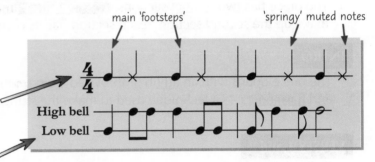

3) Over the basic surdo beat you hear many other complex syncopated, ostinato rhythms, such as this agogo bells rhythm:

4) Other common percussion instruments include: shakers (known as ganzas, caxixis, or shekeres), scrapers (the reco reco) and tambourines (pandeiros).

The **Whistle Player** is **In Charge** of a Samba Band

1) Large samba bands are controlled by a leader playing a two-toned samba whistle and a drum.

2) The whistle sets the tempo and signals call and response sections. In the call and response bits, the leader plays a rhythm (usually on a drum called a repinique) and is answered by the rest of the band.

3) The call and response sections contrast with the sections where everyone plays repeated rhythms.

4) Sometimes the whole band stops and then starts again. This is called a break.

5) Samba melodies are usually very catchy and repetitive. They also build up — parts get added on top.

Samba has been **Fused** to Make **New Styles**

1) Because of its popularity, samba has led to many new musical styles.

2) Samba is often mixed with other dance styles, e.g. tango and rumba.

3) In the 1950s, samba was fused with jazz to make a style called bossa nova.

4) It has also been mixed with soul, funk, rock and disco to create a wide range of subgenres and fusions.

Put 2nd December in your diaries — it's Brazil's National Samba Day...

Just like any type of music, the typical rhythms of samba can be changed or added to, so that it doesn't become too boring and repetitive. The rhythms on this page are common, but there are loads of others.

Esperanza Spalding — Samba Em Preludio

'Samba Em Preludio' is the final track from the album *Esperanza*, released by Esperanza Spalding in 2008.

Esperanza Spalding is an American Jazz Musician

1) Esperanza Spalding is a <u>bassist</u> — she plays acoustic and electric <u>bass guitar</u>, and <u>double bass</u>.

2) She is also a <u>singer</u> and <u>songwriter</u>, writing in English, Spanish and Portuguese.

3) She is best known as a jazz musician — she draws on <u>international influences</u> to create many <u>different</u> jazz styles, in particular <u>Latin jazz</u>, <u>Cuban jazz</u> and <u>jazz fusion</u>.

4) Spalding's version of Samba Em Preludio mixes <u>elements</u> of jazz and <u>Latin American</u> music, especially <u>samba</u>.

'Samba Em Preludio' is in Binary Form

1) 'Samba Em Preludio' is made up of 4 verses, sung in <u>Portuguese</u>. The lyrics express someone <u>pining</u> for a lost love and begging for them to <u>come back</u>.

2) The piece has two <u>distinct</u> sections. <u>Verses 1 and 2</u> make up the first section, and <u>verses 3 and 4</u> make up the second section. Each section has its own <u>unique</u> features:

INTRO

The piece opens with an <u>ad lib</u> (improvised) solo on the <u>bass guitar</u>, featuring <u>chords</u>, <u>arpeggios</u> and <u>harmonics</u> — a technique used to make the string <u>vibrate</u> to produce a <u>high</u>, <u>ringing note</u>.

VERSES 1 and 2

- Spalding sings the first two verses <u>quietly</u>, <u>slowly</u> and in a <u>free rhythm</u>. She sings <u>legato</u> and in a <u>low vocal range</u> (or <u>tessitura</u>), accompanying herself on <u>bass guitar</u>.

- The melody is in <u>B minor</u> and is based on <u>7th chords</u> in a <u>descending sequence</u>. The chords are <u>broken</u> — the notes are played one at a time, in a <u>triplet rhythm</u>.

- A 7th chord is a <u>triad</u> with a <u>7th note</u> added — this gives quite a <u>jazzy</u> feel to these verses.

- The <u>first</u> and <u>fourth chords</u> of the verse are shown here: 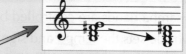 To get from the first to the fourth, Spalding moves each note down <u>stepwise</u>.

- The first and fourth chords are the same — they're both a <u>G major triad</u> with a <u>major 7th</u>. The first chord is in <u>first inversion</u>, and the fourth chord is in <u>root position</u>.

VERSES 3 and 4

- A <u>guitarist</u> now joins in. The melody changes — it has a <u>steady</u> tempo and <u>syncopated</u> rhythm.

- The guitarist then plays a <u>solo</u> over the bass guitar and <u>gentle</u> guitar chords. The two guitar lines use <u>layering</u> — when performed <u>live</u> it won't sound quite the same as the <u>album version</u>. After the solo, verses 3 and 4 are <u>repeated</u>, while the bass guitar repeats the triplets from verses 1 and 2.

OUTRO

The <u>last line</u> of verse 4 is <u>repeated</u> 3 times — the piece then finishes with <u>flourishes</u> on <u>both</u> guitars.

Desculpe, não falo português...

You don't need to speak Portuguese to tell that this is a sad piece of music. The minor key and low vocal range create a melancholy mood, and the long, drawn-out notes in verses 3 and 4 almost sound like crying.

Esperanza Spalding — Samba Em Preludio

'Samba Em Preludio' was written by two Brazilian musicians.
Esperanza Spalding then took this music and added in her own jazz elements.

'Samba Em Preludio' means 'Samba in the Style of a Prelude'

1) The music for 'Samba Em Preludio' was composed by <u>Brazilian</u>
   guitarist <u>Baden Powell</u>, with lyrics by <u>Vinícius de Moraes</u>.

2) When de Moraes first
   heard the tune, it reminded
   him of Chopin's piano
   <u>preludes</u>. There are some
   <u>similarities</u> in style:

   - Chopin's preludes explore a <u>particular mood</u>.
   - They often have an <u>improvised</u> feel.
   - They can build on two (or more) <u>different melodic ideas</u>.

3) <u>Samba</u> is an <u>up-tempo</u> dance from Brazil that
   typically uses a syncopated rhythm (see p.110).
   'Samba Em Preludio' is <u>not</u> up-tempo, but it
   does have <u>samba rhythms</u> in verses 3 and 4:

4) The <u>dynamics</u> of 'Samba Em Preludio' are very <u>different</u> to typical samba dynamics.
   Samba is <u>carnival</u> music, so it has to be <u>loud</u>. 'Samba Em Preludio' begins <u>quietly</u> with Spalding
   singing <u>softly</u>, accompanied by bass guitar. The dynamics stay quiet <u>throughout</u> the song.

Latin American and Jazz Elements are Mixed Together

There are <u>loads</u> of different <u>elements</u> and <u>ideas</u> in 'Samba Em Preludio'
that are taken from both <u>Latin American</u> music and <u>jazz</u>.

RHYTHM & TEMPO

In verses 1 and 2, the rhythm is <u>free flowing</u>, which is common in jazz.
It then adopts a steady <u>pulsing samba</u> rhythm in verses 3 and 4. It is much
<u>slower</u> than a typical samba piece, so it keeps the jazzy feel during this section.

INSTRUMENTS

- <u>Guitars</u> are often used in Latin American music, especially the <u>nylon-stringed guitar</u> that
  can be heard in this piece. <u>Bass guitars</u> are used in both <u>jazz</u> and <u>Latin American</u> music.
- Both instruments have a <u>solo</u> section, which again is a common feature of jazz.
  The piece opens with the bass guitar <u>improvising</u>. The nylon-stringed guitar has a
  <u>long</u> solo section in the <u>middle</u> of the piece, played in a Latin American style —
  techniques such as <u>tremolo picking</u> and <u>fast arpeggios</u> are used.

TEXTURE

The texture is <u>polyphonic</u> with vocal and instrument lines moving <u>independently</u> — the
<u>vocals</u> and the <u>bass guitar</u> create an obvious <u>contrapuntal</u> texture. This is heard a lot in
jazz and Latin American music. It is quite a <u>light</u> texture, as there are only two instruments
in the first two verses. At verse 3 the <u>guitar</u> joins in to create a <u>slightly denser</u> texture.

HARMONY

Spalding sometimes sings notes that <u>clash</u> with the underlying chords, which creates
<u>dissonance</u>. She also uses <u>7th chords</u>. These are both common features of jazz.

Salmon Em Preludio — my favourite Brazilian fish dish...

You could also argue that it has Baroque influences — there's counterpoint, it starts like a recitative,
the first preludes were Baroque. Classical music still has many musical fingers in many musical pies...

Other Fusions

The set works represent only two types of musical fusion. But there are loads and loads of others — salsa is one of the most popular fusions (it's pretty much a genre in its own right).

Salsa Grew Out of Son and Big-Band Jazz

1) <u>Son</u> is the traditional music of <u>Cuba</u>, which combines the music of the <u>Spanish colonists</u>, and the <u>African slaves</u> that they brought with them. Some of the <u>features</u> are:

- A basic <u>repeated rhythm pattern</u> that people can dance to is called a <u>clave</u> (pronounced *CLAH-VEY*) (see below). It's played by hitting two sticks called <u>claves</u> (pronounced *CLAYVES*) together. <u>Maracas</u> and <u>bongos</u> play complicated <u>cross-rhythms</u> and <u>polyrhythms</u> against the clave part.
- A melody played by <u>brass instruments</u> like trumpets (see p.135 for other son instruments).
- <u>Call and response</u> between a lead singer (<u>sonero</u>) and the chorus (<u>choro</u>). Lyrics are often <u>simple</u> and <u>improvised</u>.

2) Salsa grew in the <u>1960s</u> and <u>1970s</u> in <u>New York</u>, in the city's Latin American community.

3) Taking the basic structure of son, <u>salsa bands</u> added the harsher, brass-based arrangements of <u>big band jazz</u>. The <u>trombone</u> was a big focus.

4) Salsa also took inspiration from <u>Puerto Rican</u>, <u>Brazilian</u> and <u>African</u> music. It soon became popular throughout <u>Latin America</u> and <u>beyond</u>.

Clave is the Rhythm of Salsa

A common salsa rhythm is the <u>son clave</u> — it has a group of <u>three</u> notes and a group of <u>two</u>.

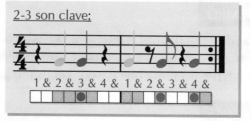

The clave might change partway through a piece.

The Structure of Salsa is Flexible

There are <u>three main chunks</u> in a salsa tune. The three different chunks can appear in <u>any order</u>, and they can all be used <u>more than once</u>.

1) In the <u>verse</u>, you hear the <u>main melody</u>, usually sung by the <u>sonero</u> or played by an instrumentalist.

2) The <u>montuno</u> is a kind of <u>chorus</u> where the sonero or lead instrumentalist <u>improvises</u> and the choro or other instrumentalists <u>answer</u>.

3) There is a <u>break</u> between choruses, called the <u>mambo</u>, with new musical material — e.g. different chords or a different melody. It's often played by the <u>horn section</u>.

4) There's usually an <u>introduction</u> and <u>ending</u>.

5) There could also be a 'break' — a bit where the main tune <u>stops</u> and just the rhythm section plays.

Here's a fairly <u>typical</u> salsa structure:

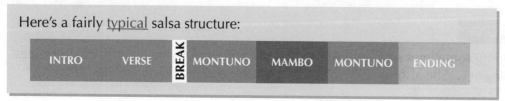

You say clave — I say clave...
Listen to some salsa and listen carefully to the rhythms — see if you can pick out the son clave.

Other Fusions

Bhangra takes traditional Punjabi music and turns it into a new type of club music.
There are also loads of other ways of creating new fusion genres.

Modern Bhangra Developed in the UK

1) Traditional <u>bhangra</u> is a type of <u>folk music</u> from the <u>Punjab</u> — a region of <u>North India</u> and <u>Pakistan</u>.

2) The key instrument is the <u>dhol</u>, a <u>double-headed</u>, <u>barrel-shaped drum</u>.
Each drumhead has a different sound. One is much <u>lower</u> than the other.

3) This is one of the <u>traditional rhythms</u> in bhangra:

DHA NA NA NA NA DHA DHA NA

The most popular rhythm for traditional and modern bhangra is the <u>chaal</u>. It's an <u>eight-note</u> repeated pattern. The quavers are <u>swung</u>, like in the blues.
NA = play the <u>small</u> drumhead. DHA = play <u>both</u> drumheads.

4) The modern bhangra style developed in the <u>UK</u> in the <u>1970s and 1980s</u>.

5) Asian musicians <u>fused</u> the <u>chaal rhythm</u> with Western styles like <u>hip-hop</u>, <u>disco</u>, <u>drum'n'bass</u>, <u>rap</u> and <u>reggae</u>. This created a whole new sound and made bhangra much more popular with <u>mainstream audiences</u>.

6) They also used Western instruments like <u>electric guitars</u> and <u>synthesizers</u>.

7) <u>Music technology</u> plays a big part in modern bhangra:

- <u>Remixes</u> — tracks with lots of different <u>layers</u> mixed together in <u>new ways</u>.
- <u>Samples</u> from other music, e.g. <u>bass lines</u>, <u>drum parts</u>, <u>words</u> or <u>other sounds</u> mixed in with the new track.
- <u>Drum machines</u> instead of the dhol.
- DJ techniques like <u>scratching</u>.

There are Lots of Other Fusions

1) <u>Son</u> and <u>jazz</u> can make salsa (see previous page). But by taking two similar elements you can end up with a completely <u>different</u> fusion — <u>Afro-Cuban jazz</u>. Salsa could be seen as <u>more Latin American</u>, whereas Afro-Cuban jazz leans more towards the <u>jazz</u> side. It is often thought of as the original <u>Latin jazz</u> fusion.

2) <u>Pop-folk</u> is a very broad term that covers a lot of different <u>genres</u>. It mixes <u>popular music</u> styles with <u>folk music</u> from <u>anywhere</u> in the world. These are often very popular in the country which they come from. For example:

- A fusion of pop music and <u>traditional Turkish music</u> is popular in Turkey. <u>Demet Akalın</u> is a successful Turkish musician who often uses this fusion.
- <u>Rock music</u> and <u>Celtic folk music</u> make a <u>Celtic rock</u> fusion. This often involves the upbeat <u>jig-type rhythm</u> of Celtic music (see p.139) and <u>strong</u>, <u>amplified guitars</u> and <u>drums</u> of rock. <u>Runrig</u> and <u>Capercaillie</u> are two very popular Celtic rock bands.
- <u>J-pop</u> and <u>K-pop</u> are two examples of East Asian music influencing <u>dance-pop music</u>. J-pop is short for "<u>Japanese pop</u>" and K-pop is short for "<u>South Korean pop</u>".

REVISION TIP

My favourite fusion is Finnish screamo stadium opera...

These types of fusion aren't strictly on your GCSE course, but you do need to know a wide range of fusion genres — they could easily crop up as an unfamiliar piece. So it's a good excuse to listen to new, exciting genres and fusions — it'll help you prepare for the exam.

Warm-up and Exam Questions

Final section, final warm-up and exam questions. Congratulations for making it this far.
But don't forget about the practice exam at the end of the book.

Warm-up Questions

1) Name three traditional Indian instruments.

2) Where is gamelan music played?

3) Where does calypso music come from?

4) What does the master drummer do in an African drum ensemble?

5) Where is Gaelic spoken?

6) List three African instruments, three Irish instruments
   and three electric instruments used in 'Release'.

7) Describe the dynamics of 'Release'.

8) Which decade is known as the 'Jazz Age'?

9) What is the main difference between Dixieland jazz and swing?

10) Name four instruments commonly played by jazz musicians.

11) What is scat?

12) Where is samba played?

13) Name three percussion instruments used in samba.

14) What is the structure of 'Samba Em Preludio'?

15) Describe the rhythm in the first verse of 'Samba Em Preludio'.

16) Which two musical styles influenced salsa?

17) Where did modern bhangra develop?

Exam Questions

Have a go at these exam-style questions.

Track 36 is an extract from 'Release' by Afro Celt Sound System.
Play the extract **three** times. Leave a short pause between each playing.

 Track 36

a) Name one Irish instrument that is playing in this extract.

.............Hurdy-Gurdy...

[1 mark]

b) What is the texture when the female voice is singing the verse?
   Circle the correct answer.

polyphonic   **antiphonal**   **homophonic**   **monophonic**

[1 mark]

Exam Questions

c)   Circle two features you can hear in this extract.

a cappella   <u>ostinato</u>   **call and response**   <u>drone</u>   **trill**

[2 marks]

d)   The mood of this extract could be described as 'reflective' and 'sombre'.
Give two musical reasons to explain how this mood is achieved.

The music is quiet as in a minor
key signature.

[2 marks]

e)   This piece is a work of fusion. How does the name of the band,
Afro Celt Sound System, reflect the musical features of this piece?

Uses both African and Celtic instruments.
Gaelic singing is used.
African vocal language singing used to
show the fusion.

[4 marks]

Track 37 is an extract from 'Samba Em Preludio' by Esperanza Spalding.
Play the extract **three** times. Leave a short pause between each playing.

(**Track 37**)

a)   Which of the following words best describes the texture of the extract?
Circle the correct answer.

monophonic   <u>**polyphonic**</u>   **heterophonic**

[1 mark]

Exam Questions

b) List three features of the extract that give it a jazz sound.

7th Chords, improvised bass guitar part and syncopated jazz rhythms.

[3 marks]

c) Explain how contrast is achieved throughout the extract.
You might want to mention the following musical features:
- Instruments
- Tempo
- Texture

The addition of guitar part. Second section sung in a lower tessitura. Section is more consist whilst the start is very disjoint. There is less dissonance in the second section to create contrast.

[4 marks]

d) i) What language are the lyrics sung in?

Portuguese.

[1 mark]

ii) The lyrics describe a person wishing to be reunited with their lost love.
How is this reflected in the music?

This is reflected through a minor key and extended note lengths.

[2 marks]

Revision Summary for Section Nine

Well, that was a pretty long section... Go through these questions and make sure you know the answer to all of them. If there are any you don't know, go back through the section and learn the answer. And then go through the questions again, to make sure you're completely comfortable with the material.

1) What is a raga?
2) Name three traditional gamelan instruments.
3) What is: a) a slendro?   b) a pelog?
4) List five different types of North American music.
5) Name a type of dance music that comes from Argentina and Uruguay.
6) What is a fusion?
7) Name three different types of African drum.
8) What is a balafon?
9) Describe mbube and isicathamiya singing.
10) What scales are folk melodies usually based on?
11) List three different types of Irish dance.
12) What different types of music do Afro Celt Sound System fuse together?
13) What is the structure of 'Release'?
14) What time signature is 'Release' in?
15) Which instruments play in the solos of 'Release'?
16) Describe the ending of 'Release'.
17) Where did jazz first develop?
18) What is the typical texture of Dixieland jazz?
19) Describe free jazz.
20) What sort of rhythms are usually used in jazz?
21) Name three fusions that have come from jazz.
22) List five techniques that could be used in improvisation.
23) What are the typical time signatures of samba?
24) What is the role of the whistle player in a samba band?
25) Name all the instruments used in 'Samba Em Preludio'.
26) List three ways in which 'Samba Em Preludio' is like a samba piece.
27) List three ways in which 'Samba Em Preludio' is like a prelude.
28) List three influences of jazz on the piece 'Samba Em Preludio'.
29) Give the two definitions of the word 'clave' in Cuban son.
30) What is: i) a sonero?   ii) a choro?
31) Describe a typical salsa structure.
32) Where does traditional bhangra come from?
33) What is a dhol?
34) Describe the chaal rhythm.
35) Give three examples of music technology used in modern bhangra.
36) Name two fusions that originate from jazz and Cuban son.
37) List three examples of pop folk fusions.

General Certificate of Secondary Education

GCSE
Music

Appraising Exam

Centre name					
Centre number					
Candidate number					

Surname	
Other names	

Time allowed: 1 hour 45 minutes

Instructions
- Write in black ink or ballpoint pen.
- Answer **all** questions in the spaces provided.
- Give all the information you are asked for, and write neatly.
- Do all rough work in this book. Cross through any work you do not want marked.

Information
- The marks are shown by each question.
- The maximum mark for this paper is 80.
- Section A has 68 marks and Section B has 12 marks.
- For each question you will need to play one or more tracks from the CD.
  You will be told how many times to play each track.
- For copyright reasons, Question 5 requires an additional resource — we recommend you have this
  prepared before you start this exam. Please read the instructions at the start of Question 5 (p.160) now.
- Read through the question before you play the track(s).
- Leave a gap between each playing to give yourself time to write.
- In Section A, you do not need to write in full sentences — you may respond using phrases and key words.
- In Section B, you should write your answer as an essay.

Instructions for playing the CD:
- There are 9 questions, covered on the CD by tracks 38-46.

Question No.	1	2	3	4	5	6	7	8	9
CD Track No.	38	39	40	41	see above	42	43	44	45, 46

- Leave some time at the start to read through the exam.
- Play the CD, one track at a time, stopping the CD after each track.
- Each question will tell you how many times the track should be repeated.
- Allow a short pause between each playing for writing time.
  After the final playing of each track, allow some time for writing.

Section A

1 You will hear an extract from 'Samba Em Preludio' by Esperanza Spalding.
Play the track **three** times.

(Track 38)

a) Which of the following words best describes the texture
during the first half of this extract? Circle your answer.

heterophonic   **monophonic**   **homophonic**   **contrapuntal**

(1 mark)

b) Identify **two** features of the extract that give it a samba feel.

....

....

....

(2 marks)

c) The piece has a key signature with two sharps. What key is it in?

....

(1 mark)

d) Which of the following best describes the melody of the extract? Circle your answer.

syllabic   **melismatic**   **chromatic**

(1 mark)

e) List and briefly describe **two** differences between the verses.

....

....

....

....

(2 marks)

Turn over

2 You will hear an extract from 'Music for a While' by Henry Purcell.
Play the track **three** times.

(Track 39)

a) In which musical period was this work composed?

....

(1 mark)

b) Suggest an appropriate tempo marking for this extract.

....

(1 mark)

c) Describe the accompaniment in this extract.

....

....

....

....

....

(3 marks)

d) Look at the opening two lines of lyrics:

Music, music for a while
Shall all your cares beguile.

With reference to the first time that these words are sung,
answer the following questions:

i)   Write down a word that is sung syllabically.

....

(1 mark)

ii) Write down a word that is sung melismatically.

....

(1 mark)

iii) What is the cadence on the words 'cares beguile'?

....

(1 mark)

e) What word describes the texture between the vocal part and the accompaniment
   in the section where the singer sings 'wondering'? Circle the correct answer.

heterophonic

homophonic

imitation

unison

(1 mark)

3 You will hear an extract from 'Killer Queen' by Queen.
Play the track **three** times.

(Track 40)

a) Which word describes the texture in the opening of the extract?

   monophonic   **heterophonic**   **homophonic**   **polyphonic**

(1 mark)

b) Name a way in which Queen used technology in the recording and production of this track.

   ....

(1 mark)

c) Name **two** guitar techniques used in the first half of this extract.

   ....

   ....

(2 marks)

d) In the phrase 'drop of a hat' in the vocal part, what is the interval
   between the notes used for 'a' and 'hat'?

   ....

(1 mark)

e) Compare the two sections of music heard in the extract. List **three** differences.

   ....

   ....

   ....

   ....

   ....

(3 marks)

4 You will hear an extract from 'Main Title/Rebel Blockade Runner' by John Williams. Play the track **three** times.

(Track 41)

a) What ensemble is playing in this extract? Tick the correct answer.

string quartet ☐

chamber orchestra ☐

symphony orchestra ☐

wind band ☐

(1 mark)

b) Which of the words below describes the beginning of the extract? Tick the correct answer.

fugue ☐

fanfare ☐

prelude ☐

sonata ☐

(1 mark)

c) This music has the performance direction '*maestoso*'. What does this mean?

....

(1 mark)

d) Describe the differences between the two halves of the extract. You should think about different musical features, such as the instrumentation, melody and texture.

....

....

....

....

(3 marks)

Turn over

5   This question is about 'Defying Gravity', from the original Broadway cast recording (2003) of *Wicked* by Stephen Schwartz. This song is sung by Idina Menzel and Kristin Chenoweth.
Unfortunately, we were unable to get permission to include this track on our audio CD.
However, it's readily available to listen to online —
you just need to listen to 4:08 – 5:05 of the recording.
Play the extract **three** times.

a) Give **two** ways in which the vocal lines in the opening of the extract
   reflect the friendship between Elphaba and Glinda.

   ....

   ....
   (2 marks)

b) Tick the box next to the word that best describes the change in dynamics
   that comes after 'friend' and before 'So if you...'.

   diminuendo   ☐

   sforzando   ☐

   marcato   ☐

   crescendo   ☐
   (1 mark)

c) Describe how the music around the phrase that starts 'look...'
   reflects Elphaba's mood at this point in the piece.

   ....

   ....

   ....

   ....

   ....
   (4 marks)

d) Suggest a word that describes the change in tempo on the phrase that starts 'everyone...'.

....

(1 mark)

e) Describe how the use of percussion changes during the extract.

....

....

....

(2 marks)

162

6   You will hear an extract from the 1st Movement of 'Sonata Pathétique' by Beethoven.
Play the track **three** times.

   a) This piece was written in the Classical era. Identify **two** aspects
of Classical music that are noticeable in this extract.

....

....
(2 marks)

   b) The first 8 bars of this extract form a phrase.
Give **one** way in which Beethoven varies this phrase during the extract.

....

....
(1 mark)

   c) Describe the use of dynamics in this extract.

....

....
(2 marks)

   d) At the time this sonata was composed, the term 'pathétique'
could be used to mean 'emotional' or 'passionate'.

   Describe how the extract fits this description.

....

....

....

....

....
(4 marks)

7 You will hear an extract from 'Music for a While' by Purcell.
Play the track **four** times.

a) Fill in the missing rhythm on the score below.

fill in the missing rhythm

(5 marks)

b) Fill in the missing pitches on the score below.

fill in the missing pitches

(5 marks)

Turn over

8 You will hear an extract from an unfamiliar piece.
The extract is from the 2nd Movement of 'Sonata Pathétique' by Beethoven.
Play the track **three** times.

A skeleton score of the extract is shown below.

a) Give one similarity and one difference between the accompaniment in bars 1-8
and the accompaniment in bars 9-16.

....

....

....

(2 marks)

b) Which word describes the use of tempo throughout this extract?
Circle the correct answer.

rubato   **accelerando**   **rallentando**   **allegro**

(1 mark)

c) i)   What is the rhythm used in the last two beats of bar 8?

....

(1 mark)

   ii)   What articulation marking would be appropriate in the last two beats of bar 8?

....

(1 mark)

d) The piece is marked 'cantabile', meaning 'in a singing style'.
Give two ways in which the word 'cantabile' reflects how this piece is performed.

....

....

....

(2 marks)

e) i)   What is the key at bar 16?

....

(1 mark)

   ii)   What is the harmonic device used in bar 16? Circle the correct answer.

pedal point   **chromatic notes**   **appoggiatura**

(1 mark)

Turn over

Section B

9   You will hear **two** extracts for this question.

You will hear an extract from the 3rd Movement of J.S. Bach's
'Brandenburg Concerto No.5 in D major'. Play the track **once**.

You will then hear an extract from the 3rd Movement of Haydn's 'Trumpet Concerto in E♭ major'.
Play the track **three** times.

Evaluate how the role of the soloist(s) differs from
the role of the accompaniment in these two extracts.

You should use your knowledge of musical elements, context and language in your response.
The scores of the solo instruments for these two extracts are on pages 168-171.

....

....

....

....

....

....

....

....

....

....

....

....

....

....

....

....

....

....

....

....

....

....

....

....

....

....

....

....

....

....

....

(12 marks)

The score for the solo instruments (flute, violin and harpsichord)
Brandenburg Concerto No.5, by J.S. Bach, 3rd Movement. Bars 233-310

Turn over

The score for the trumpet of the Trumpet Concerto in E♭ major,
by Joseph Haydn, 3rd Movement. Bars 45-124

END OF TEST

Answers

Section Two — Reading and Writing Music

Page 15 (Warm-up Questions)

1)

2) A sharp sign raises the pitch of the note (and other notes of the same pitch later in the bar) by one semitone.
A flat sign lowers the pitch of the note (and other notes of the same pitch later in the bar) by one semitone.
A natural sign cancels out a flat or sharp sign in the key signature or earlier on in the bar.

3)

4) Three beats

5) In simple time, the main beats are divided into 2, 4, 8, etc. but in compound time the beats are divided into 3, 6, 9, etc.

6) Regular, irregular and free

Page 15 (Exam Question)

Track 1

a)

(1 mark for each correct note or correct interval between two adjacent notes, up to 8 marks)

b) *(1 mark)*

c) *(1 mark)*

d)

(up to 3 marks, one for each different feature identified)

Page 21 (Warm-up Questions)

1) (semibreve)

2)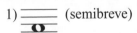

3) Dotted crotchet, one and a half beats
Quaver, half a beat
Dotted minim, three beats

4) A tie joins two or more notes of the same pitch together. A slur joins two or more notes of different pitch together.

5) Presto, allegro, moderato, andante, largo

Pages 21-22 (Exam Question)

Track 2

a) dotted notes *(1 mark)*

b) allegro *(1 mark)*

c) forte *(1 mark)*

d) energico *(1 mark)*

Section Three — Keys, Scales and Chords

Page 31 (Practice Questions)

Track 10 a) natural minor   b) melodic minor
c) whole tone   d) major

Track 11 Pentatonic (major isn't wrong, but pentatonic is more accurate)

Track 12 a) unison   b) perfect 5th   c) major 3rd
d) minor 3rd   e) major 7th   f) perfect 4th
g) minor 6th   h) augmented 4th/ diminished 5th

Track 13 a) minor 2nd   b) major 3rd   c) perfect 4th
d) octave   e) major 6th   f) perfect 5th
g) minor 7th   h) major 2nd

Page 32 (Warm-up Questions)

1) Eight

2) They tell you what sharps or flats to play.

3) They are relative scales – they have the same notes/same key signature.

4) Natural, harmonic and melodic

5) Major pentatonic

6) It includes every white and black note on a keyboard.

7) A harmonic interval.

8) Diminished 7th

Pages 32-33 (Exam Question)

Track 14

a) i)   Four *(1 mark)*

ii)   Perfect fourth *(1 mark)*

iii)   Minor third/augmented second *(1 mark)*

b) C# minor *(1 mark)*

c) Tenuto — played full length or longer *(1 mark)*

Page 40 (Practice Questions)

Track 17 a) major   b) minor   c) major

d) augmented   e) minor   f) diminished

g) diminished   h) minor

Track 18 a) root   b) 2nd   c) root

d) 2nd   e) 1st   f) 2nd

g) root   h) root

Pages 49-50 (Practice Questions)

Track 21 a) perfect   b) plagal   c) interrupted

d) imperfect   e) interrupted   f) perfect

g) imperfect   h) perfect

Track 22 a)

b) first inversion

c) plagal

Track 23 a)

b) homophonic

c) perfect

d) A

Track 24 a)

b) F sharp

c) interrupted

Track 25 a)

b) (see above)

c) Relative minor

Track 26 a)

b) E flat major

c) G minor

d) pivot chord

e) V, III

Page 51 (Warm-up Questions)

1) e.g. piano, guitar

2) I, IV and V or tonic, subdominant, dominant

3) First inversion

4) Block chords, rhythmic chords, broken / arpeggiated chords

5) Diatonic

6) Any three of the following: auxiliary notes, passing notes, appoggiaturas, suspensions, trills or other sensible answer.

7) In the middle of a piece, or at the end of any phrase except the last phrase.

8) Contrapuntal

Pages 51-52 (Exam Question)

Track 27

a) Piano *(1 mark)*

b) Alberti bass / broken chords / arpeggios *(1 mark)*

c) Imperfect *(1 mark)*

d) G major *(1 mark)*

e) Accidental *(1 mark)*

f) Staccato *(1 mark)*

g) Homophonic *(1 mark)*

Section Four — Structure and Form

Page 59 (Warm-up Questions)

1) *Conjunct* — melodies move mainly by step. Notes are a major 2nd (a tone) or a semitone apart.

Disjunct — melodies have a lot of jumps. Notes are more than a major 2nd apart.

Triadic — melodies made up of the three notes in a triad.

Scalic — melody moves up and down the notes of a scale.

2) A form where each verse has different music.

3) A repeated bass part, usually four or eight bars long that is played by the left hand on the piano or harpsichord, or by cello and double bass in an orchestra.

Pages 59-60 (Exam Questions)

Track 28

a) i) G major *(1 mark)*

ii) Minor third *(1 mark)*

b) Call and response/question and answer *(1 mark)*

c) A *(1 mark)*

Track 29

a) Baroque period *(1 mark)*

b) Oboe, bassoon, violin, viola, harpsichord. *(1 mark for each instrument, up to 2 marks)*

c) i)

(1 mark for each correct note or correct interval between two adjacent notes, up to 7 marks)

  ii) Conjunct *(1 mark)*

d) Basso continuo *(1 mark)*

e) Bassoon / Harpsichord *(1 mark)*

Section Five — Instruments

Page 76 (Warm-up Questions)

1) E.g. slide — trombone
   Single reed — clarinet or saxophone
   Double reed — oboe or bassoon
   Pizzicato — violin, viola, cello, double bass
   Wooden bars — xylophone

2) *Tremolo* — trembling sound on string instrument (fast, short, light strokes with the bow). Guitars can also produce this type of sound.
   Con sordino — 'with mute', mute placed on the bridge of string instruments to make them sound further away. Brass instruments can also be muted.
   Tenor — higher male voice.
   Falsetto — someone with a lower voice singing much higher than their normal range.

3) Acoustic guitar — e.g. played by strumming or plucking six or twelve strings.
   Electric guitar — e.g. needs an amplifier and loudspeaker to be heard.
   Bass guitar — e.g. has only four strings, is pitched lower than electric and acoustic guitar, needs amplification.

4) Baroque

5) A military band is a marching wind band, with woodwind, brass and percussion. A brass band has brass and percussion. A jazz band can include woodwind, brass, percussion and any other instruments too, and sounds quite different.

6) Piano trio — piano, violin, cello.
   Clarinet quintet — clarinet, first violin, second violin, viola, cello.

7) MIDI — musical instrument digital interface
   Sampler — record, process and play back samples of music
   Remix — mixing together samples of pop or dance music to a fast drumbeat, often speeded up
   Sequencer — computer program that records and replays many tracks of music together

Pages 76-78 (Exam Question)

Tracks 30 and 31

  a) Flute *(1 mark)*

  b) Piano *(1 mark)*

  c) Shape B *(1 mark)*

  d) The left hand of the piano has chords, the right hand melody imitates the flute part. One follows the other around. / The melodies interweave in a two-part texture at a similar pitch. / The parts are contrapuntal.
   (1 mark for each sensible comment up to a maximum of 2 marks)

  e) Flute, clarinet *(1 mark for each)*

  f) Strings *(1 mark)*

  g) Chromatic *(1 mark)*

  h) Shape C *(1 mark)*

  i) Crescendo *(1 mark)*

Section Six
— Instrumental Music 1700-1820

Page 96 (Warm-up Questions)

1) There were sudden changes in dynamics (no crescendos or diminuendos).

2) a) A small group of solo instruments.

  b) A larger group of accompanying instruments (often a string orchestra).

3) A note that clashes with a chord, but which is followed by a note belonging to the chord (usually a tone or semitone away from the first note).

4) E.g. clarinet

5) Three movements — first movement in sonata form (quick), second movement in ternary or variation form (slow), third movement in rondo, variation or sonata form (quick).

6) Exposition, Development and Recapitulation.

7) E.g. Mozart, Haydn.

Pages 96-99 (Exam Questions)

Track 32

  a) Any two of: flute, violin, harpsichord
   (1 mark for each, up to a maximum of 2 marks)

  b) Any two of: violin, viola, cello, violone/double bass, harpsichord
   (1 mark for each, up to a maximum of 2 marks)

  c) i) Imitation *(1 mark)*

    ii) Fugue *(1 mark)*

d) i) Baroque *(1 mark)*

   ii) Any three of:
   - The music is in the form of a concerto grosso.
   - There is a concertino (solo group of instruments) accompanied by a ripieno (string orchestra).
   (Award 1 mark for either of these statements)
   - The piece is played by a small chamber group.
   - The texture is polyphonic.
   - There is a continuo (played by the harpsichord, cello and violone/double bass).
   (1 mark for each, up to a maximum of 3 marks)

Track 33

a) Any two of:
   - Tempo (extract starts very slowly, then suddenly becomes much quicker after 4 bars).
   - Dynamics
   - Pitch
   (1 mark for each, up to a maximum of 2 marks)

b) The texture is homophonic — both hands move with the same rhythm. *(1 mark)*
   The music is made up of block chords. *(1 mark)*

c) Any four of the following:
   - The music is very dramatic/emotional/there are contrasting moods.
   - There is discordance.
   - It is very chromatic.
   - A large pitch range is used.
   - Sudden changes in dynamics.
   - Sudden change in tempo after the opening 4 bars of extract.
   - The opening is virtuosic.
   (1 mark for each, up to a maximum of 4 marks)

d) i) Staccato *(1 mark)*

   ii) Murky bass *(1 mark)*

Section Seven — Vocal Music

Page 116 (Warm-up Questions)

1) E.g. mass, oratorio

2) Treble, countertenor (or alto), tenor, bass

3) Grand opera, opera seria, opera buffa, opéra comique, operetta

4) A solo song in an opera, oratorio or cantata.

5) Polyphonic

6) Each character sings at a different pitch.

7) *Oedipus*

8) When a note is held over a change of chord to create dissonance.

9) Verse-chorus structure

10) In harmony, in unison, descant and call and response.

11) African slaves in America.

12) I, I, I, I, IV, IV, I, I, V, IV, I, I

13) E.g. strong beat and catchy tunes.

14) A chord made up of the tonic and the fifth.

15) Recording parts on top of each other.

Pages 116-118 (Exam Questions)

Track 34

a) Baroque *(1 mark)*

b) Ground bass *(1 mark)*

c) The word starts on a suspension, which creates dissonance. This dissonance then resolves, which sounds like it has been 'eas'd'. *(1 mark for suspension/dissonance, 1 mark for resolution)*

d) Harpsichord *(1 mark)*, cello *(1 mark)*

e) i) Melisma *(1 mark)*

   ii) To extend/illustrate the word *(1 mark)*

f) Any four of:
   - Use of word painting / melody illustrates the words / specific example of word painting.
   - Minor key.
   - Modulates to related / dominant key.
   - Vocal part and ground bass are in contrary motion / melody falls as ground bass rises.
   - Walking bass / quavers in bass part.
   - Faster / shorter note values in vocal part.
   (1 mark for each, up to a maximum of 4 marks)

Track 35

a) i) C minor *(1 mark)*

   ii) Relative minor *(1 mark)*

b) Portamento *(1 mark)*

c) Any four of:
   - Light instrumental accompaniment.
   - Short piano chords, mini guitar fills between lines, drum roll and bell.
   - 4-part harmony in the second half of the verse and in the chorus.
   - Backing vocals mainly sing 'oooh' and 'aaah' but sometimes echo the soloist.
   - Steady, on-beat rhythms / swung rhythms.
   - Layering of vocals.
   - Flanger effect on some words (e.g. laser beam).
   (1 mark for each, up to a maximum of 4 marks)

d) (Electric) guitar *(1 mark)*

Section Eight — Music for Stage and Screen

Page 130 (Warm-up Questions)

1) A lighter, more modern version of opera.

2) 4 sections of 8 bars. Sections 1, 2 and 4 use the main theme, section 3 has a contrasting theme.

3) Solo character song, duet, action song, chorus number

4) Stephen Schwartz

5) Elphaba and Glinda

6) A phrase of music that represents a character, place or emotion.

7) E.g. to link parts of the film together.

8) To create the mood of a specific time or place.

9) E.g. *Jaws, Indiana Jones, E.T. the Extra Terrestrial*

10) There is scrolling text setting the scene.

Pages 130-132 (Exam Questions)

a) i) Pizzicato *(1 mark)*

   ii) Tremolo *(1 mark)*

b) (Perfect) octave *(1 mark)*

c) Major *(1 mark)*

d) Similarities:
   Any two of:
   - Same key
   - Similar accompaniment (string quavers).
   - Similar words and melody.
   - Percussion accompaniment in both.
   (1 mark for each, up to a maximum of 2 marks)
   Differences:
   Any two of:
   - Two voices singing instead of one / voices in harmony.
   - Voice and accompaniment are much louder in second chorus.
   - Strings are lower in second chorus.
   (1 mark for each, up to a maximum of 2 marks)

e) Syncopated *(1 mark)*

Track 41

a) Triplets *(1 mark)*

b) i) Trumpet *(1 mark)*

   ii) E.g. It sounds heroic. / It sounds like a fanfare. / It sounds ceremonial. / It sounds hopeful.
   (1 mark)

c) Legato *(1 mark)*, conjunct *(1 mark)*

d) Similarities:
   Any two of:
   - Mainly brass and percussion.
   - Loud.
   - Triplet rhythms.
   - Pulse stays the same.
   (1 mark for each, up to a maximum of 2 marks)
   Differences:
   Any two of:
   - Main theme accompanied by woodwind and strings as well.
   - Fanfare is polyphonic whereas the main theme is homophonic.
   - Full orchestra is playing for the main theme.
   - It changes from 4/4 to 2/2.
   (1 mark for each, up to a maximum of 2 marks)

Section Nine — Fusions

Page 150 (Warm-up Questions)

1) E.g. sitar, tambura, tabla.

2) Java and Bali (Indonesian islands).

3) Trinidad and Tobago.

4) The master drummer leads the drum ensemble.

5) Scotland and Ireland.

6) E.g. African: djembe, kora, balafon
   Irish: Uilleann pipes, hurdy-gurdy, bodhrán
   Electric: electric guitar, bass guitar, keyboard.

7) The piece starts quietly, then gradually gets louder as more instruments are added.

8) 1920s

9) Swing is more structured than Dixieland jazz.

10) E.g. trumpets, trombones, saxophones, piano.

11) A type of improvised singing with nonsense words and syllables.

12) Brazil

13) E.g. surdo drums, agogo bells, shakers.

14) Binary form

15) Free rhythm

16) Son and big-band jazz

17) UK

Pages 150-152 (Exam Questions)

Track 36

a) Any of: bodhrán, flute, hurdy-gurdy *(1 mark)*

b) Homophonic *(1 mark)*

c) Ostinato *(1 mark)*, drone *(1 mark)*

d) Any two of:
- It uses a minor (pentatonic) scale.
- It is fairly quiet.
- It has a haunting melody.
(1 mark for each, up to a maximum of 2 marks)

e) Any four of:
- It uses African instruments.
- It uses Irish/Celtic instruments.
- It uses different types of percussion instrument, playing different rhythms, which is a feature of African music.
- One vocalist sings in English.
- One vocalist sings in Gaelic.
(1 mark for each, up to a maximum of 4 marks)

Track 37

a) Polyphonic *(1 mark)*

b) Any three of:
- It has a free rhythm at the start.
- There are clashing notes.
- The bass guitar improvises.
- It uses blue notes/the blues scale.
- The rhythms are syncopated.
(1 mark for each, up to a maximum of 3 marks)

c) Any four of:
- The second part has an additional instrument (the guitar).
- The rhythm is steadier and slightly quicker in the second part.
- The rhythms start working together instead of against each other.
- Fewer clashing notes in the second half.
- The first part is sung in a higher register than the second part.
- The first part is disjunct, the second part is conjunct.
(1 mark for each, up to a maximum of 4 marks)

d) i) Portuguese *(1 mark)*
  ii) Any two of:
- Minor key.
- Low vocal range (tessitura).
- Long, drawn-out notes.
- Sudden high notes (that sound like crying).
(1 mark for each, up to a maximum of 2 marks)

Page 154-171 — Practice Exam

1 *Track 38*

a) contrapuntal *(1 mark)*

b) Any two of:
- Free/syncopated rhythms
- Portuguese lyrics
- Spanish/Latin American guitar
(1 mark for each, up to a maximum of 2 marks)

c) B minor *(1 mark)*

d) syllabic *(1 mark)*

e) Any two of:
- The rhythm changes from free to syncopated
- The pitch changes from fairly high to fairly low
- The texture changes from contrapuntal to homophonic
- A guitar comes in for the second verse
- The second verse is slightly louder
- The second verse has a steadier tempo than the first verse
(1 mark for each, up to a maximum of 2 marks)

2 *Track 39*

a) Baroque *(1 mark)*

b) Accept any of: *largo, larghetto, adagio, andante,* or a metronome mark of 40-70 beats per minute *(1 mark)*

c) Any three of:
- The accompaniment is a continuo.
- Played by harpsichord and cello (or bass viol).
- The cello plays a ground bass.
- It has a realisation of a figured bass.
(1 mark for each, up to a maximum of 3 marks)

d) i) Any of: music, while, shall, all, cares *(1 mark)*
  ii) Any of: for, a, your, beguile *(1 mark)*
  iii) Perfect *(1 mark)*

e) Imitation *(1 mark)*

3 *Track 40*

a) Homophonic *(1 mark)*

b) Any of: layering, guitar distortion, reverb, flanger effect, studio effects *(1 mark)*

c) Any two of: picking, hammer-on, pull-off, pitch/string bend, vibrato, sliding.
(1 mark for each, up to a maximum of 2 marks)

d) Semitone *(1 mark)*

e) Any three of:
- First section is guitar solo, second section has vocal lead/guitar in accompanying role.
- No drums at start of first section, drums used throughout vocal section, with drum rolls leading into the chorus.
- In part of the guitar section, three separate guitar parts have distinct lines, all contributing to the melody (bell-effect). In the vocal section, the single vocal melody is very clear/there are close harmonies with backing vocals rather than separate melodic lines.
- Guitar section has an improvised feel, vocal section more structured.
(1 mark for each, up to a maximum of 3 marks)

4 *Track 41*

a) symphony orchestra *(1 mark)*

b) fanfare *(1 mark)*

c) Majestically *(1 mark)*

d) Any three of:

- The first half is dominated by brass instruments, with string and woodwind accompaniment. The second half is dominated by strings, with very little brass initially.
- Timpani have an important role the first half. The percussion section is much quieter in the second half — only the glockenspiel can be heard.
- In the first half the melody is quite disjunct — there are lots of jumps. The second half is more scalic/conjunct.
- In the first half, the fanfare is polyphonic, then the main theme is homophonic — it has a trumpet melody with a distinct triplet accompaniment. The second half is mostly homophonic — all the instruments play the same rhythm but different notes.
- The first half has a very dramatic feel, with driving triplets. The second half has a calmer, more legato feel.

(1 mark for each, up to a maximum of 3 marks)

5 a) Any two of:

- Positive lyrics.
- Part of it is sung in unison — this reflects their closeness.
- The part sung in harmony reflects their different characters.
- It's in a major key — this reflects their positive relationship.

(1 mark for each, up to a maximum of 2 marks)

b) crescendo *(1 mark)*

c) Any two of:

- Major key reflects positive, hopeful feelings.
- Singing in the high register reflects increasing confidence.
- Leaps in the melody, e.g. at 'look' and 'fly' show excitement and confidence.
- Loud dynamics reflect positive feelings / the dramatic nature of her decision to leave.

(For each, award one mark for a correct feature, and a further mark for a suitable justification, up to a total of 4 marks.)

d) *ritenuto* or *rallentando* (allow *rit.* or *rall.*)
   (1 mark)

e) Any two of:

- Very little percussion at the start of the extract (during Elphaba and Glinda's duet).
- Cymbal crashes during the 'look to the western sky' section.
- Percussion builds up as chorus is approached, with drums leading directly into chorus.
- Regular percussion beat as chorus begins.

(1 mark for each, up to a maximum of 2 marks)

6 *Track 42*

a) Any two of:

- Alberti bass
- Clear tune with a chordal accompaniment
- Clear, structured phrases (mostly 4, 8 or 12 bars long)
- Steady rhythm with no big change in tempo
- Use of crescendos and gradual changes in dynamics

(1 mark for each, up to a maximum of 2 marks)

b) Any one of:

- Repeated phrase with modulations to major key
- Pattern of descending mordents extended

(1 mark)

c) Any two of:

- Fairly quiet at the start, but with staccato notes louder.
- Long ascending section crescendos throughout.
- Rich chords at the end of the extract are loud.

(1 mark for each, up to a maximum of 2 marks)

d) Any two of the following:

- Minor key to represent sadness or grief.
- Rapid sections show turbulent emotions.
- Loud, *sforzando* chords at the end of the extract, which show tension or passion.
- The high legato parts at the start of the extract are interrupted by low staccato notes, which suggest dark emotions / showing contrasting emotions.
- Contrast between quiet and loud dynamics shows turbulent emotions.
- Notes ascending chromatically and with a crescendo in the second part of the extract, which represent building emotions.

(For each, award 1 mark for a correct feature, and a further mark for a suitable justification, up to a total of 4 marks.)

7 *Track 43*

a)

(1 mark for each correct note length.)

b)

(1 mark for each correct note.)

8 *Track 44*

a) Similarities — any of: both sections use broken chords, they have the same chord pattern, both use semiquavers continuously.
Differences — any of: bars 9-16 have more notes in the chords, in bars 9-16 the accompaniment has a denser texture.
(1 mark for a correct similarity, 1 mark for a correct difference.)

b) rubato *(1 mark)*

c) i) triplets *(1 mark)*

ii) staccato *(1 mark)*

d) Any two of:
- Melodic line is emphasised
- Quiet dynamics
- Legato playing
- Slow tempo
- Use of rubato
(1 mark for each, up to a maximum of 2 marks)

e) i) A♭ major *(1 mark)*

ii) appoggiatura *(1 mark)*

9 *Tracks 45 and 46*

The following points are true for **both** extracts:
- Both pieces feature a soloist or group of soloists, which is used to contrast with the full orchestra.
- The solo parts are virtuosic, which showcases the ability of the player along with the range and techniques appropriate to the instrument *(award a mark for an appropriate example)*.
- Orchestra is both to play the ritornello / main theme(s) and to accompany the solo *(award a mark for an appropriate example)*

- The roles demonstrate dynamic contrast through adding and removing instruments swapping from *p* to *f* when soloist / orchestra are playing.

The following points are true for the **Bach** extract:
- Solo part often based around arpeggio figures and mostly diatonic. The harpsichord's solo parts are often scalic.
- It is written in ritornello form — the soloists set out the main themes which are repeated.
- The piece is a fugue — the soloists set out the main themes which are repeated by the ripieno.
(N.B. Do not double credit explanation of 'ritornello' and 'fugue')

- This is a concerto grosso which means that it features a group of solo instruments — a flute, violin and harpsichord.
- The ripieno (a string orchestra) are the backing instruments and give contrast in terms of texture and dynamics along with the harmony.
- The harpsichord features in both groups. It plays the continuo in parts of the extract, but also plays with the concertino, where has a more virtuosic and ornamented role.
- The extract starts with an extended section without the ripieno, which adds emphasis to the importance of the soloists.

The following points are true for the **Haydn** extract:
- There is a single solo trumpet with a modest orchestral accompaniment, dominated by strings. This draws attention to the solo trumpet part.
- Melody features such as chromatic notes, scales, octave leaps and arpeggio figures showcase the abilities of the performer.
- These elements also demonstrate the capabilities of the trumpet, which was still developing as an instrument when the piece was composed.
- Use of fast rhythms such as semiquavers, ornamentation and use of long high notes show the ability of the trumpet player.
- The trumpet repeats the main theme for emphasis.
- The solo trumpet introduces some figures that are then played by the orchestra, which highlights the importance of its role.
- Cadenza-like passage gives the trumpet player a further opportunity to showcase their virtuosity and technical ability, developing the main themes and improvising based on them.
(Award 1 mark for each point made, or any other correct point not covered here, up to a maximum of 12 marks. If only one piece is discussed, the maximum is 6 marks.)

Index and Glossary

7th chords A **triad** with the seventh note above the **root** added. **35, 37**

12-bar blues A style of **blues** with a 12-bar repeating **chord progression**. **55, 111, 113, 143, 144**

32-bar song form A structure used in pop music, made up of four 8-bar sections. Sections 1, 2 & 4 use the main theme and section 3 uses a contrasting theme. **58**

A

a cappella Singing with no instrumental backing. **68, 109, 134, 137**

a tempo Go back to the original **tempo**. **18**

abrupt modulation A **modulation** that happens with no build-up or preparation. **44**

accelerando or accel. Speed up the **tempo**. **18**

accent A type of **articulation** that tells you to emphasise or stress a note. **14, 20, 93, 129, 137, 139, 144**

acciaccatura An **ornament** that's a very quick, 'crushed' note, played before the main note. **84**

accidental A note that doesn't belong to the **home key** of a piece, indicated by a **sharp**, **flat** or **natural**. **11, 44**

action song A song in a **musical** that tells you what's going on. A bit like a **recitative**. **121**

adagio Play at 66-76 beats per minute. A bit faster than **largo**. **18**

African music 55, 136, 137

Afro Celt Sound System 140, 141

Afro-Cuban jazz A **fusion** genre that comes from **son** and **jazz music**. **149**

agitato Play in an agitated way. **18**

agogo bells A pair of bells often used in **samba** music. **145**

Akalın, Demet 149

Alberti bass A pattern of notes — a way of playing a **broken chord**. **39, 95**

alla marcia Play in a **march** style. **18**

allargando or allarg. Slow down the **tempo** and play more broadly (and a little louder). **18**

allegro 120-168 beats per minute. Lively. **18**

all-female choir A **choir** made up of two groups of **sopranos** and two groups of **altos**. **68**

all-male choir A **choir** made up of **trebles**, **altos**, **tenors** and **basses**. **68**

alto Voice that sings roughly in the range from F below the middle C to the F at the top of the treble clef stave. **68, 101**

alto clef A clef used for mid-pitched music, usually the viola parts. **10**

American music 135

amoroso Play in a romantic, loving way. **18**

anacrusis An unaccented beat at the start of a **phrase**. **12, 138, 139**

andante 76-108 beats a minute. Walking pace. **18**

anthem Short **polyphonic** choral piece performed in Protestant churches. **104**

antiphonal A type of **texture** where two choirs or groups of instruments are singing or playing at different times. **47**

appoggiatura An **ornament** that clashes with the accompanying chord then resolves. **41, 84**

arch shape A melody that finishes the same way it started, e.g. ABA or ABCBA. **55**

aria A **solo** from an **opera** or **oratorio**. **56, 102-104**

arpeggio The notes of a chord played in succession, either going up or down. **39**

articulation How the notes are played — e.g. clear and short or long and flowing. **19**

atonal Music that's not written in a key. **26**

augmentation Increasing the length of notes to make the music sound slower. **18**

augmented interval An interval that's a **semitone** larger than a major or perfect interval. **29**

augmented triad A **triad** that has four **semitones** (a major third) between the bottom and middle notes, and the middle and top notes. **35**

auxiliary notes A type of **decoration** that's one **semitone** or **tone** higher or lower than the notes either side. **41**

B

Bach, C.P.E. 87
Bach, J.C. 87
Bach, J.S. 80, 81, 85, 86

backing vocals 109, 115

balafon A West African xylophone. **137, 140, 141**

ballad A song that tells a story. In **pop** and **rock music**, ballads tend to tell love stories. **58, 108**

bar 8, 9

bar lines 9

baritone A male voice that sings the top part of the **bass** range and the bottom part of the **tenor** range. **68, 101**

Baroque Musical style around in Europe from about 1600-1750. Strong bass and lots of **decoration**. **41, 46, 56, 57, 66, 80-87, 101-103, 106**

bass Voice that sings roughly in the range from F below the bass clef to the E just above middle C. **68, 101**

bass clef A clef used for low-pitched music — it's the bottom clef in piano music. **10, 16**

basso continuo A continuous bass part in **Baroque** music, often played on a **harpsichord** and cello. Also called a **continuo**. **57, 80**

beat 12

bebop A type of **jazz** characterised by complex harmonies and fast, **syncopated** rhythms. **142**

Beethoven 87, 90, 93-95, 105

bell effect A technique where notes are played one at a time and left to ring, to sound like a bell. **115**

bend A technique used to change the pitch of a note slightly. **20**

bhangra Modern bhangra is a fusion of traditional Indian and Pakistani music with club dance music. **149**

big band A band that plays **jazz** and **swing music**. **69, 142, 143**

binary form Form of music in two distinct sections. **81**

bi-rhythm A **polyrhythm** made up of two different rhythms. **14**

block chord Chord played by sounding all the notes at once. **39, 89**

blue notes The flattened notes in a **blues scale**. **110, 143**

blues Style of late 19th and early 20th century music from America that has sad lyrics and uses the **blues scale**. **110, 111, 142, 144**

blues scale A **scale** made by flattening the third, fifth and seventh of a **major scale**. The unflattened fifth is sometimes also played. **110**

Index and Glossary

bodhrán An Irish framed drum.
138, 139

bossa nova A style of Brazilian music based on a fusion of **samba** and **jazz**.
135, 145

Brahms 105

Brandenburg Concerto No.5
81, 83, 85, 86

brass band Band with **brass** and **percussion** sections. **69**

brass instruments Metal instruments where the sound is produced by 'buzzing' the lips.
62, 69, 71, 74, 80, 88, 93

bridge Section in a piece of music used to link two different chunks together. **58, 91-93, 109, 114**

Broadway A famous theatre street in New York. **120**

broken chord Chord that's played as a series of notes. **39, 89**

broken octave When notes an **octave** apart are played alternately — also called a **murky bass**. **95**

Bush, Kate 108

C

C clef A clef that can move up and down the **stave** — the middle point of the clef is always at middle C. **10**

cadence Pair of chords used to finish off a **phrase**. **42, 43, 92**

cadenza Section of a **concerto** where the soloist can really show off.
57, 90

call and response A short melody (the call), followed by an answering phrase (the response).
47, 55, 58, 109, 110, 143, 148

calmato Play the music so it sounds very calm. **18**

canon Where the same tune is played by two or more parts, each coming in separately and at regular intervals. The parts overlap. Also called a **round. 46, 109**

cantata A piece of music made up of **arias** and **recitatives**. **104**

Capercaillie 138, 149

carnival 145

Celtic folk music Western European **folk music** particularly popular in Scotland and Ireland. **138, 149**

Celtic rock A fusion of **Celtic folk** and **rock music. 149**

chaal Eight-note rhythmic pattern used in **bhangra**. **149**

chamber choir A small choir. **101**

chamber music Music written for small groups. It was originally played in people's houses. **70**

chamber orchestra Orchestra with small **string** and **percussion** sections, and one or two of each **wind** and **brass** instrument. **71, 101**

choir A group of singers. **68**

Chopin 93, 147

choral music Music written for **choirs**.
68, 101

chorale A hymn. **104**

chord A group of two or more notes all played at the same time. **9, 34-39**

chord progression Repeated pattern of related chords used in bass and rhythm parts, especially **ground bass**.
36

chorus Piece in an **opera**, **oratorio** or **cantata** sung by the chorus (choir).
102, 103

chorus effect An electronic effect that gives the impression of lots of singers or instruments. **75**

chorus number A piece in a **musical** sung by the whole cast. Similar to a **chorus** in **opera**. **121**

chromatic decoration 41

chromatic notes Notes that don't belong to the main **key** of a melody.
95, 126

chromatic scale 12-note scale containing all the notes (**tones** and **semitones**) within an octave. **27**

circle of fifths Madly complicated diagram showing how all the keys relate to each other. **26**

clarinet quintet Small group with clarinet, two violins, viola and a cello. **70**

classical <u>Either</u> any music that's not pop (or **jazz**, **folk**, **hip-hop**, **R'n'B**, etc.), or music composed in Europe from about 1750 to 1820. **87-95**

clave rhythm The basic rhythm of a piece of **son** or **salsa** music around which the rest of the music has to fit.
148

claves Wooden sticks used to set the **clave rhythm. 135, 148**

clavichord An early keyboard instrument. **66**

coda The final section of a piece of music.
58, 91, 94, 95, 109, 112, 122

col legno For string players — play the string with the back of the bow instead of bowing. **64**

compound time A **time signature** where each main beat can be split into three little ones. **13**

con arco Play with the bow. The opposite of **pizzicato**. **64**

con sordino Play with a mute. **64**

concept album An album where all the tracks are linked by a theme. **113**

concertino The small group of soloists in a **concerto grosso**. **81, 85, 86**

concerto Piece for an orchestra with a soloist, in three movements. **81, 87, 88**

concerto grosso A type of Baroque concerto, made up of a **concertino** and a **ripieno. 81, 85, 87**

concordance Nice sound that you get when notes that fit together are played together at the same time. **34**

conductor The person who controls an **orchestra**. **71**

conjunct Where the melody is smooth — there aren't big jumps between the notes. **28, 54**

consonance Nice sound that you get when notes that fit together are played at the same time. Also called **concordance. 34**

continuo Another name for **basso continuo. 57, 85, 106, 107**

contralto A low-range female voice.
68, 101

contrapuntal Music with two or more tunes played at the same time and woven together. Also called **polyphonic. 45-47, 80, 85, 147**

contrary motion 106

counter-subject The melodic line that follows the **subject** in a **fugue**. **85**

countertenor A high-pitched male voice. **68, 101, 106**

crescendo Get louder gradually. **19**

cross-rhythm Tension-building effect — over a few bars of music, rhythms with **accents** in different places are played at the same time. Used in African music. **14, 135, 137, 148**

crotchet A note that lasts for one beat. **12, 16**

Cubase A piece of software used as a **sequencer. 126**

cyclic form Where a common **theme** runs throughout the movements, usually in a large-scale work. **56**

Index and Glossary

D

da capo aria An **aria** in **ternary form**. 56

decoration A way of making music more interesting by adding extra notes. 41, 84

Defying Gravity 122, 123

development The second section of **sonata form** where ideas are developed. 91, 94

dhol Drum used in traditional **bhangra**. 149

diatonic decoration Decoration that belongs to the key of the melody. 41

diatonic scale Another name for **major** and **minor scales**. 89

diegetic music When the characters in a film can actually hear the music. 126

diminished chord 35, 36

diminished triad A **triad** that has three **semitones** (a minor third) between the bottom and middle notes, and the middle and top notes. 35

diminuendo Get quieter gradually. 19

diminution Shortening the length of the notes to make the music sound quicker. 18

disco Popular 70s dance style. 112, 149

discordance Horrible sound that you get when notes that don't fit together are played at the same time. Also called **dissonance**. 34, 41, 93, 107, 123

disjunct When there are big jumps between the notes of a melody. The opposite of **conjunct**. 54, 123

dissonance Another name for **discordance**. 34, 41, 93, 107, 123

distortion A guitar effect that distorts the note. 75, 113

Dixieland Jazz An early form of **jazz**. 142

DJ Disc jockey. Chooses which tracks to play on the radio or at a club. 73

djembe Single-headed African drum, played with the hands. 136, 137, 140, 141

dolce Play sweetly. 18

dot A symbol that makes a note or rest one-and-a-half times its normal length. 17

double flat A symbol that tells you to lower a note by two **semitones**. 11

double sharp A symbol that tells you to raise a note by two **semitones**. 11

double-stopping Playing two notes at the same time on a **string instrument**. 64

drone A long, held-on note, usually in the bass. 39, 134, 141, 144

drum fill A short drum solo in between sections of a piece, usually found in **pop music**. 14

drum machine An electronic instrument used instead of live drums. 72, 73, 112, 149

drum'n'bass A fusion of club dance, **jazz** and funk. 149

duet A piece for two players or two singers. 70, 121

dynamics How loud or quiet the music is. 19, 80, 87, 93, 95

E

electronic effects Effects used to change the **timbre** of instruments. 75

energico Play energetically. 18

enharmonic equivalent Notes which sound the same but are written differently (e.g. C♯ and D♭). 11

exposition The first section of **sonata form** where ideas are introduced. 91, 94

extra-diegetic music Music in a film that can't be heard by the characters. 126

F

falsetto When male singers sing notes in the female vocal range — much higher than their normal range. 68, 101, 109

fanfare A flourish, usually performed by **brass instruments**. 62, 129

fantasia A composition with an **improvised** feel. 82

feedback The noise you get when you stand too close to a speaker with a guitar or microphone. Sometimes used deliberately in **rock music**. 113

figured bass A type of notation often used for **continuo** parts. The bass notes are written on the **stave**, then numbers written underneath the notes tell the performers which chords to play. 57, 85

film music 124-129

first inversion An **inversion** of a **triad** with the third at the bottom. 37

flanger A guitar effect that sounds a bit like a **phaser** but more intense. 75, 115

flat A symbol that tells you to lower a note by one **semitone**. 11

folk music Music played by ordinary people. It wasn't usually written down — it was passed on aurally. 108, 113, 138

forte, f Loud. 19

fortissimo, ff Very loud. 19

free jazz A type of **jazz** from the 1950s and 60s with lots of **improvisation**. It didn't stick to set tempos or rhythms. 142

fugue A popular Baroque structure. It usually involves **imitation** and **counterpoint**. 81, 85, 86

fusion A musical genre formed by mixing the elements of two or more different musical styles. 135, 140-143, 145-149

G

Gaelic Traditional Celtic language spoken in Scotland and Ireland. The two main types are Scots Gaelic and Irish Gaelic. 138, 140, 141

gamelan Type of music played in Indonesia using a five or seven note scale. Also the name of the orchestra that plays this type of music. 134

gigue A 17th century dance with a regular beat and lively **tempo**. 85

giocoso Play in a light-hearted, joky way. 18

glissando A slide between notes. 20

Goethe 105

grand opera A serious **opera**, set entirely to music. 102

grandioso Play very grandly. 18

grave Play very slowly and solemnly. 94

ground bass A way of playing **variations** with a strong repeating bass part as the main **theme**. 57, 82, 83, 106, 107

H

hammer-on A guitar technique that allows you to play notes quickly and in a **legato** style. 65

Handel 47, 80, 81, 103

harmonic A technique on stringed instruments (including guitars) that produces a high, ringing note. **64, 146**

harmonic interval The difference between two notes played at the same time. **28**

harmonic minor scale 8-note scale using notes from the **minor key** <u>except for the seventh note</u>, which is sharpened by one **semitone**. **25**

harmonic progression A series of chords. Another name for a **chord progression**. **36**

harpsichord A keyboard instrument shaped like a small grand piano. It was popular in the **Baroque** period. **57, 66, 80, 81, 85-88, 106**

Haydn 81, 87-90

hemiola When the music feels like it's in triple time when it's actually written in duple time, or vice versa. **14**

heterophonic In heterophonic music all the parts have different versions of the tune. **45**

hip-hop Music with Jamaican and African-American influences and lots of rapping. **108, 135, 149**

home key The key that a piece of music starts and ends in. **44**

homophonic Where the tune is accompanied by chords, keeping to roughly the same rhythm. **45, 47, 87, 89, 95, 123**

hook A catchy tune used in **pop music** and **musicals**. **112, 121**

hornpipe An Irish dance, a little slower than a **reel**. **139**

hurdy-gurdy A string instrument with a keyboard used in **folk music**. **138**

I

imitation A phrase is repeated with little variation. Could be one instrument or voice, or two or more imitating each other. **45, 46, 83, 85, 104**

imperfect cadence A **cadence** that usually moves from chord I, II or IV to chord V. **42, 43**

improvisation Music that's made up on the spot by a performer, often based on a given **chord progression** or set of notes. It's used a lot in **jazz**. **55, 57, 142-144, 146, 148**

incidental music Music written to be performed as part of a play. **106, 120**

Indian music 55, 134

interlude A short bit of a piece of music that goes between more important parts. **114, 122**

interrupted cadence A **cadence** that moves from chord V to any chord except chord I. **42, 43**

interval The gap in pitch between two notes, played one after another or at the same time in a chord. **28, 29**

inversion (chord) Using a chord in a position other than its **root position**. **37, 38**

J

jazz Music with lots of **syncopation**, **improvisation** and quirky harmonisation. Influenced many different musical styles, such as **hip-hop** and **salsa**. **142-144, 146-149**

jazz rock A **fusion** genre of **jazz** and **rock music**. **143**

jig A fast Irish dance. **139**

J-pop Japanese **pop music**, influenced by traditional Japanese music. **149**

K

key signature Sharps or flats just before the **time signature**, to tell you what key the music's in. **11, 24-26, 44**

Keys, Alicia 108

Killer Queen 114, 115

kora A West African harp-like instrument. **137, 140**

K-pop South Korean **pop music**, influenced by traditional South Korean music. **149**

L

larghetto 60-66 beats a minute. Broad and slow, but less so than **largo**. **18**

largo 40-60 beats a minute. Broad and slow. **18**

Latin American music 147

layering Using technology to record several parts separately and layer them one on top of another. **46, 114, 115**

ledger lines Extra lines added above or below the stave, to write high or low notes. **16**

legato Play smoothly. **19**

leitmotif A phrase or piece of music that represents a person, place, time or emotion in film music or musicals. **122, 124, 126, 128, 129**

Lied A **Romantic** song for one singer and piano. The lyrics are often in German. **105**

loop Section of music repeated over and over. **46, 73, 75, 112**

M

madrigal Song from the Renaissance times for five or six singers. **104**

maestoso Play majestically. **129**

Main Title/Rebel Blockade Runner 128, 129

major key A **key** using notes from a **major scale**. **89, 127**

major scale Series of eight notes. The **intervals** between them are: **tone**, tone, **semitone**, tone, tone, tone, semitone. **24**

major triad A **triad** with an **interval** of four **semitones** between the bottom and middle notes, and three semitones between the middle and top notes. **35**

male voice choir A **choir** made up of two groups of **tenors** as well as **baritones** and **basses**. **68**

mambo A break between choruses in **salsa** music. **148**

marcato Play all the notes with **accents**. **20, 129**

march A piece of music in 2/4 or 4/4 with a regular pulse. The first (and third) beat of the bar is accented — designed to be marched to. **69, 129**

mass Piece of music sung as part of the Catholic church service. **101, 104**

melismatic A single syllable of text is sung over a succession of notes. The opposite of **syllabic**. **103, 107**

melodic interval The difference in pitch between two notes played one after another in a tune. **28**

melodic inversion Version of a tune where the intervals between notes are the same but in the opposite direction (e.g. up instead of down). **83**

melodic minor scale A **minor scale**. Like the **natural minor** but with the 6th and 7th notes raised a **semitone** going up and reverting back to the natural minor coming down. Used for composing melodies in **minor keys**. **25**

Messiah 103

Index and Glossary

mezzoforte, mf Fairly loud. **19**

mezzopiano, mp Fairly quiet. **19**

mezzo-soprano A female voice that sings the top part of the **alto** range and the bottom part of the **soprano** range. **68, 101**

middle 8 Eight bars, in the middle of a song. Has different chords and/or tune to keep you interested. **58, 109**

MIDI Stands for Musical Instrument Digital Interface — a way of connecting different electronic instruments. **72**

military band A type of **wind band** — they usually play **marches**. **69**

minim A note that lasts for two beats. **12, 16**

minor key A key that sounds sad. Uses notes from the **minor scale**. **89, 127**

minor scale Series of eight notes (the first and last notes are the same). The **intervals** between them are **tone**, **semitone**, tone, tone, semitone, tone, tone in a **natural minor** scale. **Melodic** and **harmonic** minor scales are slightly different. **25**

minor triad A **triad** with an **interval** of three **semitones** between the bottom and middle notes, and four semitones between the middle and top notes. **35**

minuet and trio Third movement of a **sonata** or **symphony**. Two sections in **ternary form** — the minuet and the trio — are put together so the overall structure of the piece is ternary too. **91, 92**

mixing When different records are mixed together. **75**

mode Seven-note scale following a particular sequence of **tones** and **semitones**. **27, 139, 144**

moderato 108-120 beats per minute. Not too fast, not too slow. Moderate speed. **18**

modulation When music shifts into another **key**, usually a related one, e.g. the dominant or **relative minor**. **44, 80, 81, 91, 95**

monophonic Music with a tune and nothing else — no backing, rhythm or harmony. **45, 47**

montuno The chorus in a **salsa** tune. **148**

mood The overall feel of a piece. **18**

mordent An **ornament** commonly used in **Baroque** music. **84**

motet Short **polyphonic** choral piece performed in Catholic churches. **104**

motif A little bit of music that's often repeated. **105**

Mozart 81, 87-90

Müller 105

multi-track Recording system that allows you to record different parts separately then play them all back together. **72**

murky bass Another name for **broken octave**. **95**

Music for a While 106, 107

musical A lighter, more modern version of **opera** that's been around since the early twentieth century. Has more talking and more dancing. **120-123**

mute Wooden, rubber or metal gadget used to dampen the sound of **brass** and **string instruments**. **62**

N

natural A symbol that cancels out a **sharp** or a **flat**. **11**

natural minor scale A minor scale using the notes of the **minor key** (and no funny accidentals like the **melodic** and **harmonic** minors). **25**

nu jazz A **fusion** genre made from **jazz**, **electronic dance**, **funk** and **soul music**. **143**

O

octave The distance from one note to the next note up or down with the same letter name. **28, 95**

octave effect An electronic effect used to create octaves higher or lower than the note played. **75**

octet Piece in eight parts, or a group with eight players or singers in it. **70**

Oedipus **106**

opera Drama set to music. **90, 102, 103, 120**

opera buffa A type of **opera** with light, everyday themes. **102**

opéra comique Form of **opera** with some spoken **recitatives**. **102, 120**

opera seria A type of **opera** with serious, often mythological themes. **102**

operetta A small **opera**. **102, 120**

oral tradition Passing on music by playing and listening — not writing it down. **136, 138**

oratorio Bible stories set to music. Oratorios are **sacred**. A bit like **opera**, but not acted out and with a religious theme. **101, 103**

organ A large keyboard instrument that makes sound by blowing air through pipes. **66, 80, 85**

ornament Short extra notes that add some **decoration**. **80, 84, 87, 91, 144**

ostinato A musical pattern which repeats over and over again, like the bass part in **ground bass**. **57, 83, 127**

overture A one-movement piece for **orchestra**, usually written as an introduction to an **opera** or ballet. **90**

P

parallel motion When two or more parts move with the same **interval** between them. **45**

passing note A type of **decoration** — a note that links the two notes before and after it. **41**

patron People who paid composers to write music. **88**

pause A rest in the music, usually more than a beat long. **18**

pedal note A held-on or repeated note, often in the bass part. Also called a **pedal point**. **39, 86**

pedal point Another name for a **pedal note**. **86**

pentatonic scale 5-note scale used in **folk music**. A major pentatonic uses notes 1, 2, 3, 5 and 6 of an ordinary **major scale**. A minor pentatonic uses notes 1, 3, 4, 5 and 7 of a **natural minor scale**. **27, 138**

percussion instruments Instruments that make a sound when you hit or shake them. **67, 71, 74, 88**

perfect cadence Chords V and I played at the end of a section or piece to round it off. **42, 43, 107**

performance dances Traditional dances that the audience watch rather than join in with. **139**

pesante Play in a heavy style. **18**

phaser A guitar effect that creates a 'whooshing' sound. **75**

phrase Sort of like a musical sentence — they're sometimes marked with a curved line above the music. **42**

pianissimo, pp Very quiet. **19**

piano, p Quiet. **19**

Index and Glossary

piano (instrument)
66, 74, 87, 93, 94

piano trio A piano, a violin and a cello. **70**

picking On a guitar, plucking one string at a time. **65**

pitch shifting An electronic effect used to bend a note or add harmony. **75**

pivot chord Chord that belongs to two **keys**. It's used to shift a piece of music from one key to another (**modulate**) because it sounds OK in both. **44**

pizzicato 'Plucked'. A way of playing a string instrument. **64**

plagal cadence Cadence going from chord IV to I. **42, 43**

plainsong An unaccompanied **modal** melody with no fixed rhythm, typically sung in church by an **all-male choir**. Also called plainchant. **101**

polyphonic Musical **texture** where two or more tunes are played at the same time and woven together. **45-47, 80, 85, 87, 89, 142**

polyrhythm Two or more contrasting rhythms being played at the same time. **14, 135, 137, 148**

pop Popular music. **58, 124, 125**

pop-folk A **fusion** genre made from **pop** and **folk music**. **149**

portamento When a singer slides from one note to another. **20, 109, 115**

power chord Chord made up of the tonic and the fifth. Used in **rock music**. **113**

prelude A piano piece, originally the bit that came before the main piece. **Romantic** composers wrote some preludes as stand-alone pieces. **81, 147**

preparation The first of three notes in a **suspension**. **41**

presto 180-200 beats per minute. Really fast. About as fast as it gets. **18**

primary chord Root note chord, and chords IV and V. These are the easiest ones to harmonise with. **36**

Pro-Tools® A piece of software used as a sequencer. **126**

pull-off A guitar technique that allows you to play notes quickly and in a **legato** style. **65**

Purcell, Henry 80, 106, 107

Q

quartet Piece in four parts, or a group with four players or singers in it. **70**

quaver A note that lasts for half a beat. **12, 16**

Queen 114, 115, 120

question and answer A bit like **call and response** — one part sings or plays a phrase (the question) and another part responds (the answer). **47, 139**

quintet Piece in five parts, or a group with five players or singers in it. **70**

R

raga A **scale** of 5-8 notes used in Indian classical music. **134, 144**

ragtime A type of music popular in early 20th century America with **syncopated** rhythms. **Jazz** music came from ragtime. **142**

rallentando, **or** *rall.* Slowing down gradually. **18**

range The set of notes that a voice or instrument can play. **54, 68**

recapitulation The third section of **sonata form** where the main ideas are played again. **91, 94**

recitative A song performed in operas, **oratorios** and **cantatas**. It tells the story and moves it along. **102-104**

reel A quick and lively **folk dance** with straight (undotted) quavers. **139**

reggae A form of Jamaican music. **135**

relative major Every **minor key** has a relative major key which has the same **key signature**. E.g. C major is the relative major of A minor. **25, 26**

relative minor Every **major key** has a relative minor key which has the same **key signature**. E.g. A minor is the relative minor of C major. **26, 44**

remix Version of a song altered electronically in a studio — usually to make it easier to dance to. **73, 149**

requiem A **mass** for the dead. **101**

resolution The last of the three notes in a **suspension**. **41**

rest A break in the music — different rest symbols will tell you how long the break should be. **16**

retrograde Version of a tune where the composer takes all the notes and puts them in reverse order. **83**

retrograde inversion Version of a tune that's both **retrograde** <u>and</u> an inversion. **83**

reverb A guitar effect that adds an echo to the sound. **75**

rhythmic chords Chords played in a rhythmic way so you get rhythm and harmony. **39**

rhythm'n'blues 110

riff Repeated phrase played over and over again. Used in **jazz**, **pop** and **rock music**. **58, 109**

ripieno The group of accompanying instruments in a **concerto grosso**. **81, 85, 86**

risoluto Play in a confident, decided way. **18**

ritenuto, *rit.* Holding back the pace. **18**

ritornello A musical form where the main **theme** is returned to regularly. **81, 86**

rock A popular music form that usually involves amplified instruments, strong rhythms and **power chords**. **113**

Romantic Musical style which was around from about 1820 to 1900. The music describes a story or powerful emotions. **93-95, 105**

rondo A way of structuring music so you start with one **theme**, go on to a new one, go back to the first one, on to another new one, back to the first one, on to a new one... as many times as you like. **81, 92**

root chord Chord with its **root note** at the bottom. **38**

root note The note a chord originates from, e.g. in a C major chord, the root note would be C. **37, 38**

root position A **triad** that hasn't been **inverted** (the **root note** is at the bottom). **37**

round Another name for a **canon**. **46**

rubato, **or** *rub.* Be flexible with the pace of the music. **18, 93**

S

sacred music Church music. **101, 103, 106**

salsa A type of Latin American dance music. It's a fusion of **jazz** and Cuban **son**. **135, 148**

samba A type of Brazilian carnival music. **135, 145, 146**

Index and Glossary

sampler Electronic equipment for storing and altering sounds. **73**

sampling Adding other people's tunes, rhythms or voices to your own music. Used a lot in club dance music. **73, 75, 149**

SATB Short for 'sopranos, altos, tenors, basses', the four sections of a standard choir. **68**

scale A set pattern of notes all from the same key. The most common ones in Western music are major and minor scales. **24, 25**

scalic Similar to conjunct. A smooth melody that moves up and down a scale. **28, 54**

scat A type of improvised singing used in jazz, with nonsense words and syllables. **144**

scherzo Lively third movement of a symphony or sonata. Wakes the audience up in time for the final movement. **91, 92**

Schumann 105

Schwartz, Stephen 122

Scotch snap A rhythm used in Scottish dances where an accented semiquaver is followed by an unaccented dotted quaver. **17**

second inversion An inversion of a triad with the fifth at the bottom. **37**

semibreve A note that lasts for four beats. **16**

semiquaver A note that lasts for one quarter of a beat. **12, 16**

semitone The gap in pitch between e.g. A and A♯, E♭ and E or B and C. On a piano keyboard, any two notes, black or white, immediately next to each other are a semitone apart. **9, 24, 25, 27**

septet Piece in seven parts or group with seven players. **70**

sequence Technique used in recording club dance — building up a song by layering lots of tracks over one another. **72, 112**

sequence Also a repeated musical pattern where the starting note moves up or down each time. **83, 86, 124**

sequencer Electronic equipment which can record, edit and play back MIDI files and usually audio. **72, 112**

sextet A piece for six players or six singers. **70**

sforzando, sfz A sudden, strongly accented note. **20, 93**

sharp A symbol that tells you to raise a note by one semitone. **11**

simple time Time signature with two, three or four basic beats. **13**

singer-songwriter Someone that writes and sings their own songs. **108**

sitar Large, long-necked string instrument used in Indian music. **134**

slur Curved line joining notes of different pitch. Means you should go smoothly from one to the next. **19**

social dances Traditional Irish dances that people join in with. **139**

solo A common feature of jazz and rock music where one instrument or singer plays on its own or over accompaniment. **114, 115**

solo character song A song in a musical sung by one character. A bit like an aria in an opera. **121**

Somewhere Over The Rainbow 122

son Dance style which combined Spanish and African music, based on rhythm patterns called claves. Salsa evolved from son. **135, 148**

son clave A clave rhythm used in son — the beats are grouped into a 3 and a 2, or the other way round. **148**

sonata Piece of music in three or four movements for a soloist or duet. **87, 90, 91**

sonata form Piece of music with an exposition, a development and a recapitulation. **87, 91, 94**

Sonata Pathétique 94, 95

song cycle A collection of Lieder. **105**

sonority The nature or quality of a sound. **74**

soprano Voice that sings roughly in the range from middle C to two octaves above that. Some singers can go even higher. **68, 101, 106**

sospirando Play or sing in a sighing sort of way. **18**

space opera An epic drama set in space. **128**

Spalding, Esperanza 146, 147

staccato Play each note short and detached from the ones either side. **19**

Star Wars 124, 128, 129

stave The five lines that music is written on. **9**

step dancing A form of Irish performance dance with complicated footwork. **139**

stepwise When a melody moves in steps. **28, 54**

Sting 108

stretto A technique in a fugue where the subject is overlapped. **86**

string instruments Instruments with strings. Fairly obvious really. **64, 65, 71, 74, 80, 88**

string quartet Two violins, a viola and a cello. **70**

string trio A violin, a viola and a cello. **70**

strophic form Type of structure where the music is the same in every verse. Only the lyrics change. **56, 105, 138, 140**

structure The way a piece of music is organised. **56, 81, 82, 87, 89-92, 138**

strumming On a guitar, playing more than one note at a time. **65**

subject The main idea of a piece of music. **85**

suite A set of dances from the Baroque period, or an orchestral arrangement of music from an opera or ballet. **81, 90**

surdo drums Drums used in samba to set the beat. **145**

suspended chord A chord where the third is replaced by a second or a fourth. **123**

suspension A series of three notes that clash with the chord then lead back into a harmony. It is also the name of the second note in the series. **41, 107**

swing music A type of jazz from the 1930s and 40s that could be danced to. **69, 120, 142, 144**

swung rhythm 110, 142, 143

syllabic Every syllable of text is sung to a single note. The opposite of melismatic. **103, 107, 114, 123**

symphony Long piece of music, in three or four movements, for a full orchestra. **87, 90, 91**

syncopation The accents are shifted from the main beat to a weaker beat. E.g. in 4/4 time the main accent usually falls on the first beat — in syncopated 4/4 time you could move the accent to, say, the second beat. **110, 123, 142**

synthesiser Electronic equipment for creating new sounds. **72, 75, 149**

Index and Glossary

T

tabla Pair of drums used in Indian classical music. **134**
tablature A way of writing guitar music — each line represents a string and the numbers show which frets to press. **65**
talking drum 136, 140
tambura Similar in shape to a sitar, but with only four metal strings. Used as a backing instrument in Indian classical music. **134**
tango A passionate Latin American dance. **135**
Tchaikovsky 93
tempo The pace or speed of the music. **18**
tenor Voice that sings roughly in the range from the C below middle C to the G above. **68, 101, 106**
tenor clef One **octave** lower than a **treble clef**. **10**
tenuto Play the note for its full length, or slightly longer. **19**
ternary form Piece in three sections. The first and last are much the same. The second's a bit different and in a different (but related) key. **56, 81, 86, 87**
tessitura The **range** of a singer's voice. **68**
texture The way different parts are woven together. **45-47, 89**
The Erl King 105
The Wizard of Oz 122
theme Musical idea. The bit you hum. In **theme and variation** and **rondo** forms this is the bit that gets repeated. **56, 82**
theme and variation form First you hear a simple tune. After a short pause you hear a **variation** on the tune. Then there's another pause and another variation, another pause, another variation, etc. **82, 87**
third inversion An **inversion** of a chord with the seventh below a standard **triad**. **37**
through-composed form Type of **structure** where the music is different in every verse. **56, 105, 113**
thumb piano A small African instrument. **137**
tie A curved line that joins two notes of the same pitch, so when they're played they sound like one note. **17**
Tierce de Picardie When a piece in a minor key finishes with a major chord (e.g. a piece in A minor finishes with an A major chord). **43**
timbre The type of sound an instrument makes. Also known as tone colour. **74, 75, 93, 141**
time signature Numbers at the beginning of a piece that tell you how many beats there are in a bar. **12, 13**
timpani A large **percussion instrument** often used in **orchestras**. Also called kettledrums. **67, 88**
tonal Music that's written in a specific **key**. **80, 89**
tone The gap in pitch between e.g. A and B, E flat and F or G and A. One tone = two **semitones**. **9, 24, 25, 27, 74**
tonic key The **key** a piece starts in. **44, 91**
treble Boy who sings at **soprano** pitch. **68, 101**
treble clef A clef used for higher-pitched music — it's the upper clef in piano music. **10, 16**
tremolo Play in a trembly, nervous sounding way. **64, 123, 127, 147**
triad 3-note chord which uses a **root**, a third above and a fifth above. **34-37**
triadic A melody that moves using notes of the triad. **54**
trill Twiddly **ornament**. **84, 86**
trio Second part of a piece in **minuet and trio** form <u>or</u> a piece for three players or three singers. **70**
trionfale Play in a triumphant, confident-sounding way. **18**
triplet Three notes played in the space of two. **17**
tritone Uncomfortable-sounding interval of three tones. **29, 125**
turn Another twiddly **ornament**. **84**

U

Uilleann pipes Irish bagpipes. **139-141**
unison Everyone plays or sings the same notes at the same time. **45, 47, 101, 109, 129, 139**
upbeat Another name for an **anacrusis**. **12**

V

variation Either a recognisable version of the main **theme** of a piece, or a self-contained piece of music in its own right based on a single theme. **57, 82**
verse-chorus structure Structure used in **pop** songs. Verses have the same melody but the lyrics change each time. Choruses have a different tune to the verse but the words don't change. **58, 109, 112, 114, 122**
vibrato When singers make their voices wobble, giving a richer sound. String instruments can produce a similar effect too. **64, 74, 109**
virginal A table-top version of a **harpsichord**. **66**
vivace 168-180 beats a minute. Very lively. **18**
Vivaldi 80, 81
voice 68, 74, 109

W

Wagner 93
walking bass A bass part that moves in **crotchets**, usually either in step or **arpeggios**. **39, 106**
West End Theatre district in London. **120**
whistle An instrument often used in **samba**, usually to lead the band. **145**
whole tone scale 6-note scale with a **tone** between each note and the next. **27**
Wicked 122, 123
Williams, John 124, 128, 129
wind band A fairly large band made up of **woodwind**, **brass** and **percussion**. **69**
wind quintet A group made up of a flute, a clarinet, an oboe, a horn and a bassoon. **70**
woodwind instruments Instruments that make a sound when you blow them (not including **brass** instruments). **63, 71, 74, 80, 88**
word-painting Where the music matches the words or action. **103, 107, 123**
work song **Folk** songs sung by labourers, to keep spirits up and help them work as a team. **110**
world music A term used to describe traditional music from around the world. **134, 135**

Acknowledgements

The publisher would like to thank the following copyright holders for permission to reproduce material:

Track 1
Caro Nome, from *Rigoletto*, by Verdi.
Performed by the Slovak Philharmonic Orchestra.
Licensed courtesy of Naxos Rights US Inc.

Track 2
Oboe Concerto No. 3 in G minor, by Handel.
Performed by the City of London Sinfonia.
Licensed courtesy of Naxos Rights US Inc.

Tracks 3-13
Composed and performed by Sam Norman.
© 2010 Coordination Group Publications Ltd.

Track 14
Prelude in C♯ Minor, Op. 3, No. 2, by Rachmaninov.
Performed by Idil Biret.
Licensed courtesy of Naxos Rights US Inc.

Tracks 15-26
Composed and performed by Sam Norman.
© 2010 Coordination Group Publications Ltd.

Track 27
Sonatina 3, Op. 36, *un poco adagio*, by Clementi.
Performed by Sam Norman.
© 2010 Coordination Group Publications Ltd.

Track 28
St Louis Blues #2, by WC Handy.
Performed by Louis Armstrong.
Licensed courtesy of Naxos Rights US Inc.

Track 29
Courante, from *Suite No. 1 in C major*, BWV 1066, by J.S. Bach.
Performed by the Cologne Chamber Orchestra.
Licensed courtesy of Naxos Rights US Inc.

Track 30
Le Merle Noir, by Messiaen.
Performed by Patrick Gallois & Lydia Wong.
Licensed courtesy of Naxos Rights US Inc.

Track 31
Flight of the Bumble Bee, by Rimsky-Korsakov.
Performed by the CSR Symphony Orchestra.
Licensed courtesy of Naxos Rights US Inc.

Tracks 32 & 45
Brandenburg Concerto No. 5, BWV 1050, 3rd movement: *Allegro*, by J.S. Bach.
Performed by the Swiss Baroque Soloists.
Licensed courtesy of Naxos Rights US Inc.

Tracks 33 & 42
Piano Sonata No. 8 in C Minor, Op. 13, "Pathétique",
1st movement: *Grave — Allegro di molto e con brio*, by Beethoven.
Performed by Boris Giltburg.
Licensed courtesy of Naxos Rights US Inc.

Tracks 34, 39 & 43
Music for a While, from *Oedipus*, Z. 583, by Henry Purcell.
Performed by Carolyn Sampson, Anne-Marie Lasla and Laurence Cummings.
Licensed courtesy of Naxos Rights US Inc.